BADER'S
SPITFIRE WING

BADER'S SPITFIRE WING

TANGMERE 1941

DILIP SARKAR
MBE, FRHistS

BADER'S SPITFIRE WING
Tangmere 1941

First published in Great Britain in 2022 by
Air World
An imprint of
Pen & Sword Books Ltd
Yorkshire – Philadelphia

Copyright © Dilip Sarkar, 2022

ISBN 978 1 39901 705 3

The right of Dilip Sarkar to be identified as Author of this work has been asserted by him in accordance with the Copyright, Designs and Patents Act 1988.

All photographs Dilip Sarkar Archive.

A CIP catalogue record for this book is available from the British Library.

All rights reserved. No part of this book may be reproduced or transmitted in any form or by any means, electronic or mechanical including photocopying, recording or by any information storage and retrieval system, without permission from the Publisher in writing.

Typeset by SJmagic DESIGN SERVICES, India.

Printed and bound in the UK by CPI Group (UK) Ltd.

Pen & Sword Books Limited incorporates the imprints of Atlas, Archaeology, Aviation, Discovery, Family History, Fiction, History, Maritime, Military, Military Classics, Politics, Select, Transport, True Crime, Air World, Frontline Publishing, Leo Cooper, Remember When, Seaforth Publishing, The Praetorian Press, Wharncliffe Local History, Wharncliffe Transport, Wharncliffe True Crime and White Owl.

For a complete list of Pen & Sword titles please contact

PEN & SWORD BOOKS LIMITED
47 Church Street, Barnsley, South Yorkshire, S70 2AS, England
E-mail: enquiries@pen-and-sword.co.uk
Website: www.pen-and-sword.co.uk

Or

PEN AND SWORD BOOKS
1950 Lawrence Rd, Havertown, PA 19083, USA
E-mail: Uspen-and-sword@casematepublishers.com
Website: www.penandswordbooks.com

Contents

Introduction   vi
Author's Note & Glossary   viii

Chapter One	The Non-stop Offensive	1
Chapter Two	Der Kanaljäger	34
Chapter Three	Tangmere Wing War Diary 18 March – 8 August 1941	50
Chapter Four	'He never stood-down himself…'	174
Chapter Five	'Break! For Christ's Sake BREAK!'	179
Chapter Six	'Nothing is certain, nor ever will be'… or is it?	204
Chapter Seven	Bader's Bus Company: Still Running	224

Appendix 1	238
Appendix 2	251
Appendix 3	255
Appendix 4	260
Appendix 5	283
Acknowledgements	286
Bibliography	288
Other books by Dilip Sarkar	291
Index	293

Introduction

Group Captain Sir Douglas Bader was made a household name during the Second World War and in 1956, upon publication of Paul Brickhill's globally best-selling but romanticised Bader biography *Reach for the Sky*, and Daniel Angel's film of the same name, starring Kenneth More, which hit the silver screen a year later. The swashbuckling, legless, Douglas Bader arguably remains the most famous RAF pilot of the war. Indeed, the world over he is held in a very special esteem and affection by the public, and remains an inspiration and example on many levels, not least to the amputee disabled community.

In the introduction to *Bader's Big Wing Controversy, Duxford 1940*, I wrote that:

> This book, however, is not a romanticised tale. It is based upon factual evidence – which often departs substantially from the popular narrative – and investigates a distasteful thread of the Battle of Britain story. While Bader was not personally intending disloyalty, as such, to his Air Officer Commander-in-Chief, Air Chief Marshal Sir Hugh Dowding, he was, as Lord Dowding later commented, 'the cause of a lot of the trouble'. In his burning desire to propel 242 Squadron and himself, their leader, into the forefront of the action, the newsworthy but naïve acting squadron leader found himself used by darker forces, men with axes to grind and personal ambitions to further.

All of that holds true regarding that particular tale, which is essential reading prior to this, *Bader's Spitfire Wing: Tangmere 1941*.

A few months after the Battle of Britain, by day Fighter Command adopted an offensive posture, 'reaching out' and taking the war across the Channel to

INTRODUCTION

the Germans in north-west France. This optimistic scenario was welcomed by the Command, and morale was high. In the spring of 1941, frontline day fighter squadrons became Spitfire-equipped, and organised into wings of three squadrons, based at each sector. A new post was created, that of 'Wing Commander (Flying)' – the wing leader. All of this was underpinned by the experience of Squadron Leader Douglas Bader and his 'Big Wing' of Battle of Britain days, and unsurprisingly 'Dogsbody' was among the first wing leaders appointed, choosing Tangmere, on the south coast. The scene was set for derring-do, and that summer saw a relentless round of operational flying, especially after Hitler invaded Russia on 22 June 1941, and Fighter Command increased the pressure, in order to pin down German air force units in the west, and hopefully draw other units away from the Ostfront, to support the Soviets. So it was that the 'Non-stop Offensive' also became a political expedient, making it impossible to abandon or reduce when heavy losses suggested that the plan was failing. Nonetheless, Fighter Command was eager for battle – and there was no shortage of aerial combat that heady summer.

Down at Tangmere, Wing Commander Bader immensely inspired most but, although respected by all, was far from universally liked; as always, this unique, swashbuckling, legless, leader remains, in many ways, an enigmatic and elusive character. Nonetheless, his ability to put steel in a man and imbue them, through his own example, with his own enthusiasm was astonishing. Unfortunately, the great man was brought down over France and captured on 9 August 1941 – most likely the victim of 'friendly fire', as explained, in detail, in this book.

For many who flew under Wing Commander Bader that heady summer – whatever the actual outcome of the 'Non-stop Offensive' – it always remained the most inspirational and exciting period of their lives. Heavily myth-laden and romanticised during the immediate post-war period, this book deconstructs the macro and micro events of that 'season', as they affected Fighter Command as a whole and the 'Tangmere Wing of all the talents' in particular. Here we have shone Churchill's 'flickering lamp' of history on those far-off days, attempting to maintain a certain currency for the human experience, the courage, the sacrifices involved – including the enemy, so close, just across the Channel.

For the survivors of 'Bader's Bus Company', this book arguably represents the last word on that bloody summer of 1941. Indeed, there could never be another like it.

Dilip Sarkar MBE FRHistS

Author's Note & Glossary

The aviation-minded reader will notice that I have referred to German Messerschmitt fighters by the abbreviation 'Me' (not 'Bf', which is more technically correct), or simply by their numeric designation, such as '109' or '110'. This not only reads better but is authentic: during the Battle of Britain, Keith Lawrence, a New Zealander, flew Spitfires and once said to me 'To us they were just "Me's", "109s" or "110s", simple, never "Bf".'

In another attempt to preserve accuracy, I have also used the original German, wherever possible, regarding terms associated with the Luftwaffe, such as:

Eichenlaub	The Oak Leaves, essentially being a bar to the Ritterkreuz.
Experte	A fighter 'ace'. Ace status, on both sides, was achieved by destroying five enemy aircraft.
Freie hunt	A fighter sweep.
Gefechstand	Operations headquarters.
Geschwader	The whole group, usually of three gruppen.
Geschwaderkommodore	The group leader.
Gruppe	A wing, usually of three squadrons.
Gruppenkeil	A wedge formation of bombers, usually made up of vics of three.
Gruppenkommandeur	The wing commander.
Jagdbomber ('*Jabo*')	Fighter-bomber.
Jagdflieger	Fighter pilot.
Jagdgeschwader	Fighter group, abbreviated JG.
Jagdwaffe	The fighter force.
Jäger	Hunter, in this context a fighter pilot or aircraft.
Kampfflieger	Bomber aircrew.
Kampfgeschwader	Bomber group, abbreviated KG.
Kanal	English Channel.

AUTHOR'S NOTE & GLOSSARY

Kanaljäger	Channel Fighters.
Katchmarek	Wingman.
Lehrgeschwader	Literally a training group, but actually a precision bombing unit, abbreviated LG.
Luftflotte	Air Fleet.
Oberkanone	Literally the 'Top Gun', or leading fighter ace.
Oberkommando der Wehrmacht (OKW)	The German armed forces high command.
Ritterkreuz	The Knight's Cross of the Iron Cross.
Rotte	A pair of fighters, comprising leader and wingman, into which the Schwärm broke once battle was joined.
Rottenführer	Leader of a fighting pair.
Rottenhund	Wingman
Schwärm	A section of four fighters.
Schwärmführer	Section leader.
Seelöwe	Sealion, the codename given to Hitler's proposed seaborne invasion of England.
Seenotflugkommando	Luftwaffe air sea rescue organisation.
Stab	Staff
StabSchwärm	Staff flight.
Staffel	A squadron.
Staffelkapitän	The squadron leader.
Störflug	Harassing attacks, usually by lone Ju 88s.
Stuka	The Ju 87 dive-bomber.
Sturzkampfgeschwader	Dive-bomber group, abbreviated StG.
Vermisst	Missing.
Zerstörer	Literally 'destroyer', the term used for the Me 110.
Zerstörergeschwader	Destroyer group, abbreviated ZG.

Each geschwader generally comprised three gruppen, each of three staffeln. Each gruppe is designated by Roman numerals, i.e. III/JG 26 refers to the third gruppe of Fighter Group (abbreviated 'JG') 26. Staffeln are identified by numbers, so 7/JG 26 is the 7th staffel and belongs to III/JG 26.

Rank comparisons may also be useful:-

Gefreiter	Private 1st Class
Unteroffizier	Corporal, no aircrew equivalent in Fighter Command.
Feldwebel	Sergeant

BADER'S SPITFIRE WING

Oberfeldwebel	Flight Sergeant
Leutnant	Pilot Officer
Oberleutnant	Flight Lieutenant
Hauptmann	Squadron Leader
Major	Wing Commander
Oberst/Oberstleutnant	Group Captain

RAF Abbreviations:-

AAF	Auxiliary Air Force
AASF	Advance Air Striking Force
A&AEE	Aeroplane & Armament Experimental Establishment
AFC	Air Force Cross
AFDU	Air Fighting Development Unit
AI	Airborne Interception radar
AOC	Air Officer Commanding
AOC-in-C	Air Officer Commanding-in-Chief
ATA	Air Transport Auxiliary
ATS	Armament Training School
BEF	British Expeditionary Force
CAS	Chief of the Air Staff
CFS	Central Flying School
CGS	Central Gunnery School
CO	Commanding Officer
DCAS	Deputy CAS
DES	Direct Entry Scheme
DFC	Distinguished Flying Cross
DFM	Distinguished Flying Medal
DSO	Distinguished Service Order
E/A	Enemy Aircraft
EFTS	Elementary Flying Training School
FAA	Fleet Air Arm
FIU	Fighter Interception Unit
FTS	Flying Training School
ITW	Initial Training Wing
LAC	Leading Aircraftman
MRAF	Marshal of the Royal Air Force
MSFU	Merchant Ship Fighter Unit

AUTHOR'S NOTE & GLOSSARY

NCO	Non-Commissioned Officer
OC	Observer Corps
ORB	Operations Record Book
OTC	Officer Training Corps
OTU	Operational Training Unit
PDC	Personnel Distribution Centre
RAFVR	Royal Air Force Volunteer Reserve
RFS	Reserve Flying School
RN	Royal Navy
RNAS	Royal Navy Air Service
RT	Radio Telephone
SASO	Senior Air Staff Officer
SEAC	South East Asia Command
SOO	Senior Operations Officer
SSC	Short Service Commission
UAS	University Air Squadron
US	Unserviceable

Chapter One

The Non-stop Offensive

When Air Marshal Sholto Douglas took over from Air Chief Marshal Sir Hugh Dowding as Fighter Command's Air Officer Commanding-in-Chief on 25 November 1940, his most pressing problem that winter was not daylight operations – but the German night Blitz on British cities. Five days previously, the *Daily Telegraph* had reported that 'those in a position to know predict with some confidence that mass raids by moonlight will become so costly that the enemy will be largely forced to abandon them, as they have the large-scale daylight attacks'. Fighter Command's new chief, however, was not among those apparently predicting with 'confidence' a rapid and decisive defeat of the German night-bombers. Far from it.

Indeed, on the night of 14/15 November 1940, the Luftwaffe's Operation Mondscheinsonate ('Moonlight Sonata') had left the ancient city centre of Coventry in ruins – by dawn, the famous Gothic cathedral was a burned-out shell; 4,300 homes were destroyed and two-thirds of the city's buildings were damaged, including two hospitals and a third of Coventry's factories. Worse, at least 568 people were killed, with 863 seriously injured. So desperate was the destruction wrought, in fact, that Nazi Reich Minister

Air Marshal Sholto Douglas, whose main priority when taking over Fighter Command in November 1940 was defeating the German night bombers – whilst looking ahead to an aggressive offensive daylight policy for the New Year.

of Propaganda, Joseph Goebbels, trumpeted the phrase 'Coventration'. The success of the Coventry raid was partially due to the British failure to disrupt the enemy X-Gerät radio navigation beams – and emphasised the ongoing inadequacy of Britain's night defences. At night, the Luftwaffe was able to roam over Britain in comparative safety, the trade-off being that nocturnal bombing was generally less accurate than by day. While Coventry became synonymous with the suffering of British cities that dreadful winter, many others were hit – including London, Southampton, Liverpool, Birmingham and Bristol. By November 1940, the German night offensive was the greatest threat to Britain, so when he took over at Bentley Priory, Air Marshal Douglas knew full-well that defeating the night-bombers was his 'first responsibility' – not day-fighting at that time – and considered this 'a mammoth and worrying task'.

Before the Second World War, the main investment had been on the bomber force, air power doctrine revolving around the concept that 'the bomber will always get through'. What comparatively little spending there had been on fighters rightly prioritised the new Hurricane and Spitfire, both short-range daylight interceptors. The Boulton-Paul Defiant, a two-man turreted fighter, however, proved unsuitable for daylight operations, suffering grievous losses during the Battle of Britain, so during the winter of 1940 this type joined the twin-engine Bristol Blenheim, and purpose-built Bristol Beaufighter, the latter type just starting to reach the squadrons, as a night-fighter. The main problem, though, was that radar only looked out, towards France, and so when an enemy aircraft crossed the British coast and headed inland, it could not be tracked. During daylight, the progress of enemy formations could be seen and reported by the Observer Corps on the ground and pilots in the air – but this did not apply once the cloak of darkness fell. Ultimately, Airborne Interception (AI) radar sets were installed in night-fighters, and deficiencies with ground radar overcome – but all of this took time – and so day-fighters were pressed into the nocturnal role. The idea was that on 'Fighter Nights', Spitfires and Hurricanes would fly at medium altitude, separated by height intervals and entering the target area via a 'gate' in the searchlight beams. The pilots involved hoped for a visual sighting of a German bomber, but these proved rare, and very few were brought down in this way. Indeed, so urgent was the hour that David Denchfield, an RAFVR sergeant-pilot who had joined 610 'County of Chester' Squadron as a replacement pilot towards the Battle of Britain's end, recalled that 'After notching up just an hour's night-flying, we were declared "Night Operational"!'

THE NON-STOP OFFENSIVE

Air Vice-Marshal Johnnie Johnson, a lowly pilot officer in 1941, also recalled these nocturnal sorties:

> We never became proficient in this kind of work, largely because the requirement itself was a basic contradiction of all our training. During the day we fought and lived as a team, and this was the very essence of our squadron and wing formation. When we climbed our Spitfires into the darkness we were oppressed not only by the strange loneliness of our solitary flights but by the thought of our own severe limitations in the task ahead.

Nonetheless, three Hurricane squadrons were pressed into the full-time night-fighter role, while the Beaufighter crews grappled with their mysterious on-board radar sets and learned this new, deadly trade of killing enemy bombers in the dark. The Spitfire, however, with its narrow-track undercarriage, was unsuited to night operations, although hundreds of such 'Fighter Night' sorties were flown. The Spitfire's superiority, with its high-altitude ability, had been recognised during the critical combats of 1940, and the type's future lay not in Britain's murky night skies, chasing phantoms, but in daylight skies.

In December 1940, Air Marshal Douglas had every reason to anticipate a resumption of Germany's mass daylight air attacks when the weather improved the following spring or summer, so although preoccupied with the vexing night battle, Fighter Command's AOC-in-C still had to give consideration to, and provide resources for, day-fighting. At the Battle of Britain's conclusion, Fighter Command's strength was 55½ squadrons; Douglas now informed the Air Ministry that eighty were required to defend Britain. So large a fighter force, however, would have dislocated plans for other Commands, and so a compromise was reached at sixty-four fighter squadrons (by April 1941). By the end of 1940, Fighter Command had 1,243 pilots, increasing to 1,655 by early 1941. Lord Beaverbrook, the press magnate made Minister for Aircraft Production, had energetically organised the supply of fighters, especially the all-important Spitfire at the new Castle Bromwich Aircraft Factory, near Birmingham, which would ultimately produce the majority of the 22,000 built. Operational training units expanded, increasing the flow of pilots, and help continued to arrive from the Empire and Commonwealth, in addition to American volunteers and those squadrons formed from foreign nationals, including French,

'Big Wing' protagonist Air Vice-Marshal Leigh-Mallory (centre) took over 11 Group in December 1940 – and soon had Fighter Command re-organised into wings of three Spitfire squadrons based at each sector station.

Belgians, Czechs and Poles, all continuing the fight. Certainly, the future appeared more optimistic than the previous year – even if still somewhat uncertain and overshadowed by the night Blitz.

In his 1948 despatch on operations at this time, Air Marshal Douglas makes the point that although it was officially decided that the Battle of Britain concluded on 31 October 1940, in reality there was no abrupt cessation of the fighting. On the contrary, in addition to the night attacks, early in November the Germans resumed attacking shipping by day in the Channel and Thames Estuary. These raids lasted a fortnight – but brought another argument to a head: on the one hand the aerial protection requirements of shipping, and on the other, defending aircraft factories. The latter were best defended by fighters deployed forward of the targets, but convoys were a different matter, ideally requiring resource-heavy and tiring, tedious, standing patrols over the sea. Fortunately, the matter naturally dissipated when the enemy conveniently gave up this latest tack. In November 1940, eleven ships had been sunk within RAF fighter range, four in December but only two in January 1941.

From November 1940 onwards, the Germans continued with their daylight fighter and fighter-bomber sweeps, which had been employed during the Battle of Britain's final phase. Because of the lower air temperatures, however, these incursions were made slightly lower down, to avoid highly visible condensation trails, and consequently were slightly less demanding to intercept. These raids ceased in mid-December, resuming on a reduced scale in February 1941. In the meantime, lone Ju 88s continued their Störflug operations, harassing attacks on the British aircraft industry, using cloud cover to safely reach and withdraw from their targets. Although too infrequent to have any particular material effect, these raids did put Fighter Command under pressure to provide local protection for Lord Beaverbrook's factories. Although the main aerial battle was being fought after dark, clearly Fighter Command also remained under pressure to defend Britain in daylight – and the dreadful night attacks were perceived by Air Marshal Douglas and his staff to be 'a softening up ... for an invasion of Britain in the spring of 1941'. Although the crisis of summer 1940 had passed, the spectre of a seaborne invasion, therefore, remained a constant shadow.

Before Air Marshal Douglas left the Air Ministry to take up his new appointment at Fighter Command, however, he met with Air Chief Marshal Charles 'Peter' Portal, the Chief of the Air Staff (CAS), to discuss the future of day fighting. Portal had recently been visited by the service's first CAS, the so-called 'Father of the RAF', Lord 'Boom' Trenchard. Before the Second World War, Trenchard, a confirmed 'Bomber Baron', thought so little of fighters that he considered them 'necessary only to keep up the morale of one's own people'. Now, the former CAS insisted that the fighters' time had come, and, with the Battle of Britain won, it was time for Fighter Command to go over to the offensive and 'lean towards France', advocating sweeps across the Channel similar to tactics used over the Western Front during the First World War. At first, Air Marshal Douglas was not convinced, pointing out that those operations were costly, and that cross-Channel operations were likely to be 'too severe for the results that we would be likely to achieve'. Portal instructed Douglas to produce a report on the matter, which he did, writing 'a very full appreciation with the object of proving that a policy of offensive patrols over northern France was not a good one'. Afterwards, however, Douglas had a rethink, concluding that his 'arguments were pretty feeble', and that they actually supported the prospect that 'an offensive policy for fighters against the German air force in northern France was the right one'. Consequently, Douglas had to inform Portal that he had changed his tune, and was, after all, 'in favour of Trenchard's idea'. Nonetheless, Douglas knew that caution would have to be exercised, and that his fighters

Pilot Officer C.A.W. 'Bogle' Bodie of 66 Squadron, pictured at Kenley during the Battle of Britain – who, with Flight Lieutenant Christie made history on 20 December 1941, when the pair flew the Non-stop Offensive's first 'Mosquito' raid.

must not 'just go belting over there looking for trouble'. On 21 October 1940, the Air Staff then formally directed Fighter Command to prepare for these offensive fighter operations. So it was that soon, Air Marshal Douglas's young pilots would start 'carrying the war to the enemy'.

On 20 December 1940, Flight Lieutenant Christie and Pilot Officer Bodie of 66 Squadron crossed the Channel at low-level and strafed the enemy airfield at either Berck or Le Touquet. This 'Mosquito' raid set the scene, in fact, for the New Year ahead.

On Christmas Day 1940, Air Marshal Douglas held a conference of squadron commanders at Fighter Command HQ, at which the new 'Non-Stop Offensive' was outlined:

> Broadly speaking the plan, which we now adopted, visualised two kinds of offensive operations. In cloudy weather, small numbers of fighters would cross the Channel under cover of the clouds, dart out of them to attack any German aircraft they could find, and return similarly protected. In good weather fighter forces amounting to several squadrons at a time, and sometimes accompanied by bombers, would sweep over northern France. The codenames chosen for these operations were respectively 'Mosquito' (later changed to 'Rhubarb' to avoid confusion with the aircraft of that name) and 'Circus'; but in practice it was necessary to restrict the name 'Circus' to operations with bombers, and fulfilling certain other conditions...
>
> Rhubarb patrols began on 20 December 1940, and provided valuable experience alike for pilots, operational commanders, and the staffs of the formations concerned. I encouraged the delegation of responsibility for the planning of these patrols to lower formations, and many patrols were planned by the pilots themselves with the help of their Squadron Intelligence Officers.

It was obvious from the start that in many cases pilots engaged on these patrols would not meet any German aircraft, and that being so they were authorised to attack ground targets. Air Marshal Douglas, however, emphasised that the primary objective was the destruction of enemy aircraft.

On 27 December 1940, Air Vice-Marshal Keith Park was replaced as AOC-in-C 11 Group, covering London and the south-east, by 'Big Wing' protagonist, Air Vice-Marshal Sir Trafford Leigh-Mallory, formerly AOC 12 Group. Air Marshal Douglas was 'quite happy' about Leigh-Mallory's appointment, but 'knew that his strong personality led him to be somewhat self-opinionated, and while not himself particularly prickly, he did have the habit of raising the hackles of other people. Some found him arrogant and apt to lay down the law on his own assumption that he always knew the right answers.' Previously, Douglas and Leigh-Mallory had served together as majors, commanding squadrons on the Western Front during the First World War, and the previous summer had both been key players in the 'Big Wing Controversy' (see *Bader's Big Wing Controversy: Duxford 1940*), so were well-known to each other. Leigh-Mallory summed up the new offensive outlook: 'We have stopped licking our wounds. We are now going over to the offensive. Last year the fighting was desperate. Now we're entitled to be cocky.'

Operations on a large scale began on 9 January 1941, when five RAF squadrons – sixty fighters – swept uneventfully over France. At the time, Wing Commander David Cox was an RAFVR sergeant-pilot in 19 Squadron, and remembered that:

> When only fighters appeared the Germans were content to stay on the ground and let Fighter Command waste fuel. To provoke the enemy, Blenheim bombers (of 2 Group, Bomber Command) joined the Offensive, and later even four-engine Stirlings. This resulted in quite a sharp reaction from the German fighters.

These operations' component fighter squadrons deployed thus:-

> <u>Close Escort</u>: Surrounding and remaining with the bombers at all times.
>
> <u>Escort Cover</u>: Protecting the Close Escort fighters.
>
> <u>High Cover</u>: Preventing enemy fighters getting between the Close and Escort wings.
>
> <u>Target Support</u>: Independently routed fighters flying directly to and covering the target area.
>
> <u>Withdrawal Cover</u>: Fighters supporting the return flight, by which time escorting fighters would be running short of fuel and ammunition.

> Fighter Diversion: A wing, or even wings, eventually, creating a diversionary sweep to keep hostile aircraft from the target area during 'Ramrod' operations, this being similar to a Circus but involving the destruction of a specific target.

During the Battle of Britain, Group Captain A.B. 'Woody' Woodhall had been Station Commander and Duxford's 'Boss Controller', who wholeheartedly supported the 'Big Wing' concept and was a personal friend of both Air Vice-Marshal Leigh-Mallory and Squadron Leader Douglas Bader. In his memoir, *Soldier, Sailor, Airman Too*, he wrote that these mass fighter formations of 1941 were:

> a formidable force, and some wag christened it the 'Beehive', because the sedate bomber formation, flying in perfect formation and surrounded by a weaving mass of faster Spitfires, looked just like a swarm of bees circling their parent hive – and so 'Beehive' became its code name.

On 10 January 1941, Circus No 1 was despatched against ammunition supplies hidden in the Forêt de Guines. Blenheims of 114 Squadron were closely escorted by the Hurricanes of 56 Squadron, forward support being provided by the North Weald Hurricane squadrons: 242 and 249. 302 Squadron's Hurricanes and 610 Squadron's Spitfires flew target support; the Spitfires of 41, 64 and 611 Squadrons were high cover, and finally 74 and 92 Squadrons' Spitfires brought up the rear. This represented some 120 fighters and six bombers, and was a complete reversal of the defensive role previously undertaken by Fighter Command – and one for which Hurricanes and Spitfires, intended as short-range interceptors, were not designed or intended. It was Fighter Command's pilots who now faced a two-way Channel crossing on a single engine with limited fuel, and combat either over the sea or enemy-occupied territory. On this initial operation, I and II/JG 53 responded and engaged the RAF fighters: one Hurricane and a Spitfire were destroyed for no German loss – rather setting the scene for the 'season' ahead. On that day, Squadron Leader Bob Beardsley was also an RAFVR sergeant-pilot, flying with 41 Squadron:

> I was flying with another experienced sergeant pilot as 'Arse-end Charlie'. We were in the coastal area, heading outbound, when I saw six Me 109s in my rear-view mirror. Before I could

Sergeant Bob Beardsley, of 41 Squadron, who was shot-up on Circus No 1, 10 January 1941.

give a warning, I received the 'full dose' from their leader. This attack damaged my aileron control and my radio would not transmit. However, by chance the E/As did not follow me down as I dived frantically to catch up with the squadron. My other 'rear-guard' had not seen anything happen to me, and as I was unable to contact the squadron I tagged on behind, at the same time discovering that I had neither guns nor flaps. Obviously, the pneumatic system had been damaged. I let the squadron land at Hornchurch and flew a large circuit; with no ailerons it must have been clear that I was in trouble! Thank heavens that the engine was undamaged. I blew down the undercarriage, using the emergency bottle and landed safely on flat tyres! I was met by the fire engine and driven back to dispersal to be greeted by the Flight Commander with 'Where the hell have you been, and where is your aircraft?', most definitely not the 'How are you, old chap?' that I thought the situation merited! When he finally realised the situation and condition of the aircraft (Category 3, written-off) he was somewhat mollified! I was rather hacked off as it was *my* aircraft!

THE NON-STOP OFFENSIVE

A 2 Group Blenheim – the mainstay bomber type used in the Non-stop Offensive of 1941.

Fighter Command lost two aircraft on Circus No 1, whereas not a single Me 109 was destroyed. One of the RAF pilots baled out and was picked up from the cold sea by an Air Sea Rescue (ASR) launch. He was lucky. At this time, ASR remained in its infancy, and yet the RAF aircrews now faced two sea-crossings per sortie. Flight Lieutenant Ron Rayner was yet another RAFVR sergeant-pilot in 1941, serving with Bob Beardsley on 41 Squadron:

> Crossing the water with one engine was always a concern, and of course we monitored our fuel gauges very carefully. It was noisy, flying a Spitfire, but with the flying helmet strapped tight the ears were almost sealed by the ear pieces' rubber rings, which helped. Anyway, once a combat started the R/T chattered away constantly, until we touched down and switched off. These early Spitfires had no cockpit heating, so we had to take steps to protect against the cold. My mother knitted me some woollen stockings which I used to pull up over my legs at high altitude. Flying a Spitfire was also a very physical business, especially when in formation, which required constant jiggling about of the control column. Regarding range, this depended on the use of throttle, and of course combat used up more petrol. When

attacked, you would automatically go into a step climbing turn, pushing the throttle forward for maximum boost as you did so. After an operational flight I suppose we were tired, but we were fit and just glad not to be in the infantry!

Circus No 2 went ahead on 2 February 1941, with Blenheims of 139 Squadron targeting Boulogne docks. The Intelligence Report from the Biggin Hill Squadrons relates events:

> Twelve Spitfires of 66 Squadron and twelve Spitfires of 74 Squadron took off from Biggin Hill at 1325 hrs to meet 92 Squadron over West Malling at 10,000ft before sweeping from Dungeness to Boulogne.
>
> 66 Squadron, after making the indicated rendezvous ran into the cloud at 15,000ft in mid-Channel and Blue Section became detached. They made three sweeps from Boulogne to Cap Gris-Nez and back, then patrolled Calais-Dunkirk and back at 19,000ft but saw no E/A. Flak seen in Calais area and light flak bursting at 6–10,000ft was seen. No balloons were seen. 66 Squadron landed at Biggin Hill by 1450 hrs.
>
> 74 Squadron swept Boulogne at 19,000ft and sighted six Me 109s in that area, slightly beneath them flying north-east. Squadron Leader Malan dived to attack 4 Me 109s which he sighted at 12,000ft flying north, opening fire from astern and above at 300 yards, closing to 200 yards, he delivered two 4-second bursts. The E/A had dived and Squadron Leader Malan broke away at 4,000ft, watching the Me 109 dive into the sea just outside Boulogne Harbour. His engine developed a glycol leak, but he nursed it back to Hawkinge, landing at 1430 hrs.
>
> Meanwhile, Sergeant Payne, Red 1, made a quarter attack on one E/A with a 3 second burst from 600 yards, resulting in the E/A diving steeply emitting blue smoke from the engine. Red 1 dived after him, giving a further 6 second burst, and closing to 50 yards he saw some bullets striking the water and then pulled out to avoid hitting the sea. P/O Chesters confirms that this E/A crashed into the sea in flames about five miles NW Boulogne. P/O Smith turned after an Me 109 which had passed under Red Section, going north, whereupon the enemy

aircraft turned steeply to starboard. P/O Smith was inside his turn and opened fire at about 200 yards, continuing to fire until he had closed right up. He last saw the Me 109 at a height of 1,000ft, diving steeply towards the sea. P/O Spurdle, Yellow 3, reports that he saw a large splash and a cloud of brownish smoke in the area in approximately this position, so a probably destroyed casualty is claimed by P/O Smith.

Squadron Leader E.J.C. Michelmore, attached to 74 Squadron as supernumerary and flying No 2 to the CO, the legendary Squadron Leader A.G. 'Sailor' Malan, was missing.

Circus No 3 was flown three days later, a raid on the notorious enemy airfield at St Omer. 610, 65 and 302 Squadrons from Tangmere flew top cover, the former reporting Me 109s stalking the 'Beehive' after the target had been successfully bombed. Between St Omer and the French coast, the Me 109Es of I/JG 3 pounced on 610 Squadron. It was a day that Sergeant David Denchfield would never forget:

> I was on readiness on the morning of 5 February 1941, and mid-morning the CO popped his head into 'B' Flight to say 'Released from 1300 to 0900 hrs tomorrow morning.' As we all gave vent to various sounds of appreciation, he then smiled and said, 'That's after we get back from St Omer, take-off 1200.' Then followed a fairly basic briefing. We would follow 302 Squadron to Rye, climb up through the 10/10ths cloud to about 15,000ft and join up with seven other fighter squadrons, where we would be top but one (having Tangmere's 65 Squadron above us). The whole shooting match would then escort twelve Blenheims to St Omer, where they would cause great alarm and despondency with their 250lb bombs. 610 would fly in a vic of three vics, each of three aircraft with Green Section slipping into the boxes.
>
> We went for lunch at 1139 hrs and after this I walked out to my Spitfire, 'DW-P', and asked my rigger to top the tanks up after he'd completed his pre-op engine run. He knew full well why I'd asked: as 'weaver' I would use an awful lot of fuel, and we only had about 1¾ hours of endurance at best. After checking 'P' it was back to dispersal to empty our pockets, for security reasons, and hear any last-minute instructions.

Incidentally, some three weeks previously we all had to hand in our working tunics, and when returned each had an escape silk map sewn into a shoulder, and a compass needle threaded on a cotton sewn into one of the front seams. Naturally we had to search for them, and look at them. Consequently our sewing was hardly as neatly done and I do remember thinking that only an idiot would think there was nothing wrong with one of my shoulders: it was lumpy!

While we were waiting, strapped into our aircraft for the CO to signal the start-up, one of the 'Erks' [groundcrew] came up to push two letters into my hand, and without thinking I rammed them in my tunic pocket. These were to cause me some concern later that day until I was able to flush them in pieces down the loo. One each from Paddy and Fred, giving their unit and address! The CO's Merlin coughed into life, and almost immediately the other eleven engines were adding their share to the noise and slipstream wind. Then, section-by-section, we all lurched over to near 'A' Flight's dispersal, formed up in our vics of three vics with the fourth vic of Green Section out to port of Blue, on the port side, and took off towards Chichester Cathedral to the south-west.

As we flew out the CO ordered Green Section to go into the box – Green 1 and 2 were now rear of Red and Yellow Sections respectively. It wasn't the most comfortable of formations as we were following 302, who had taken off just before us, were about a mile behind and at a pedestrian 160 mph, rather than our normal 180 mph, so everything felt most sloppy. The CO told us to keep close and climb to 15,000ft, so into and up through the murk we went; the cloud base was at about 1,500ft and it was solid up to around 12,000. I suppose twelve props must have churned it up well for I could see all Blue Section quite easily, and caught glimpses of Red 3 beyond. Quick glances at my instrument panel showed a nice easy climb, so I relaxed, hoping Red 1 would not become disorientated!

We broke into brilliant sunshine and climbed to our Angels 15 (15,000ft), by which time we were orbiting Rye and waiting for the off. The strange thing was I could see no aircraft above us, and weirdly the cloud over England ended at the coast in an almost vertical cliff edge, leaving the skies over the Channel and France completely cloudless. The Channel to the east looked ridiculously narrow, and the skies over the snow-clad French landscape were broodingly ominous. As usual, the sun glare blinding out of the clear blue made looking to the southeast difficult. God only knew what nasties were moving into its hidey-hole, and as we circled Rye for a good five minutes at least we certainly gave them plenty of time get ready for us. I guess, like me, that the others had their gun-sights switched 'on', their gun firing buttons turned to 'fire' and their hoods slid back for better visibility. And I bet they were sweating cobs too.

Eventually, as we seemed to fly more or less in an easterly direction, the CO gave 'Elfin aircraft – search formation – weavers – go!' and so I, like Pilot Officer Fenwick behind Yellow Section moved to be about 100ft above Blue Section and just behind, and commenced swinging backwards and forwards across them in a series of elongated 'S' turns as we made towards Boulogne. I still couldn't see 65 Squadron above us, although they could have been outside my arc of vision. However, from what Pilot Officer Hill later told me, only his Section turned up intact after climbing up through the cloud, and was the only 65 formation to sit where they should have been.

Weaving was quite energetic. The extent of my 'beat' was from just to port of Blue 3 across to almost behind Red 3 – as we were in search formation with aircraft about four spans apart this would be about 100 yards, or a fraction more. Starting from the left-hand side I would fly angled across to the right-hand side, searching up and down to the rear as I did so. At the right-hand side there would be a quick glance down to check I was still positioned safely above Green Section (approaching this point I would have already made sure I and Green 2 were not on a collision course), and then a steep left-hand turn to get me on the outward trip when once again I would be searching to the rear. Then a steep right-hand turn started the cycle all over again … and so on, and so on. In retrospect there wasn't much time for searching, due to the need to be continually steep turning and checking position. I have since felt it would have been better to have had one aircraft weaving above and the other below, for then the beat would have been over some 250 yards giving a far longer search time. The weavers were known as 'Arse-end Charlies', sometimes more politely 'Tail-end Charlies'. At the end we most certainly were, and must have been right 'Charlies' to get stuck with the job! Of course the other ten aircraft had a far quieter time, flying straight and level and looking only inwards so they could keep position with the Section Leader and watch for trouble at the same time.

Just after crossing the French coast I reported some contrails up to port and slightly to our rear, but they extinguished almost immediately, so whatever it was had moved either above or below the contrail level. I had no idea where we were – there was no time to look at the map which was left folded in my left boot – but we must have been near the target (the airfield of St Omer), when I caught a flash way up behind as I was about to start the steep turn back towards the centre once more. I held off the turn to have a good check, and then turned back, only to see the squadron a good 800 yards or so away in front, as my extended run had taken us apart. As speed in regaining position seemed to be vital (it was not clever to be on one's own in enemy skies), I did a quick left and right steep turn, during which I had a good 'shufti' behind, and then 'slung the coal on' and went fast, to get back with the rest.

I was about halfway back and about to have another look behind, when there was a sudden staccato vibration and sparks seemed to erupt out of my port wingtip. My 'Bloody hell!' and steep left-hand turn only just beat a violent clang from up front, at which the rudder pedals suddenly lost all feel and became seemingly disconnected from the rudder. As the nose fell away the cockpit filled with a white mist accompanied by the foul smell of glycol and 100-octane fuel. I let the nose go on down, hoping whatever it was couldn't follow and that the mist would clear before it became a problem (I remembered the unseen white-hot debris from the exhausts, and in the context of the fuel smell didn't have a lot of confidence in the immediate future).

The mist rapidly went however, and I was able to ease out of the steep diving turn to edge slightly west of north while weaving like mad one way and the other to clear my tail, and

THE NON-STOP OFFENSIVE

able now to check damage. The port wingtip was mangled, the rudder just a useless uncontrollable flap, the radiator and oil temperatures were perhaps a little too high, and the elevator perhaps a bit less than precise. However, she was still flying and I was at about 9,000ft, having lost the rest in the diving turn, and thinking it might be an uncomfortable ride home.

Over the next few minutes the radiator and oil temps showed a gradual but steady rise, and I found the cause of the petrol smell: nearly twenty gallons of fuel were sloshing about in the belly of the fuselage under my feet. I now knew why my lower legs were so cold – on the ground I later found the insides of my flying boot and my trouser legs were absolutely saturated with the damn stuff. On checking the fuel gauge, the top tank was empty so that had clearly been hit as had the glycol tank or piping.

By now I was having to accept a gradual height loss in order to maintain the 290 mph desirable as the Merlin seemed not to be giving its best, and another cause of disquiet was the ever-increasing amount of tail heavy trim having to be wound on to stop the nose from dropping. Looking in my rear-view mirror I thought I could see strips of fabric trailing from the elevators – the view was not all that clear, but if it was so could have accounted for the effect on the aircraft.

Some six minutes after being hit we were down to maybe 6,000ft with the radiator temp almost in the red. I could see the Channel, and had seen the Blenheims pass about 1,000ft above me, clearly on their way home and going like the Devil. My thought was that my Spitfire would never reach the Channel and I wasn't about to try to put her down – not with all that petrol washing around – so like a good Boy Scout I prepared by disconnecting my helmet leads and ramming them securely into my parachute harness straps, and then released my Sutton harness so I was unattached to the aircraft. There seemed little point in doing anything else as I'd run out of scope in playing with pitch control and throttle, and when all throttle movement had been used she was clearly going to go in only one direction, even if the overheating didn't do it first, which was …. down!

I decided to stand on the seat and then kick the stick forward to throw me out, but my planning came to naught. A most expensive sounding noise came from up front, accompanied by darkish smoke and jets of flame, and as I started to stand, letting go of the stick, dear old 'P' helped me to the last. She threw her nose violently down and I shot up and out like the cork from a bottle! And then there was only a flickering jumble of sky and snow as I obviously somersaulted, until I yanked the ripcord. What a relief to be right way up, and even greater to look up and check the beautiful white canopy fully open. My right boot had disappeared as I was launched from the aircraft, so the landing itself – on one foot to save my unbooted one was a bit of a thud, but there I was in the middle of a snow-covered, iron-hard, stubble field!

The only cover in sight was a clump of bushes maybe 100 yards away and up a slight slope. They were not leafed and even a mouse would have laughed at them, but I couldn't be a chooser so I dragged myself and 'chute up there, where there was snow about eighteen inches deep, into which I pushed the 'chute and the mike etc from my helmet. I then attempted to 'shoe' my right foot by tying the oxygen tube in such a fashion as to hold the helmet around my foot; this worked reasonably well.

I was now aware I hadn't had a pee since early in the morning, and was thus engaged, crouched behind these silly little bushes, when two uniforms walked through a field entrance some 250 yards away. I finished my pee lying down! It was to no avail – they walked straight up to me, and as I stood up the one with the gun said 'For you the war is over' (and I thought they only said that in things like the *Hotspur* and *Magnet* comics – we live and learn!). It was all very friendly and we walked as a small group down to the opening they'd come through, meeting on the way a French boy of about 8 years old who asked my age. Although I understood him perfectly my answer of '21' was given using all eight fingers and two thumbs twice and a bit!

We got into the Ford V8 they'd arrived in, and drove, perhaps, 400 yards to where the remains of poor 'P' were smoking. She had impacted on the side of the road, which was sunken slightly below the field level, and all that could be seen was a rather buckled tail assembly sitting on top of a mass of jumbled scrap metal in what was clearly a damn great hole. I could see nothing identifiable in this mess – no sign of seat, panel, oxygen bottles, no nothing, and I guessed it was my good fortune not to be with it all umpteen feet down. Broken chunks of main plane lay at the side together with the broken remains of eight Browning .303 machine guns, barrels snapped, and eight ammo boxes with sides peeled back to show the indentations of the cartridge rims on the inside surfaces, looking almost like a machined finish. Ammunition lay everywhere. Loose wreckage lay all over the road and elsewhere – I picked up the tail wheel from 200 yards away, inside an adjacent field!

She (Spitfire N3249) was manufactured by Vickers Supermarine at Woolston near Southampton in December 1939, being in one of the earliest batches made. She had flown with 92 and 602 squadrons, and with 92 had scored over France during the Dunkirk evacuation in the hands of Bob Stanford-Tuck. She had the original type of undercarriage retraction via a lever in a box on the right-hand side to select 'up' or 'down', and out of the same box a lever with which to pump up the hydraulic pressure to effect the required change. As pumping with the right hand caused the left hand (on the stick) to make sympathetic pumping actions also, one could always tell the new boys as they climbed away from take-off in a series of steps. We had all done it. The more recent aircraft had instead a single lever only, with the hydraulics supplied from an engine-driven pump.

Leaving 'P' to her lonely roadside grave (until 1991 when we found and recovered her) we drove to the airfield at St Omer, barely ten minutes away, and I was decamped outside what looked like a haystack but which was in fact a building. The adjacent hut disgorged a load of about twelve Luftwaffe pilots, who, one by one, came to attention in front of me and then saluted. Of course I had to reciprocate. At that time there was a fair degree of mutual respect between us, mirroring that of the First World War. Anyway, I was treated with extreme courtesy and had my own personal guide appointed – an English-speaking German pilot recovering from a perforated eardrum. In the crew room I was introduced to the pilot who shot me down, Major Oeseau, who became one of the top-scoring pilots before losing his life in 1944. We spoke for a couple of minutes with my escort as interpreter, and then I signed his cigarette case in pencil for him to have engraved over. There were six other English names there from, I should think, the battle in France in 1940. After I'd turned out my pockets, ignoring the two letters mentioned earlier, I was taken on a tour of their part of St Omer airfield. We went to a clothing store where he gave me a brand-new German flying boot for my right foot. He wouldn't make it the pair, so from then until we marched out of Fallingbostel in 1945 I wore odd flying boots!

Returning to the crew room, I met Pilot Officer Hill, who had been in the sole 65 Squadron Section to get into place (as he told me). Later, when we were on our own, he said the 109s went through their Section as if they weren't there, and then doubtless down on to us! He had some cannon shell splinters in his back and was somewhat sore. He didn't know what had happened to the other three, but was not too hopeful. He later became a top antique dealer in London, and in 2008 the business was sold for millions!

We spent the rest of the afternoon in what was a reasonably comfortable lounge, interrupted at times by 'Goons' (Germans) who were claiming ever increasing numbers of RAF aircraft shot down. I think they finally racked it up to nineteen, but wouldn't say where the other PoWs were – it seemed inconceivable to us that if that number were down we were the only ones alive. I believe our people admitted five, which sounds in the right order. Then they transferred us to the pilots' quarters in a large, old country house about 10 minutes' drive away. This was the Abbe Notre Dame at Wisques. Next day it was off to Germany and Poland for a four-year journey around the PoW camps…

On this day, III/JG 3 had scrambled from St Omer in time to climb above the escorting Spitfires, diving upon the RAF fighters, destroying three Hurricanes and three Spitfires, while II/JG 26 from Abbeville shot down another Spitfire. Unfortunately for David Denchfield, now a prisoner, he would go down in history as one of the Non-Stop Offensive's first casualties.

THE NON-STOP OFFENSIVE

Above: Luftwaffe personnel examining the crash site of Sergeant David Denchfield's 610 Squadron Spitfire, N3249, DW-P, shot down near St Omer on Circus No 3, 5 February 1941.

Right: Sergeant Denchfield had been shot down by Oberleutenant Walter Oesau, and was amongst the first RAF casualties of the Non-stop Offensive, spending the remainder of the war as a prisoner.

Although 65 Squadron's Flying Officer 'Paddy' Finucane and 611 Squadron's Pilot Officer Barrie Heath both claimed Me 109s destroyed, the Germans actually suffered no loss. This is worth examining in more detail, because overclaiming became a constant theme of these operations.

From 13 August 1940 onwards, Fighter Command's process for accrediting claims concerned three categories:

> Category 1: 'Destroyed' – all cases when an enemy aircraft was unquestionably destroyed, having exploded or seen to crash, for example, or forced-down and captured.
>
> Category 2: 'Probably Destroyed' – when a combat had to be broken off and the target not seen to crash but known to be so damaged as to make survival unlikely.
>
> Category 3: 'Damaged' – when an enemy aircraft was clearly seen to be damaged but not destroyed.

The speeds achieved by the still comparatively new monoplane fighters meant that by its very nature air fighting was often a confusing business, however, especially when many aircraft were engaged, it being so easy for the speed of combat to deceive the human eye. Moreover, several pilots could attack an enemy aircraft simultaneously but independently, unaware that they alone were not solely responsible for the target's fate – meaning that same enemy machine could be claimed and credited multiple times. During the Battle of Britain, RAF Intelligence Officers were sometimes able to visit the crash sites of enemy aircraft destroyed, assisting with the verification process, but this was impossible with these combats now being fought over enemy occupied France. Indeed, these engagements were often fought at medium to high altitude, above cloud. Because the Me 109 enjoyed the benefit of a fuel-injected engine, which was unaffected by gravity and did not cut-out in a dive, the German pilots did two things to capitalise on their fighters' technical advantage. Firstly, they strove to enjoy the height advantage, only attacking when tactical conditions were favourable, as Wing Commander David Cox recalled:

> The 109s used to sit right up there, then suddenly dive through our formations, very fast, firing as they went, then gone. Because we could turn tighter than the 109 the German pilots

THE NON-STOP OFFENSIVE

didn't want to engage in dogfights, as it were, so instead used this very effective method – which I dubbed the 'Dirty Dart'.

Secondly, when attacked, the Me 109 pilot's standard evasive manoeuvre was to dive, very fast, ramming the throttle forward. Because the Spitfire and Hurricane's Merlin engine had a gravity-fed carburettor, they would momentarily cut-out in a steep dive, allowing the 109 to gain ground. As the enemy pilot rammed his throttle forward, black smoke was emitted from his engine's exhausts – leading the pursuing RAF pilot to believe that he had fatally hit his target, which was now diving vertically, at high speed and apparently on fire. All too often, however, the 109 would disappear into the cloud layer far below, pull up and rejoin the fray – while the RAF pilot believed that, on balance, his target had crashed.

Sergeant Bob Morton, of whom more later, flew Spitfires in action over France that year and commented that:

> Although we maintained strict radio silence on the way across, the enemy fighters generally got wind of our approach and were waiting near their ceiling by the time we crossed the coast. This meant that they could gain speed far in excess of ours in a long dive, come up rapidly behind us, get in one long burst and break away. To avoid this, one Spitfire pilot in each section had to fly with his chin on his shoulder, watching his tail. This naturally did not make for good formation flying; the four aircraft sections quickly split up into pairs when the action began, but almost every pilot found himself unaccompanied after a

Sergeant Bob Morton of 616 Squadron: 'My mother asked me to have a photograph taken for her, so I did!'

time. At that point the Me 109s which had split up the Spitfire formation would begin climbing to engage loners. In the subsequent scraps we were disadvantaged in several ways, in the matter of claims, for example. To claim an enemy aircraft destroyed, one had to have seen one of three events:-

1. The aircraft concerned striking the ground or sea.
2. The pilot baling out.
3. The aircraft bursting into flames.

The first was almost impossible; most of our fighting was carried out above 10,000ft and no one would be fool enough to keep his eyes on an aircraft he had shot at, or follow it down. The second took time to occur, and other aircraft were likely to be shooting at the attacker as the Germans always worked in pairs. As for the third, although in the 1969 film *Battle of Britain* every German aircraft fired at immediately burst into flames and exploded after a few seconds, I never saw either of those events take place.

By mid-February 1941, these offensive operations had cost Fighter Command at least twenty-five aircraft destroyed, eighteen pilots killed, three wounded and five captured. That month, RAF fighter pilots, in response, had claimed 15½ enemy aircraft destroyed, three probables and fourteen damaged – although actual German losses were substantially less. Nonetheless, it was obvious that things were not going as well as had been hoped, leading Air Marshal Douglas to admit that while 'our idea was to fly over the other side and leap on the enemy from a great height in superior numbers, instead … it looks as though we ourselves are being leapt on'. Unfortunately, this too would become a constant theme of the Non-stop Offensive – which was not simply a strategic undertaking: it was also political.

Although supported by her Empire and Commonwealth, Britain was desperate for America to enter the war against the Axis powers – but this was long before both the more recent 'Grand Alliance' and 'Special Relationship'. Indeed, in addition to the American War of Independence (1776 – 1783), Britain and America had gone to war against each other once more in 1812, and nearly did so in 1861, during the American Civil War. Between then and the First World War, the two countries had largely ignored each other. Insofar as many Americans were concerned, Britain, their former colonial master, was their natural enemy, had been since 1776, and although ultimately allies in the First World War, this ill-feeling continued. Most Americans wanted no part in the Second World War, because the fighting in Europe was no threat to America's national security. Hundreds of 'isolationist' groups pressured Washington to remain neutral, isolationism from events in Europe having become a popular American foreign policy between the wars. From 1935 onwards, this attitude was cemented by the Neutrality Acts, a series of laws preventing America becoming embroiled in another European war or supplying arms to belligerent nations. By the summer of 1940, Joseph P. Kennedy, the American Ambassador in London, certainly believed this to be a wise move, as from what he could see, Britain was in the process of losing a war it could not win. The American President, Franklin D. Roosevelt, however, was sympathetic to Britain's plight, but public opinion was overwhelmingly supportive of continued Isolationism. The President's 'Destroyers for bases' deal on 2 September 1940, which provided Britain fifty destroyers in return for bases in British territory, angered the American public and actually violated the Neutrality Acts. It was a very sensitive situation, but Churchill was desperate for American aid. By January 1941, determined to help Britain, Roosevelt had initiated 'Lend-lease', a programme under which America could legitimately provide Britain and her allies with food, oil and materiel, in return for leases on bases in Allied territories. For Britain, this aid was absolutely essential. On the wider stage, British cities were being hammered by German bombers, British forces were fighting in North Africa, Malta was besieged in the Mediterranean, and the German U-boat campaign was becoming increasingly successful. Although, thanks to 'the Few', Britain had held out in 1940, and remained in the war, there was little good news to persuade Americans to abandon Isolationism and fight with Britain against Germany. Nonetheless, it was crucial that Britain projected an optimistic image and outlook – and in that respect, in spite of losses, the Non-stop Offensive, reaching out and taking the war across the Channel to France, was essential. This was another, indirect, reason that the policy had to be vigorously pursued.

Certainly, there was no lack of enthusiasm among Fighter Command's squadrons for the coming 'season'. The change in command and winter period also provided an opportunity for a reorganisation, as rested squadrons relieved tired units and returned to the front line. Flying from Kenley in 11 Group, during just one week in August 1940, 616 'South Yorkshire' Squadron had lost seven Spitfires with four pilots killed; withdrawn to rest and refit in 12 Group, having received replacements the unit had contributed to some 'Big Wing' operations towards the Battle of Britain's end, before hunkering down for the winter at Kirton-in-Lindsey, Lincolnshire, training new pilots, intercepting 'X-Raids' and flying the endless round of convoy protection patrols over the North Sea. By February 1941, Squadron Leader H.F. 'Billy' Burton and his pilots were keen to return to the fray down south. Johnnie Johnson was a pilot officer at the time and wrote that:

> Late one February evening, Billy Burton walked into the dispersal hut with welcome news: we were to fly south in a few days and if all went well remain in 11 Group for the spring and summer. We gathered round and plied him with questions. Where was our new home? Biggin, Kenley, North Weald, Hornchurch or Northolt? But he shook his head at all these

The Three Musketeers: from left, Pilot Officers 'Nip' Hepple, Roy Marples and Johnnie Johnson of 616 Squadron at Kirton in January 1941.

THE NON-STOP OFFENSIVE

Right: Squadron Leader HF 'Billy' Burton, a Cranwell Sword of Honour recipient and the exceptional commander of 616 Squadron.

Below: Flight Lieutenant Ken Holden, a tough Yorkshireman and commander of 616 Squadron's 'A' Flight.

Burton's job after the Battle of Britain was to re-build 616 Squadron at Kirton in preparation for a return to the front line; those identified are, rear row, second left: Sergeant Bob Morton; fifth left: Flight Lieutenant Ken Holden; sixth: Pilot Officer 'Nip' Hepple; seventh: Squadron Leader Billy Burton; eight: Flight Lieutenant Colin MacFie; nine: Sergeant Sid Mabbett; ten: Sergeant Jerrold Le Cheminent; extreme right, Pilot Officer Pietrascovich; front row: from extreme left: Sergeants Sellars, Brewster, n/k, (with dog): Flying Officer 'Buck' Casson, Sergeant McCairns, Pilot Officer Proctor and Sergeant Jenks.

guesses. Then someone said 'Tangmere?', and the CO laughed and nodded, and a ripple of excitement ran through our small company.

We all knew Tangmere. A pleasant sunny airfield crouching at the foot of the South Downs, only separated from the coast by a small span of flat Sussex land. It was one of Fighter Command's established airfields and for many years a home for fighter squadrons. In our world Tangmere was already a tradition, for its squadrons had gained great distinction during the fighting of the previous year, when they had routed many an enemy raid. Now we would strive to add to that tradition and at the same time gain a reputation for our squadron. These were our thoughts on that bleak February evening in Lincolnshire. But they were unspoken.

THE NON-STOP OFFENSIVE

'I'll take the squadron down to Tangmere next Wednesday,' said the CO. 'We're relieving 65 Squadron, who will bring our Spit Is back here. We'll take over their Spit IIs at Tangmere. We'll have better aircraft and be right in the front line. If the Huns come across again like they did last year, we'll have our work cut out. If not, then the form is that we'll carry our offensive to France. So, there'll be plenty of excitement.'

In November 1940, Alan Baldwin had been posted to Tangmere, that most famous of fighter stations:

I would never have contemplated service life as a career, but when it became obvious that war was likely I joined the RAFVR, a decision I never regretted.

'You'll see plenty of action at Tangmere,' said the RAF sergeant as he examined our travel warrants at Victoria Station, adding as an afterthought, 'That is if you survive.' I was one of a party of eight Aircraftman 2nd Class, all medical orderlies posted to the Station Sick Quarters after a six-week course at a Medical Training Depot attached to a hospital in Cambridgeshire.

We arrived to find the Sick Bay, like many of the other buildings, completely destroyed. Following the bombing, many of the Station's operations had been dispersed and most personnel were accommodated off the Station. Sick Quarters were at Westfield House, Fontwell, and it was there that we spent our first night. The next morning we were returned to Tangmere, where I was to remain for three years.

With the Sick Bay destroyed, the decontamination building had become the centre of operations for the medical branch, and it was there I was sent. An ambulance had just pulled up outside the entrance

Alan Baldwin, of Tangmere's Station Sick Quarters.

and an airman, with medical lapel badges on his collar, jumped down from the front. He called to an orderly and together they took a stretcher from the ambulance. I went to help, and saw that the casualty was a pilot with a broken neck. 'You'll get used to it', one of them said. So began those three eventful years.

Except for those who remained at the Station on night duty, we cycled back to Fontwell each evening. An ambulance and driver were on duty there all night, so that we could immediately be rushed to Tangmere in an emergency. Westfield House was a double-fronted house standing in its own grounds, overlooking Fontwell racecourse. The garden was still being looked after by an elderly gentleman. It seemed an oasis of calm in the midst of ongoing turmoil.

The house had been converted to Sick Quarters and an extension forming a large ward was added. One of the ground-floor rooms, at the front of the house, was a ward for officers, the other was the Station Dental Surgery. The kitchen was used to prepare meals for patients and the medical and nursing orderlies. The staff – NCOs, airmen and WAAFs – all ate together in an adjoining room. The remainder of the downstairs rooms were used as sleeping quarters. On the first floor was an office and other rooms were used as wards. This provided a pleasant and relaxed atmosphere after a day on the camp, and was within easy reach of Chichester, Arundel and Bognor. There were several country pubs within cycling distance and there was always plenty of male and female company.

I was not married at the time and, although surrounded by airfields, my parents lived in the comparative safety of rural Norfolk, so I had no domestic worries or problems, as many serving men had. I can look back on those days as a very interesting experience, and one I would not have missed.

On 26 February 1941, Squadron Leader Billy Burton's 616 Squadron arrived at Tangmere and relieved 65 Squadron. At the time, a tour of duty was considered to be a maximum of 200 hours operational flying, although it was accepted by the Air Ministry than 100 hours in some busy sectors was the equivalent of 200 in a quieter area – and Tangmere was busy. Interestingly, the RAF statisticians predicted that a day-fighter pilot had a 27 per cent chance of surviving a first tour, but only 7 per cent of safely completing a second; 20 per cent of casualties, it was reckoned, became PoWs. These figures, however, were far from the minds of Billy Burton and his pilots upon excitedly arriving at Tangmere, as Johnnie remembered:

> Our first day at Tangmere was spent in a visit to the operations room, meeting the controllers and staff... the senior intelligence officer, who gave us a long talk on the Luftwaffe's order of battle, escape and evasion techniques and an appraisal of the new Me 109F. This latest model was similar to the E version but had rounded wingtips and was overall more curvaceous than the angular *Emil*. The F also lacked tail struts, and so actually looked similar to a Spitfire. The F also had improved armament, a higher ceiling of 36,500ft, and top speed of 396 mph at 22,000ft. This, it seemed, was to be our main adversary.

616 Squadron now enjoyed the benefits of the latest Spitfire, the Mk IIA, as Johnnie explained:

> The chief difference between the Spitfire II and the I was installation of the Rolls-Royce Merlin XII engine in the former, providing extra power and benefiting from the automatic Coffman cartridge starter... Either De Havilland or Rotol constant-speed airscrews were fitted to our new Spitfires, which gave a marked improvement in climb and ceiling.

A Spitfire Mk IIA of 65 Squadron at Tangmere in February 1941 – these aircraft were taken over by 616 Squadron, which swapped its obsolete Mk IAs with 65 Squadron, which it relieved on 26 February 1941.

The Spitfire Mk IIA remained armed with eight .303 Browning machine-guns, whereas the Me 109F enjoyed the benefits of both machine-guns and cannon. The fighting of 1940 had quickly highlighted the Me 109's advantage in having such dual armament, whereas the Spitfire Mk I lacked cannon. 20mm Hispano-Suiza cannons were mounted in a small number of Mk Is, designated Mk IBs, and allocated to 19 Squadron at Duxford. Because of the Spitfire's thin wing section, however, the cannon had to be side-mounted, leading to innumerable stoppages, as the wing flexed in combat and feed mechanisms jammed. This put pilots at great risk, because these aircraft had no back-up machine-guns. Ultimately the pilots lost confidence in these aircraft, which were replaced by standard machine-gun Spitfires. The matter had since been resolved through the fitting of aerodynamic blisters to the upper and lower wing surfaces, enabling correct mounting of the cannon and accommodating the intended ammunition drum. This was progress, but each of the two cannons weighed 96lbs, and their ammunition more than trays of rifle-calibre machine-gun bullets, and yet these machines, designated Mk IIB, were powered by the same Merlin XII that powered the lighter IIA. Consequently, the IIB, which, unlike the IB, did also have four machine guns, was slightly under-powered, another matter requiring redress. Going forward, 616 Squadron would find itself operating both IIAs and Bs.

There were also broader changes. The Spitfire's versatility and superior performance led to it being recognised as the RAF's primary day fighter. From early 1941, front-line units became increasingly Spitfire-equipped, until the Hurricane had been completely replaced in the day fighter role. Air Marshal Douglas had also restructured Fighter Command so that each sector station accommodated a wing comprising three Spitfire squadrons. It was also decided to create a new post, that of 'Wing Commander (Flying)', whose sole responsibility was to lead his wing in the air, unfettered by ground-based issues. As Johnnie Johnson later recalled, this was 'every fighter pilot's dream job'. As early as 7 December 1940, while still AOC 12 Group, Air Vice-Marshal Leigh-Mallory had drawn up a provisional list of the first 'wing leaders' to be appointed. It will come as no surprise to the reader that top of that list was Douglas Bader, at that time still commanding 242 Squadron and previously leader of the 'Big Wing'. A firm Leigh-Mallory favourite, Bader was even given the choice of which wing he wanted: he chose Tangmere, on the basis that it was far enough from London for the capital's social delights not to distract his pilots. Back then, Air Marshal Sir Denis Crowley-Milling was a young pilot officer who had served in 242 Squadron under Bader's leadership throughout the Battle of Britain; he remembered that when 'DB' was promoted and posted to Tangmere, 'We were all very disappointed to see him go. He had really put the squadron through its paces and built up a splendid fighting unit from a bunch of mainly Canadians – and a "Bolshie" lot they were to begin with!'

A new era, however, was about to begin.

Above left: The legless Wing Commander Douglas Bader was given his choice of Wing – and chose Tangmere, near Chichester, in March 1941.

Above right: Also amongst the first Wing Commander (Flying) appointments was the legendary South African A.G. 'Sailor' Malan, who became Biggin Hill's first Wing Leader.

Chapter Two

Der Kanaljäger

To better understand the RAF fighter pilots' experience of the Non-stop Offensive of 1941, it is necessary to have an appreciation of the enemy faced across the Channel, in north-west France.

During the First World War, Germany had clearly demonstrated the excellence of both its fighter aircraft and pilots, producing arguably the most famous of them all: Rittmeister Manfred Freiherr von Richthofen, universally known as the 'Red Baron' on account of his crimson aircraft. At the 1919 Versailles Peace Settlement, however, the German air force was forbidden, as the victorious Allies sought to so severely limit Germany's military that the nation could never again threaten peace. With the Nazis having come to power in Germany during 1933, however, two years later the Führer, Adolf Hitler, revealed to a disbelieving world his new Luftwaffe – which had been secretly rebuilding since 1923 in Russia, far beyond prying Western eyes, behind the Urals. A year later, the newly reconstructed German Wehrmacht, including the Luftwaffe, fought in the Spanish Civil War, on the side of the fascist dictator General Franco.

By early 1937, the German presence in Spain amounted to the Condor Legion, commanded by General Hugo Sperrle. Far-sightedly, this expeditionary force included a fully integrated tactical air force with fighter, bomber and ground-attack units, supported by transport, army liaison and reconnaissance units. Jagdgruppe (Fighter Group) 88 represented the fighter contribution, comprising four Staffeln (squadrons) of Heinkel biplane fighters. Initially successful, J88 later experienced stiff resistance from Loyalists equipped with Soviet machines. In April 1937, the 2nd Staffel of J 88 (2/J 88) was the first unit to receive the new Me 109 monoplane fighter – which swiftly demonstrated its marked superiority.

In order to share the Spanish combat experience, Luftwaffe personnel were frequently rotated, as Franco's war became a melting pot for trying and testing new weapons and tactics. Thus, on 24 May 1937, Oberleutnant

DER KANALJÄGER

Werner Mölders replaced Oberleutnant Adolf Galland as Staffelkaptän (Squadron Leader) of 3/J Jagdgeschwader 88. Both young officers were to become synonymous with modern air fighting. Mölders soon realised that tactics applicable to biplane fighters were irrelevant to the fast monoplane Me 109. The basic fighter formation employed by virtually all nations was a 'V' shaped formation of three aircraft, the leader at the apex. In the RAF, this was known as the 'Vic', to the Germans, the Kette. The theory behind this formation dated back prior to air-to-air communications, when pilots had to formate closely on their leader so as to recognise hand signals. It was now found that pilots were spending too much time concentrating on formation flying, and insufficient searching for the enemy – and modern aerial communications were such that hand signals were no longer necessary.

The solution came when Mölders replaced the Kette with the Rotte, a pair of fighters, leader and wingman, which flew some 200 metres apart in a loose, line abreast, stepped-up formation, each protecting the other and able to search the sky without fear of collision. The leader's job was to jockey for position and get the shot, the wingman to protect his leader's tail, so that he could focus on getting the kill, confident that an enemy would not attack his rear. Expanding upon this, two Rotten became the Schwärm, two pairs operating as a section, the aircraft occupying the same position as the four fingers of an outstretched hand, each, again, 200 metres apart and stepped-up. When battle was joined, the four aircraft broke into two fighting pairs. This sounds simple – but it was actually so forward-thinking that it remains the basic concept for fighter combat even today.

In Spain, the Germans also perfected their new Blitzkrieg tactics, which was essentially bombers flying ahead of the advancing army to neutralise enemy positions, clearing the way for armour and troops, while fighters ensured aerial superiority over the battlefield. After success in Spain, the Blitzkrieg was

Werner Mölders (115 victories): the 'Father of Modern Air Fighting' and a totally dedicated professional.

unleashed against Poland on 1 September 1939, and three weeks later it was all over, the Germans victorious. Britain and France declared war on Germany two days after Hitler invaded Poland, Britain sending troops and aircraft to France, awaiting an attack on the west. After a quiet winter, on 9 April 1940, Germany invaded Norway, the Luftwaffe supporting amphibious landings. On 1 May 1940, Hitler was able to trumpet another resounding victory. Then, on 10 May 1940, the long-awaited punch westwards came, when Germany invaded the Netherlands, Belgium, Luxembourg and France. Two days later Leige fell, the panzers crashing across the Meuse at Dinant and Sedan; the following day, after heavy aerial bombardment, Rotterdam fell and the Dutch surrendered. On 14 May 1940, the German fighter pilots recorded their most successful day, with 814 sorties producing ninety victories over Sedan. Over France, the Me 109 met the Hawker Hurricane for the first time, which although more able than any of the obsolete types thus far encountered, was no match for the German fighter.

By 26 May 1940, with the Belgians collapsing to the north, the French to the south, their vaunted Maginot Line outflanked, the British Expeditionary Force was left with no option but to retire on, and evacuate from, Dunkirk. During the subsequent air fighting over the Belgian and French coast, the Me 109 met the Spitfire for the first time, which Air Chief Marshal Dowding had so determinedly preserved for this critical moment, finding this British fighter a worthy adversary. Nonetheless, the 109 possessed certain technical advantages, and cannon, but the Germans greatest advantage was their combat experience. By 3 June 1940, the Dunkirk evacuation was over, and soon after France, that once great military power, surrendered. One thing above all had made this German victory possible: the Me 109's complete dominance over the battlefield.

Now, Hitler was unexpectedly presented with the opportunity to mount a seaborne invasion of southern England – a huge amphibious operation for which the Germans were unprepared, and as a pre-requisite to which aerial superiority was critical. Understandably the German fighter pilots were sublimely confident in their ability to defeat Fighter Command. The story of what became known as the Battle of Britain is well-known and often told, so I will not repeat it here. Suffice to say that largely chained to the close bomber escort role, the Jagdflieger did not force the required decision – but when they were able to fly free-range fighter sweeps – Freie Hunt – their ability and experience was violently demonstrated. Indeed, there was a period in October 1940 when the German fighters did achieve ascendancy, when able to operate independently. One cannot help wonder at the outcome had this

DER KANALJÄGER

always been the case. As it was, innumerable of the Few went to their deaths because Fighter Command lacked the Germans' combat experience and still rigidly flew the suicidal vic of three. Although wise squadron commanders began their own experiments – 74 Squadron's Squadron Leader Sailor Malan, for example, favouring the section of four in line astern as a more flexible alternative to the vic – the RAF fighter squadrons still largely adhered to this outdated practice. Clearly, therefore, the Germans enjoyed an immense advantage in combat experience and tactics. When the Non-stop Offensive began in 1941, nothing had substantially changed.

As late as 1938, Hitler had actually steadfastly believed that there would be no war with Britain, whose Empire he much admired. The dictator's territorial ambitions lay eastwards, and just as the Battle of Britain began, in July 1940, Hitler made the far-reaching and, as it turned out, ultimately disastrous decision to invade Russia. German historians argue, in fact, that from that point on, the war in the west was no longer a priority for Hitler. The night Blitz on British cities continued until May 1941, and the following month, on 22 June 1941, Hitler at last invaded Russia, hoping for another swift and victorious campaign. In preparation for this, the majority of Luftwaffe units on the Kanalfront were transferred east, leaving Sperrle, by now a Feldmarschall, the sole air commander in the west. So it was that only Sperrle's Luftflotte (Air Fleet) 3 remained to meet the Non-stop Offensive – with just two Jagdgeschwadern (Fighter Groups), Major Adolf Galland's JG 26 'Schlageter', and Major Wilhelm Balthasar's JG 2 'Richthofen'. Between them, Galland and Balthasar were responsible for defending Reich territory from the Netherlands to the Bay of Biscay. The Kanalfront Jagdfliegerführer, or 'Jafü' (Fighter Leader), General Theo Osterkamp, an ace in both world wars, ordered the two Kanalgeschwardern Kommodoren (Channel Group Commodores) to inflict maximum losses upon the enemy, while preserving their own limited resources in the process. Indeed, this sounds extraordinarily similar to Air Vice-Marshal Park's brief during the Battle of Britain, emphasising the reversal of circumstances.

Named after the Red Baron, JG 2 Richthofen considered itself the premier German fighter group, its personnel wearing a prestigious cuff title bearing the great ace's name. Throughout much of the Battle of Britain, JG 2 had operated from bases, temporary and otherwise, in north-west France, including the great cornfields of Beaumont-le-Roger, and the former French Air Force aerodrome at Le Havre. In late August 1940, along with the other Me 109 groups, JG 2 relocated to the Pas-de-Calais, ready for the assault on London, flying from Théville, Mardyk and Oye Plage.

BADER'S SPITFIRE WING

Oberstleutnant Adolf Galland (103 victories), Kommodore of JG 26, was well-known for his penchant for large cigars!

Afterwards, JG 2 returned to its original area further west, where it remained to meet the Non-stop Offensive in 1941. Each Jagdgeschwader comprised three Gruppen (wings), each of three Staffeln. Each Gruppe was designated 'I', 'II' or 'III', and each staffel within its group numbered 1–12 (so 5/JG 2, for example, represents the group's fifth squadron, and the second squadron of three belonging to the second group). Each Geschwader had its own Stabschwärm (Staff Flight), led by the Geschwaderkommodore, usually a major, including the adjutant, technical and operations officers. Each Gruppe was commanded by a Gruppenkommandeur (Wing Commander), a Hauptmann, and each Gruppe had its own Gruppenstabschwärm. An operations headquarters existed at both Geschwader and Gruppen level, the Geschwadergefechsstand and Gruppengefechsstand respectively. Each of the three Staffeln within a Gruppe were commanded by a Staffelkapitän, usually an Oberleutnant and an office directly comparable to an RAF squadron leader. Every Geschwader also had its own Ergänzungstaffel, an extra squadron providing operational conversion and training for replacement pilots.

Each Staffel was subdivided into three Schwärme, sections of four, each further divided into two Rotte, or pairs. Individual aircraft within each Staffel were marked from 1 onwards, painted or outlined in the Staffel's designated colour and painted forward of the national cross on the fuselage. The marking aft of said cross indicated the aircraft's Gruppe: no marking for I, a horizontal or vertical bar for II, and a wavy line for III. Both the Geschwaderstabschwärm and Gruppenstabschwärm used a system of black and white chevron, horizontal bar and vertical symbols identifying to which officer each aircraft belonged. After 28 August 1940, engine cowlings, rudders and wingtips were also painted yellow or white to assist easy identification in the air. Contrary to popular belief, therefore, at the time and even now, yellow-painted German fighters were not from an elite unit. White denoted the first Staffel in each Gruppe, red the second, and

DER KANALJÄGER

Me 109Fs of JG 2's Stabsstaffel at Beaumont-le-Roger in 1941.

JG 2's Kommandbunker at Beaumont-le-Roger, 1941.

yellow simply the third. This colour coding was very important, because German air-to-air and air-to-ground communications early in the war were poor. For example, fighter pilots could talk to each other in the air, but not to the ground or to the bombers they may be escorting. All of JG 2's aircraft bore the Geschwader emblem, a white or silver shield bearing a large letter

Above left: Major Wilhelm Balthasar (40 victories on the Kanalfront and seven in Spain), Kommodore of JG 2.

Above right: The coveted Ritterkreuz, seen here with additional Oak Leaves, Swords and Diamonds – a level of recognition few aspired to.

'R' in red, while 1/JG 2 fighters also sported a 'Bonzo Dog', and 3/JG 2 a blue pennant bearing a dagger and word 'Horrido' – the German hunter's traditional victory cry.

On 16 February 1941, Major Wilhelm Balthasar was appointed JG 2's Kommodore. Balthasar was one of the leading Experten, and a 'Spaniard', having fought in Spain, where he scored his first victory, flying a Russian-built I-16 Rata, on 20 January 1938. Six months' later, while serving at home with JG 2, Balthasar received international acclaim for a record-breaking endurance flight around Africa. During the Battle of France, while commanding 7/JG 27, he astonishingly destroyed nine aircraft in one day, on 6 June 1940. A week later, he became only the second Luftwaffe serviceman to be awarded the Ritterkreuz – the coveted Knight's Cross – by which time he was Germany's most successful fighter pilot in the western campaign. During the Battle of Britain, Hauptmann Balthasar was Kommandeur of III/JG 3 and badly wounded on 4 September 1940, when attacked by Spitfires. His return to duty was as JG 2's Kommodore.

DER KANALJÄGER

JG 2, in fact, boasted a number of Experten among its pilots, including long-serving adjutant Oberleutnant Erich Leie, who, as a Stabsoffizier (Staff Officer) flew in the Kommodore's Stabschwärm. Egon Mayer, who had joined JG 2 in December 1939, was another, who would go on to become the first Experte to achieve 100 victories on the Kanalfront. Kurt Buhligen had begun his career as a mechanic, servicing 3/KG 4's He 111, and so impressed his Staffelkapitän, Hauptmann Hermann Kell, that he was recommended for Jagdflieger training; Kell was clearly a perceptive leader, as Buhligen also went on to achieve over 100 victories in the west. Another popular Jagdwaffe (Fighter Arm) personality was the Kommandeur of III/JG 2 in 1941, Hauptmann Hans 'Assi' Hahn, who would destroy 68 RAF aircraft before being posted to Russia in November 1942.

The Reichsluftfahrtministerium (RLM, the Air Ministry) went to great lengths, in fact, to verify, or otherwise, every Abschuss (aerial victory). Unlike the Allied air forces, kills could not be shared, and victories only awarded for aircraft destroyed, not those probably so or damaged. For confirmation, every Abschuss had to be witnessed, which was an inflexible requirement, unless the wreck of the enemy aircraft could be found and examined. The Viktor

Above left: JG 2's adjutant, Oberleutnant Erich Leie (121 victories).

Above right: JG 2's Egon Mayer, the first Kanaljäger to achieve 100 victories on the Kanalfront.

Above left: The Kommandeur of III/JG 2, Hauptmann Hans 'Assi' Hahn (108 victories, 68 of which were in the west).

Above right: Walter Osesau (127 victories), who succeeded Wilhem Balthasar as Kommodore of JG 2.

had to provide the exact location and submit the claim to his immediate supervisory officer for initial verification or rejection. If approved, the report was then forwarded to the Geschwaderstab, which made out its own report before forwarding both papers to the RLM, which would then check the circumstances and if ultimately awarded, notify the unit concerned – a drawn-out process which could take up to a year. When cross-referencing German combat claims with actual Allied losses, they are remarkably accurate – far more so than Fighter Command's. Many are surprised at this, given the high scores of German fighter pilots, which ran into the hundreds in respect of certain individuals, which seems incredible considering that the RAF's officially top-scoring ace recorded 38½. The reason for this disparity, however, is that early in the war the Jagdflieger were opposed by obsolete fighters, such as those of the Polish and French air forces, so achieved many comparatively easy victories, and this scenario was amplified during the initial years of fighting in Russia. Moreover, as the war ground on, the Germans, what with the sheer numbers of Allied aircraft, had more targets to shoot at. The overall accuracy of the German claims is therefore not in doubt.

The other Kanalgeschwader, JG 26, had an equally impressive combat record. Having received its Me 109s in November 1937, and originally

DER KANALJÄGER

designated JG 234, the unit's honour title was awarded in December 1938, the group being named after Albert Leo Schlageter, a German patriot executed by the French in 1923 after blowing up a section of railway in protest against Allied forces occupying the Rhineland, the area of Germany in which the unit was based. On 1 May 1939, the Geschwader was redesignated JG 26 and a new emblem was painted on the Schlageter 109s: a black Gothic 'S' on a white shield. 8/JG 26 added the cartoon character 'Adamson' to their machines, while 9/JG 26's fighters bore the fierce red griffin, or Höllenhund (Hellhound).

Instead of participating in the Polish campaign, JG 26 remained at home to protect Germany's western flank. During the attack on the west, it supported Army Group 'B', which invaded the Netherlands, flying Freie Hunten ahead of the advancing German troops – achieving aerial superiority on day one. JG 26 then participated in the invasion of Belgium and the Dunkirk air battles, moving to the Pas-de-Calais before joining the attack on the main French army further south. The battle won, JG 26 found itself at Villacoublay, a large former French air force base just west of Paris. When the French surrendered at Compiégne on 22 June 1940, II/JG 26's Me 109s had the honour of patrolling overhead. Afterwards, the entire Geschwader retired to the Rhineland and prepared for the air assault on England. On 21 July 1940, JG 26 returned to the Pas-de-Calais,

9/JG 26's crimson 'Hell Hound' visible on the Me 109E of Staffelkapitän Oberleutnant Gerhard Schöpfel at Caffiers, a large cornfield in the Pas-de-Calais used as an airfield during the Battle of Britain.

using temporary airfields, such as the huge cornfield at Caffiers, home of III/JG 26, the Kommandeur of which, Adolf Galland, was promoted to Major and became Kommodore on 22 August 1940. In command of III/JG 26 Galland was succeeded by another Experte, Hauptmann Gerhard Schöpfel, who, just four days previously, had destroyed four 501 Squadron Hurricanes over Canterbury in just two bloody minutes. Having been heavily engaged during the Battle of Britain, during the late autumn of 1940, JG 26 withdrew from the Pas-de-Calais to Abbeville, where, on Christmas Day, Hitler himself dined at the Geschwader's chateau HQ. On 9 February 1941, the unit again returned to Germany for refit, its place in France taken by JG 53. During this period, Galland began re-equipping with the new Me 109F, the Geschwaderstabschwärm and III/JG 26 receiving the improved Messerschmitt in March 1941. There were insufficient Fs available to re-equip the entire Geschwader, however, so certain elements of JG 26 flew their old Emils until summer 1941.

The Me 109F – the Franz – was a much better aircraft than the Emil. With redesigned radiators, flaps and ailerons it was also more aesthetically pleasing, with rounded wingtips and a streamlined nose profile including a large, rounded, spinner, a smaller rudder and no tail struts. Powered by the DB601E, which used lower octane fuel and provided a top speed of 390 mph at 20,000ft, the 109F's service ceiling was 37,000ft and range 440 miles. The F-2 enjoyed the additional benefit of the ingenious nitrous oxide injection system, known as 'Ha Ha', giving the aircraft extra, exceptional,

A yellow-nosed Me 109F of 8/JG 26 on the Kanalfront during mid-1941.

boost. The two engine-mounted MG 17 machine-guns, firing through the propeller arc, were retained, but provision was made for a single 15mm or 20mm firing through the propeller boss. The F-1 was armed with an engine-mounted MG FF/M 20mm cannon manufactured by Oerlikon, but the F-2, which became available in quantity shortly afterwards, was armed with the 15mm Mauser MG 151. To sight his target the pilot had a Revi/12C reflector gunsight; a thumb-button on his control column fired the cannon, and a finger trigger discharged the machine-guns. The MG 151 used high explosive, armour-piercing and incendiary ammunition, firing 700 rounds per minute, while the Rheinmetall-Borsig MG 17's rate of fire was 1,180 rounds per minute. Interestingly, as in Fighter Command, there was debate among the Experten over the relative merits and otherwise of the cannon and machine-gun armament. The Me 109E had been armed with two machine-guns and two 20mm cannons, so the F was more lightly armed. Galland argued that this was a retrogressive step, given that the new Spitfires were more heavily armed, and that wing-mounted cannon were better for the novice. Mölders, however, favoured the lighter armament, which reduced weight and thereby increased agility. By any standards this was an impressive fighter and arguably represented the zenith of the Ein-Hundert-Neun series.

Many German pilots had been air-minded youngsters introduced to gliding as members of the Deutscher Luftsportverband (LDV), ostensibly a sporting club providing air experience. Luftwaffe pilots' training was similar to the RAF's. What was dissimilar was that German fighter pilots, unlike their RAF enemies, were not rested after a tour of a specific period in the front line, but remained on active, operational, duty until such time as either incapacitated by wounds or killed. There was certainly some merit in this, because although operational flying could be exhausting, the German pilot was always familiar with current operational conditions and kept his 'eye' in. This indefinite period of operational flying is another reason for the German aces' greater individual scores. Conversely, RAF fighter pilots were rested after 200 operational hours' flying, usually instructing at an operational training unit for several months. Without the thrill of combat flying, all too many got their adrenalin-rush from unauthorised low-level aerobatics and other stunts – and paid the ultimate price. Upon return to an operational squadron, inevitably operational conditions would have changed, and so the RAF pilot had to adjust to the increased tempo involved – a dangerous time, during which they were vulnerable. Another difference between the two was that Luftwaffe airmen were all full-time professionals, whereas the RAF comprised regular airmen and the amateur volunteers of the part-time AAF and RAFVR. In various ways, therefore, the opposing air forces were quite different in composition, operation and structure.

One advantage the Germans had was that since 1940, the Luftwaffe had paid much more attention to air-sea rescue operations than the RAF, the Seenotflugkommando flying He 59 floatplanes and searching for downed aircrew. The German fighter pilots' lightweight and incongruous lifejacket, the Schwimmveste, was superior to the comparatively bulky RAF 'Mae West' equivalent, and could be inflated either orally or via activating a pressurised cartridge. The German example also carried packets of fluorescein, which, when exposed to water, surrounded the airman with a bright yellow dye. Also, a bright yellow skullcap was often worn over the flying helmet as an extra precaution and aid to visibility if the wearer ended up in the Kanal. Even in summer, survival time in the cold English Channel was one to two hours, so early discovery and rescue was essential. The Germans also positioned rescue buoys, known as 'Lobster Pots' by the RAF, in the sea, each containing four bunks and essential items that may be required by a downed airman. The British, however, had only a rudimentary air-sea rescue organisation early in the war, operating just eighteen high speed launches. Frequently, RAF pilots, if they were lucky, were rescued by chance, by a passing vessel.

On 1 April 1941, JG 26 was ordered to return to France, over the next few days basing itself in Brittany and providing aerial protection to the battlecruisers *Scharnhorst* and *Gneisenau*, which were recently returned from a successful Atlantic sortie. On 4 April, Major Galland and Oberfeldwebel Robert Menge flew from Düsseldorf to Brittany. refuelling at the French coastal airfield of Le Touquet, the temptation to sweep the British south-east coast was too much. At 5,000ft over Dover, the Me 109 pilots ambushed two 91 Squadron Spitfires, despatching both in a high-speed, diving, pass, before continuing their journey to Guipavas. On 15 April, Galland and Leutnant Westphal headed for Le Touquet to attend General Theo Osterkamp's forty-ninth birthday party. With a basket of lobsters and several bottles of champagne stowed behind his seat, Galland again led his Rottenhund on a cheeky sweep of Dover. This time, the two 109s met the 12 Group Wing, up from Wittering on a Channel patrol. The wing leader, Wing Commander Coope, ordered the wing to climb through cloud over Dover. Coope, however, became separated from his squadrons and was spotted by Westphal, who alerted his leader. Firing from astern,

DER KANALJÄGER

Galland hit Coope's Spitfire in the wing and fuel tank, a shell also ripping apart the pilot's parachute pack. Fortunately, the Wittering wing leader crash-landed back at Manston, shaken but unharmed. Over Dungeness, Galland found the Wittering wing still on patrol, although no doubt puzzled by their leader's disappearance. Westphal's guns jammed but Galland shot down a Spitfire, which crash-landed at Hawkinge, and wounded the pilot of another. Although 65 Squadron's Flying Officer Paddy Finucane claimed an Me 109 destroyed during the encounter, both Galland and Westphal returned to France unscathed. The JG 26 Kommodore had now recorded his 60th kill.

There was little action in Brittany, however, so JG 26 was delighted to receive orders on 31 May 1941 for its return to the Pas-de-Calais. Soon, Galland's Führerungsverband (Lead Formation) was operating from Audembert, on the coast near Wissant and just two miles from Osterkamp's Jafü 2 HQ. Hauptmann Rolf Pingel's I Gruppe went to Clairmarais, near St Omer; Schöpfel's IIIrd to Ligescourt, north-east of Abbeville, near the Somme estuary's mouth, and Hauptmann Walter Adolf's Me 109E-equipped I/JG 26 further north, to Maldegem in western Belgium. Unlike Wing Commander Bader, Oberst Galland, as he now was, would not fly exclusively with one unit, his Geschwaderstabschwärm rotating those it operated with.

Oberstleutnant Galland, who succeeded his friend Mölders as General der Jagdflieger, prepares for a sortie in his Me 109E at Audembert, February 1941.

BADER'S SPITFIRE WING

Aerial victories recorded on the rudder of 'Dolfo' Galland's Me 109.

By doing this, the Kommodore was able to maintain first-hand knowledge of the strengths and weaknesses of the units in his command.

Like JG 2, there was no shortage of Experten among Galland's pilots. Hauptmann Schöpfel ranked among Germany's most successful Kanaljäger, receiving his Ritterkreuz on 9 September 1940. Oberleutnant Gustav 'Mickey' Sprick, Staffelkapitän of 8/JG 26, was another Ritterkreuzträger, having been among the first to receive the award for twenty victories. Josef 'Pips' Priller, like Sprick, also received the Ritterkreuz in October 1940, and was destined for an impressive wartime career. Older than most of his Kameraden at 30, Hauptmann Johann Schmid, of Galland's Geschwaderstab, like Schöpfel was among the most experienced Experten on the Channel coast. There were many others and no shortage of enthusiasm to engage the enemy.

Clearly, in 1941, the German fighter pilots responding to Alarmstarts in north-west France included many highly experienced and successful individuals, equipped with a superb aeroplane and excellently led. Tactically, everything was in their favour, because strategically there were no targets in France crucial to the overall German war effort, meaning that the Me 109 pilots could gain altitude and only intercept when circumstances were entirely favourable to them, and, as already related, they maximised on their mount's technical advantages in making attacks. With the RAF aircrews facing two sea-crossings and the likelihood of capture if brought down over France, the Non-stop Offensive was never going to be a pushover.

Beyond doubt, in 1941, the Kanaljäger represented a highly experienced and motivated, well-equipped – and formidable – enemy.

Thus the die was cast.

DER KANALJÄGER

Above left: Galland at Audembert on 24 September 1940, when Kommandeur of III/JG 26, with Oberleutnants Gerhard Schöpfel (40 victories) and Joachim Müncheberg (135 victories), the trio being JG 26's first experten awarded the Ritterkreuz (Knight's Cross) – for 20 aerial victories apiece.

Above right: Another Ritterkreuzträger and dangerous opponent was Oberleutnant Gustav 'Mickey' Sprick, Staffelkapitän of 8/JG 26 (31 victories).

Above left: Older than most of his Kameraden at thirty, Hauptmann Johann Schmid (45 victories), of Galland's Geschwaderstab, was amongst the most experienced *Experten* on the Channel coast.

Above right: Made Kommandeur of I/JG 26 in July 1941, Hauptmann Johannes Seifert received the Ritterkreuz and achieved 57 aerial victories before being killed in action.

Chapter Three

Tangmere Wing War Diary
18 March – 8 August 1941

<u>18 March 1941</u>
On 18 March 1941, Wing Commander Douglas Bader reported to Tangmere's Station Commander, Group Captain Jack Boret, taking up his new appointment as the first wing leader and second-in-command of this famous fighter station. Given the Non-stop Offensive's objective – 'to establish air superiority over the enemy in his own country' – doubtless the swashbuckling Wing Commander Bader had rarely been happier.

At Tangmere, Bader found 145 Squadron, commanded by Squadron Leader Jack Leather, and Squadron Leader Billy Burton's 616 Squadron, while Squadron Leader John Ellis's 610 Squadron was dispersed to the nearby Westhampnett satellite airfield. Having served as a rigger during the Battle of Britain at Biggin Hill, and afterwards at Acklington, AC1 Harold Mead was with 610 Squadron when it had arrived at Westhampnett in December 1940:

Wing Commander Douglas Bader DSO DFC, Tangmere Wing Leader.

The West Sussex location was idyllic. Our new Station at Westhampnett had been a farm pre-war and efforts were made to keep it looking that way. A converted cowshed was our Mess, and our landing strip was edged with a camouflaged tarmac perimeter. This was destined, post-war, to become Goodwood airport, and today our old perimeter is Goodwood motor racing circuit. There were a few extraneous buildings and certainly not the cluster of permanent structures and hangars we see there today. We had a low profile, just a couple of corrugated Nissen huts for use as the pilots' crew room and overnight accommodation for groundcrews on Dawn Readiness duty. All the remaining personnel were billeted up the hill on the Goodwood race course. Although being in the uninsulated, timber-built No 1 Tote in winter wasn't exactly five-star Hilton accommodation, it was comforting to think that any sneak night-time bombing raids on our 'drome would be unlikely to pinpoint us there.

All of the Tangmere Sector's squadron commanders had flown with distinction during the Battle of Britain and were decorated with the DFC. Indeed, Harold Mead describes his CO, Squadron Leader Ellis, as 'a legend'. The Hurricanes of 302 (Polish) Squadron, which had flown in Bader's 'Big Wing' during the Battle of Britain, commanded by Squadron Leader Piotr Laguna, were also based at Westhampnett, while Beaufighter night-fighters could be found at Tangmere. The 'Wingco' was already well familiar with 616 Squadron, which had also flown in his controversial 'Big Wing', and had a ready affinity with the unit's CO, Squadron Leader Billy Burton, who was also a Cranwellian. For these reasons, Bader chose to base himself with, and lead his Wing at the head of, 616 Squadron, although according to Brickhill in his *Reach for the Sky* yarn, it was because 616 had 'the least battle experience'. That may have been a fact, but it was not why the new wing leader chose to lead with Billy Burton's squadron.

According to Pilot Officer Johnnie Johnson, 'Bader based himself with us at Westhampnett, and led the wing with us, because he already knew us and there was the Cranwell connection with Billy, the bond of which cannot be underestimated.'

Howard Frizelle Burton was born on 21 June 1916 at Letchworth, the third son of Major Louis Burton, an artillery officer killed on active service in 1917. Educated at Bedford, in 1934 'Billy', as he was universally known, achieved a King's Cadetship to RAF Cranwell, with outstanding marks. Upon passing out in December 1936, Burton was awarded that year's coveted Sword of Honour – the only blade, as things turned out, inscribed 'Edward VIII'. Pilot Officer Burton's first posting was to fly Gloster Gauntlet biplane fighters with 46 Squadron at Kenley, before moving with the unit to Digby, where his CO, Squadron Leader Dickie Barwell, assessed the young pilot's ability as both a fighter pilot and navigator as 'above the average', and 'exceptional' in 'Air Gunnery'. In June 1938 came promotion to flying officer and the same high standard maintained. By March 1939, Burton was an acting flight lieutenant and posted to 12 Group HQ on operations staff duties. Four days after the declaration of war, Flight Lieutenant Burton took over 'B' Flight of 66 Squadron, Duxford's second Spitfire squadron. During the Battle of France, Burton shared a He 111 on 12 May 1940, and destroyed another over Dunkirk on 2 June in addition to damaging a Ju 88 on 19 June. That month also saw Burton marry Jean, the only daughter of Air Commodore E.D.M. Robertson, a decorated First World War pilot, of Ashstead, Surrey. With the Second World War exactly one year old, Burton was promoted to squadron leader and given command of the decimated and demoralised 616 Squadron at Coltishall, then moved to Kirton. This was immediately after the unit's battering at Kenley during the Battle of Britain, and Burton's job was to rebuild the squadron into an effective fighting unit. Later that month, the squadron supplied a flight to participate in Big Wing operations, hence the association with Bader.

Originally a unit of the Auxiliary Air Force, locally raised in South Yorkshire, by now, as the result of casualties and the arrival of replacements, the identity of all auxiliary squadrons had very much changed – with 616 being no exception. The last serving original auxiliary pilots were Flight Lieutenant Ken Holden, commander of 'A' Flight, and his second-in-command, Flying Officer Hugh 'Cocky' Dundas – a veteran at 21 – and Flying Officer L.H. 'Buck' Casson, who had also survived the Kenley ordeal. Around these men, Burton built a new team, his replacement pilots being mostly volunteer reservists like Pilot Officers Johnnie Johnson and Philip 'Nip' Hepple, Sergeant-Pilots Bob 'Butch' Morton and Sydney 'Thug' Mabbett, and those from the Commonwealth, such as Sergeant Jeff West. Thanks to the war, the previously snobbish and exclusive AAF squadrons had become an eclectic mix of diverse backgrounds and personalities. 616 Squadron

TANGMERE WING WAR DIARY 18 MARCH – 8 AUGUST 1941

Above left: Squadron Leader Billy Burton DFC, with whose 616 Squadron 'Dogsbody' based himself at Westhampnett and led at the head of the Tangmere Wing.

Above right: Flying Officer Hugh 'Cocky' Dundas, who narrowly escaped death during the Battle of Britain and was immensely inspired by 'Dogsbody', in whose leading section he flew as No 3.

was, in fact, now a happy one, as Group Captain Sir Hugh Dundas (as he later became) recalled many years later:

> We were happy at Tangmere from the start…. I had been shot down during the Battle of Britain, baling out and injuring my shoulder. When I resumed operations, 616 Squadron was contributing to the five-squadron strong Big Wing. Given my earlier experience I was not unnaturally a little anxious. On our first patrol, Bader's voice came over the radio. To my amazement this legless man, flying into battle, was calling up Woodhall to arrange a game of squash! I was absolutely astonished! This calmed my nerves no end. With such a man leading us, how could I come to any harm? His arrival at Tangmere and decision to lead the wing with 616 Squadron was welcome indeed from my perspective.

There was, however, a negative implication concerning 'Dogsbody' exclusively leading the Tangmere Wing with 616 Squadron, as Johnnie Johnson recalled:

> Because Douglas always flew at the head of our squadron, our CO, Billy Burton, was unhappy as he never got to lead his own squadron. I do not think it was necessary for Douglas to do this. Later in the war, when I was a wing leader, I flew with all of my squadrons in rotation, although I'd keep the same Number Two in each one. It would definitely have been better for the Tangmere Wing had Douglas done this too.

19 March 1941

On 19 March 1941, Wing Commander Bader flew a 616 Squadron Spitfire Mk IIA, QJ-A, for fifty minutes to gain 'experience on type'.

Squadron Leader Sir Alan Smith, then just another lowly VR sergeant-pilot, inevitably known to all as 'Smithy', vividly recalled that day:

> Sitting in readiness at dispersal I heard the roar of a Spitfire as it dived low, climbed, did a half-roll and lowered its undercarriage while inverted, rolled out, side-slipped and made a perfect landing. Out of the cockpit climbed Wing Commander Douglas Bader, who walked with his distinctive gait into dispersal. The Wing Commander introduced himself and said he would be leading the Tangmere Wing, and explained that he would do so with 616 Squadron. He obviously knew Flying Officer Hugh 'Cocky' Dundas and Pilot Officer Johnnie Johnson, and said 'You'll be Red Three, Cocky, and you, Johnnie, will be Red Four.' Looking around he caught my eye and said 'Who are you?'
>
> 'Sergeant Smith, Sir,' I replied.
>
> 'Right, you fly as my Red Two and God help you if you don't watch my tail!'
>
> I couldn't believe my ears, it was like God asking me to keep an eye on heaven for him! Flying with Douglas, Cocky and Johnnie was to become the greatest experience of my life and I considered myself quite the most fortunate pilot in the RAF.

TANGMERE WING WAR DIARY 18 MARCH – 8 AUGUST 1941

Above left: Sergeant Alan Smith of 616 Squadron, who often flew as Dogsbody 2.

Above right: Sergeant Alan Smith and 616 Squadron's Intelligence Officer, Flying Officer 'Spy' Gibbs.

Sergeant Smith's car, appropriately named 'Fear Not', which 'died of old age and ran on 100 octane fuel'.

BADER'S SPITFIRE WING

The Wing Commander placed care of his personal Spitfire in the hands of 616 Squadron's 'A' Flight, which the impressionable Flying Officer Dundas, already in awe of his legless leader, considered 'an extraordinary stroke of luck…. So there began a close personal association between us which lasted throughout that fateful summer and beyond.' Bader's first seven flights as wing leader, between 19 and 25 March 1941, were made in 616 Squadron Spitfires QJ-A, B, D and J.

Sergeant Bob Morton recalled that his first sighting of Wing Commander Bader, 'who was already something of a legend, was sitting on the radiator of Billy Burton's car holding a shotgun, while the CO drove him erratically across the field in pursuit of rabbits!'

Unsurprisingly, as the three-squadron Spitfire wing concept was new, Wing Commander Bader discovered that his new command had never actually flown together as a cohesive formation. This had to be put right, quickly, and so a programme of hard training was swiftly devised. Moreover, the AOC, at first, would not authorise wings to cross into France, so the only hope of action was to sweep the Channel, hoping to encounter German fighters on a similar mission. These sorties Bader dubbed 'Snoops'.

At 1520 hrs on the afternoon of 19 March 1941, 610 Squadron took off from Westhampnett to patrol Hastings at 30,000ft, with 616 Squadron, up from Tangmere, leading and positioned slightly below. At the head of 616 Squadron was Wing Commander Bader, leading elements of his new wing for the first time. It would be a memorable sortie, if only for the wrong reason.

Upon reaching the patrol line, the condensation trail height was found to be 25,000ft, so instead of climbing to Angels 30, 610 Squadron descended to just below Angels 25. Consequently, any aircraft above the Spitfires would produce a highly visible white 'smoke' trail and be easily spotted. This positioning, with 610 providing top cover and 616 flying just below, would remain the standard procedure throughout Bader's tenure as Tangmere wing leader.

On this patrol, the 610 and 616 Squadron paired formation swept the Channel three times before ordered to Beachy Head (codename 'Diamond'). As the Spitfires crossed the Sussex coast, flying in vics line astern, Me 109s of II/JG 53 pounced on 610 Squadron from above. Sergeant Payne spotted the front-end of an Me 109 in his rear-view mirror, immediately half-rolling and diving away, pursued by the enemy fighter, before cleverly throttling right back so that the German overshot – enabling the British pilot to rake the 109's belly with a three second burst. Pressing home his attack, Payne saw his target's cockpit area engulfed in smoke and flames, watching with satisfaction the 109 crash into the sea about five miles off the French

TANGMERE WING WAR DIARY 18 MARCH – 8 AUGUST 1941

From left: 616 Squadron's Flight Lieutenant Colin MacFie, Flying Officer Hugh Dundas, Pilot Officer 'Nip' Hepple, and Squadron Leader Billy Burton.

Pilot Officer Johnnie Johnson replaces his CO in the line-up. On 19 March 1941, Johnson embarrassed himself by shouting 'Lookout!', upon sighting three Me 109s, causing the whole Tangmere Wing to break – and provoking a rebuke from his Wing Leader.

coast. While other 610 Squadron pilots engaged the 109s inconclusively, Hauptmann Bretnütz shot down Sergeant Eade, who forced-landed near Hailsham. There was, however, another story attached to this combat.

In his logbook, Squadron Leader Burton wrote 'Wing patrol with 610, led by Wing Commander Bader. "Johnno" gave alarm: "Look out!"' This was an embarrassment Pilot Officer Johnnie Johnson would never forget:

Flight Lieutenant Ken Holden with his 'A' Flight of 616 Squadron; standing, from left: Sergeant McCairns, Pilot Officer Hepple, Holden, Pilot Officer Johnson, Sergeant Mabbett; kneeling, from left: Sergeant West (NZ) and Sergeant Brewer.

Flight Lieutenant Colin McFie, commander of 616 Squadron's 'B' Flight, who had flown Spitfires during the Battle of Britain with 611 Squadron, but would soon become a prisoner of war.

Suddenly I spotted three lean 109s only a few hundred feet higher than our formation and travelling in the same direction … I should have calmly reported the number, type and position of the 109s to our leader, but I was excited and shouted 'Look out, Dogsbody!' The other pilots … weren't waiting for further advice from me. To them, 'look out' was a warning of utmost danger – of the dreaded 'bounce' by a strong force of 109s. Now they took swift evasive action and half-rolled, dived, aileron-turned and swung out in all directions.… In far less time than it takes to tell, a highly organised wing was reduced to a shambles and the scattered sections could never be re-formed in time to continue the planned flight. I was the last to land, for I had realised the error and knew the consequences would be unpleasant. They were all waiting in the dispersal hut.

'Close the door, Billy,' ordered Bader. And then:

'Now who's the clot who shouted "look-out"?'

I admitted being the guilty party.

'Very well. Now tell us what we had to "look-out" for?' demanded the angry Wing Commander.

'Well, sir, there were three 109s a few hundred feet above…'

'*Three* 109s!' interrupted Bader. 'We could have clobbered the lot. But your girlish scream made us think there were fifty of the brutes behind.'

This public rebuke hurt deeply, but it was well justified, for our first operation had been a complete failure, thanks to my error. Bader went on to deliver an impromptu lecture on tactics … since he was quick to forgive, he gave me an encouraging grin when he stomped out of the dispersal hut. I never forgot this lesson.

21 March 1941

In his log book, Wing Commander Bader recorded 'Snoop up Channel', but there was no action.

AC1 Harold Mead, Flight Mechanic 'A', 'B' Flight, 610 Squadron:

Before long, Wing Commander Bader had everyone else emulating his quick off the ground style of take-off … brakes on hard, throttle wide open, tail up and then release brakes to get maximum surge (preferably without nosing down and bending the prop!) and immediately up with the undercart, inducing lift before the wheels were quite clear of the ground. This was followed by a momentary, heart-stopping, sink earthwards before sweeping upwards in a long, climbing, curve. Risky, maybe, but it was a great technique. It was one learned more slowly by some than others and sometimes with expensive results.

23 March 1941
On this day, a tragedy struck when 19-year-old Pilot Officer Irvine Scott Owen Gaze, an Australian pilot of 610 Squadron, was killed on a routine training flight when his Spitfire flew into a hill at West Dean, Sussex. Also serving on the squadron at the same time was elder brother, Tony, twenty-one, who would go on to become both a fighter ace and accomplished racing driver.

24 March 1941
Another uneventful 'snoop'.

27 March 1941
Wing Commander Bader practised aerobatics in a brand-new Spitfire Mk IIA, P7966, which would become his personal mount for some time. This was an aircraft called 'Manxman', presented by the Isle of Man to

Wing Commander Bader's famous Tangmere Wing Spitfire, Mk IIA, P7666, 'D-B'.

TANGMERE WING WAR DIARY 18 MARCH – 8 AUGUST 1941

the Air Ministry under the auspices of Lord Beaverbrook's enormously popular 'Spitfire Fund'. On the fuselage was painted 'DB', it being the wing leaders' privilege to have their initials adorn their aircraft, the wing commander's pennant, and beneath the exhausts, the famous nose-art of Hitler's backside being kicked by a flying boot, similar to that which had appeared on Bader's 242 Squadron Hurricane. The aircraft had a Rotol airscrew with spinner and under-surfaces appearing in 'sky' paint, while upper-surfaces were camouflaged green and brown; the following month, a sky 'day fighter band' was added, encircling the fuselage immediately forward of the tail section.

Pilot Officer Johnnie Johnson:

> Of course, we faced that summer with the prospect of a renewed Battle of Britain-type assault, but Douglas would rub his hands together and say 'Let the buggers come, we've got the wing and the cannon now, bloody good show old boy, and if they don't come, we'll go over there, won't we?' To say he was enthusiastic about getting on with the war and engaging the enemy was an understatement.

A colour cine-gun being fitted to P7666, in which photograph the Wing Commander's famous nose-art, which previously adorned his 242 Squadron Hurricane, can clearly be seen.

BADER'S SPITFIRE WING

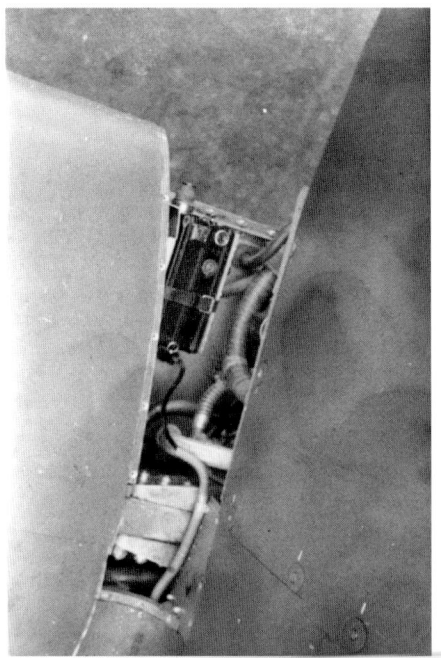 

Above left and above right: Views of the cine-gun camera which was synchronised to film whenever the guns were fired, recording results.

Johnnie's reference to Bader's enthusiasm for the cannon is interesting. Sir Alan Smith once told me that:

> I found aerial gunnery quite difficult. Unlike Johnnie and some of the country lads who had grown up with a shotgun in their hands, shooting game on the wing and thereby learning early the art of deflection shooting, as a townie I had never fired a gun before. The majority of RAF fighter pilots were in a similar position to me, so standards of marksmanship were variable. Probably similar for the Germans too, I suspect.

The eight machine-guns of the Spitfire Mk IIA produced a shot-gun effect, scattering rounds over a comparatively large area of sky. This, Bader believed, gave the average fighter pilot a better chance of hitting his intended target than the 20mm cannon, which, with its slower rate of fire, required greater accuracy. While the pilots of his wing flew variously the machine-gun-armed Mk IIA, and cannon and machine-gun armed IIB, and in due course more powerful VB, Bader's personal preference was for the

TANGMERE WING WAR DIARY 18 MARCH – 8 AUGUST 1941

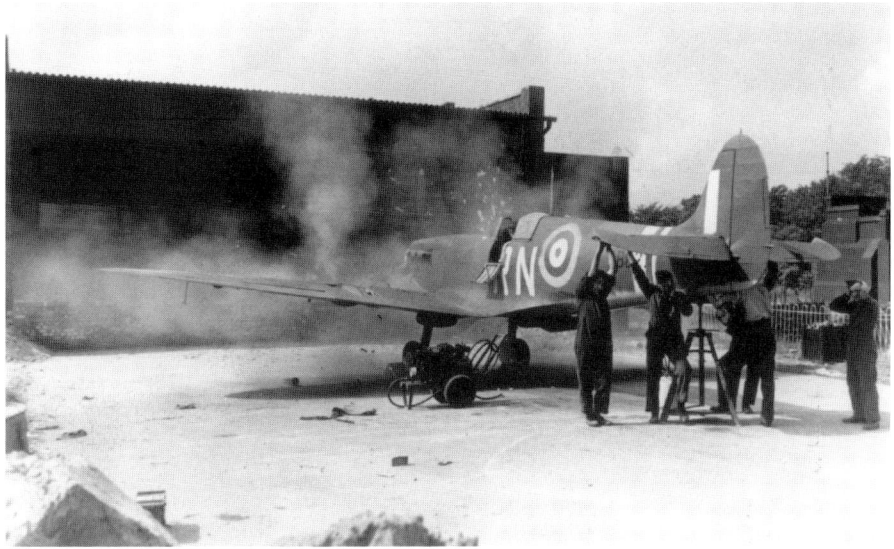

A cannon-armed 72 Squadron Spitfire testing its guns at Biggin Hill in 1941. Wing Commander Bader preferred the shot-gun effect of eight machine-guns to the cannon's slower rate of fire, which required greater accuracy.

Browning gun. Consequently, the wing leader exclusively flew the Mk IIA, before eventually updating to W3185, one of only 124 machine-gun-armed Mk VAs built. Johnnie, however, later remarked that:

> Douglas was wrong about the cannon in the hands of the average squadron pilot. With two cannon and four machine-guns we had the best of both worlds and could select on the oblong, contoured, gun button whether to fire only cannon or machine-guns, or both together. The cannon's slower rate of fire did need more accurate shooting, but the extra destructive power made it an essential weapon and gave us parity with the enemy.

28 March 1941
As the result of 'hostile bombing', some 400 airmen were dispersed from Tangmere and billeted at Goodwood racecourse.

Pat Goodenough was a member of 616 Squadron's groundcrew:

> When I joined 616 Squadron, we had biplanes, Hawker Hinds and Gloster Gauntlets. When I returned from a course on

BADER'S SPITFIRE WING

Rolls-Royce Merlin engines at St Athan, we had re-equipped with Spitfires. These new aircraft landed at over 90 mph, it was hard to believe they had so much speed and power. Most of the new airfields appeared to be built on swamps, because if the aircraft taxied off the concrete runway or perimeter track, they just sank in the mud. Then several airmen would drape themselves over the rear fuselage while the pilot opened up the throttle, the Spitfire then travelling back to the runway on its tailwheel. Pilots were often in a hurry and sometimes did not stop to let us off. Many an airman had bruises to show for it!

The Spitfires were modified with such frequency that before we received information about a modification, another had already taken its place. Of course, we were bombed at Tangmere and ground staff performed such duties as fire pickets, and dawn and dusk security patrols of the airfields. All in all they were exciting times, but we only lived from day to day. We lost Spitfires too, but received replacements very quickly. I think it was the pilots' morale that counted most.

Above and opposite: A section of Tangmere Wing Spitfires takes off from Westhampnett on a sweep, snapped by RAF photographer Norman Jenkins who was present to record the fitting of the new colour cine-gun camera.

George Reid was also one of 616 Squadron's 'erks', having previously served on 145 Squadron:

> The Squadron had only recently moved to Westhampnett and so we slept at Goodwood racecourse until something more permanent could be found. 616 then sent me on a course to Fort Dunlop in Birmingham, studying tyres and mixings. I returned a 'boffin' on oleo legs and tyres, so my time with 616 was as a kind of undercarriage and tyre inspector. I was not very popular for I wandered around the flights and aircraft

Squadron Leader Billy Burton walking in after a sweep – wearing a German schwimmveste, a highly prized trophy and more efficient than the RAF's 'Mae West'.

Above left and above right: Wing Commander Douglas Bader in his element at Westhampnett, outside 616 Squadron's dispersal hut.

and had the authority to make a Spitfire unserviceable. All the chaps had to do then was taxi over to the blister hangar and the fault would be put right.

When 616 Squadron had arrived at Tangmere, it shared the airfield with 610, another auxiliary squadron, which had been in residence since 15 December 1940.

Flight Lieutenant Peter Ward-Smith was a sergeant-pilot in 610 Squadron that summer:

> When Wing Commander Bader took over at Tangmere we realised that something big was in the offing, but never this air offensive on the Big Wing scale.
>
> Our take-off-point for one of the first attacks was the small airfield behind Beachy Head. We stooged around waiting for other squadrons to join up, then the whole mass headed for France, covering Blenheim bombers detailed to knock hell out of the shipping in Brest, although of their successes no one would say.
>
> At first there was little reaction from our enemy, or so we thought, but on this and subsequent sweeps one or two of the squadron would fail to return. We put this down to high-flying Me 109s diving through the formation and picking off the odd aircraft as they went.
>
> On one occasion we flew through intense flak which rocked my Spitfire. I remember looking back and seeing the whole sky filled with dirty brown puffs. I remember thinking, 'Christ! Have we really just flown through that lot?!' Another time I saw a 109 formating alongside me. I got behind him but

Sergeant Peter Ward-Smith of 610 Squadron.

realised that to open fire would spatter my pals. When the 109 broke away I followed him down, against strict instructions, of course, but could not catch up and lost him near the ground. I met intense flak and not finding any other suitable target I high-tailed it north and eventually hit the Channel in great danger of running out of fuel. Unable to reach an airfield, I landed on the Dymchurch Marshes. It was deemed impossible to take-off, so I had to make my way back to base by train.

LAC Cliff Airey was a Flight Mechanic (Engines) on 610 Squadron:

My role was a lesser one but I am nevertheless proud of having served on 610 Squadron, of which time I have proud memories of having been personally involved with so many heroes.

One thing I seem to recall about Wing Commander Bader is that he said polished buttons glinted far too brightly. As a result, orders came round that there was to be no more button cleaning. Eventually our battledresses were fitted with black plastic buttons, an unimportant point but perhaps of interest.

Sergeant Ward-Smith at readiness, Westhampnett 1941.

TANGMERE WING WAR DIARY 18 MARCH – 8 AUGUST 1941

Above left: Flight Lieutenant Ronnie Hamlyn DFM (standing, centre) and his Flight of 610 Squadron, including Sergeant Ward-Smith (kneeling at right).

Above right: Cliff Airey pictured when a sergeant later in the war.

> I found it such a thrill when you replied to my letter and stirred my memory by mentioning names like Johnnie Johnson and 'Crow' Milling. It reminded me of those dispersal days on readiness, awaiting the scramble call, having the parachutes hanging on the wing for the pilot to run into, starting up and generally helping ensure that 'your' aircraft got away okay in the shortest possible time. Usually, the Spitfires went off in a line of three across the grass. Then the waiting, the hoping and relief when 'your' Spitfire returned. The inspections and checks I would recall, giving particular attention to see if the throttle had broken the locking wire to go 'through the gate', if so, requiring further work on the Rolls-Royce 45 Merlin engine before the aircraft could be returned to operational service.

610 Squadron's Administration Clerk was Harry Jacks:

> While 610 Squadron operated out of Westhampnett there were a couple of events which caused Wing Commander Bader to blow his 'stack' and use very strong language to senior officers

at Group HQ. On one occasion a signal was received ordering the Wing Commander to exchange his Vauxhall staff car for a smaller eight hp model, and second, another signal arrived ordering him to return to Group inventory one of his two aircraft, either his black-painted night-flying Hurricane or his Spitfire. It is my recollection that neither instruction was acted upon!

AC2 Alan Baldwin, of Station Sick Quarters recalled the night attacks on Tangmere:

With the improved weather came renewed activity by enemy raiders. In March 1941 there were night raids on Tangmere over a period of four or five nights. The Officers' Mess was damaged, as was the Sergeants' Mess. Of the few barrack blocks that were occupied at night, one was destroyed and two damaged. Seven airmen were killed and a dozen or more injured. I remember taking some of them by ambulance to Goodwood House, which was being used as a hospital. Also, around this time, some planes were destroyed on the ground.

As the routine work of the Station went on, there was a feeling that busy times lay ahead. All around there were signs of expansion, with additional landing ground, aircraft and personnel. A new Spitfire Wing, with Wing Commander Bader in charge, had been formed, and he led attacks on France. The fact that we were now taking the initiative and attacking the enemy, instead of being tied to defending our own shores gave the whole Station a good feeling.

Two of 616 Squadron's groundcrew with a German incendiary bomb dropped the previous night.

TANGMERE WING WAR DIARY 18 MARCH – 8 AUGUST 1941

Bomb damage at Tangmere, March 1941.

Flight Lieutenant Holden and Flying Officer Dundas inspect bomb damage – the night raids were a real problem at that time.

The night raids, however, were a real concern and essential work was in progress to camouflage the runways. Unfortunately, no amount of berating by either Group Captain Woodhall or Wing Commander Bader could encourage the workers to greater industry, and the work proceeded at a snail's pace. Incensed, Bader called a golfing pal who happened to be a Fleet Street journalist, and soon an article appeared in the *Sunday Express* highlighting the plight of squadrons on an unnamed aerodrome being put at risk due to the camouflage workers' 'sloth'. Consequently, Woodhall and Bader received a visit from the Under-Secretary of State for Air, Sir Archibald Sinclair, who was well-known to both officers, the purpose being to give them a 'rocket' over the publicity. Sinclair was told, in short order, to take his 'rocket' back to the Air Ministry – and the work was completed within the week.

2 April 1941
The 11 Group AOC Air Vice-Marshal Leigh-Mallory visited Tangmere during the afternoon, touring dispersal points and the Sergeants' Mess. After an overnight stay in Chichester, or 'Chi' as it was more commonly known by Tangmere personnel, the AOC inspected the kitchen and airmen's dining hall of 610 Squadron, and Sergeants' Mess at Westhampnett. At the Officers' Mess, he addressed 610 Squadron's pilots, two of which, Flight Lieutenant Norris and Sergeant Ballard, had destroyed a Ju 88 over the sea at 0700 hrs that morning.

Air Commodore E.W. 'Peter' Merriman was a sergeant-pilot, who joined 610 Squadron at Westhampnett in April 1941:

> We NCO pilots frequented the Unicorn pub in Chichester, and returned from some of our sorties thereto with various road signs which then littered the garden of our billet, 'Fisher's Cottage', until retrieved by the police, when the whole thing would just repeat itself. I remember that one day Tony Gaze produced a shotgun with which he blasted huge holes in the metal stovepipes attached to some outdoor boilers. On seeing this, Joe Doley asked if the shot would penetrate his steel helmet, to which Gaze replied 'I don't know, put it on and we'll see!' He did, and a huge dent appeared on the helmet, beneath which was a very stunned Joe Doley! There was also a troop of light tanks based on the airfield, commanded by a lieutenant, which we used to drive with great enthusiasm! I remember also that we used to take the cordite from .303 and 20mm rounds to make bombs and rockets, albeit without much success. Finally, I recall that often upon returning from a sortie we would land at Beachy Head, where there was a sort of NAAFI hut from which we could buy oranges.

TANGMERE WING WAR DIARY 18 MARCH – 8 AUGUST 1941

Right: Flying Officer Dundas digging his vegetable patch at Westhampnett, whilst Pilot Officer Johnson and Flight Lieutenant Holden look on.

Below: Sergeant E.W. 'Peter' Merriman of 610 Squadron.

Above: Sergeant Merriman and his groundcrew at the NCO pilots' billet, 'Fisher's Cottage'.

Left: Fisher's Cottage.

TANGMERE WING WAR DIARY 18 MARCH – 8 AUGUST 1941

There was a new arrival for 616 Squadron, Sergeant-Pilot Jeff West, a replacement pilot from New Zealand; in his diary, West wrote: 'Reported to Adjutant at 0930. Met CO and Flt Cdr. Allotted to 'A' Flight, issued with parachute. Had tea – good Mess, chicken dinner. Army Ordnance Corps chatted to whole Squadron.

3 April 1941
The Tangmere Sector entertained another VIP, Group Captain HRH The Duke of Kent, to whom 302 Squadron presented a Polish eagle made of Perspex from a Ju 88 destroyed by the squadron.

4 April 1941
616 Squadron's 'Kiwi', Sergeant Jeff West, wrote in his diary:

> A clear day. Walked into camp from our new billet, had breakfast and reported to flights. Had a flip in a Spitfire II – a marvellous job with stacks of power. Went up in formation after 6 pm, had a recon flight. Hampdens in this morning. Did not know any of the crew. Paid at 11.30 am, £6-10-0. Paid Mess bill, 1/-. Came to Chi at 8 pm. Stag's Head, Unicorn and a couple of other pubs. No shops open for supper after 9.30 pm. Had a cup of tea at YMCA. Caught bus back to camp.

6 April 1941
A day of Rhubarb operations. At 1450 hrs, Squadron Leader Ellis and Sergeant Page of 610 Squadron took off, a few minutes later crossing the French coast at St Valéry, just below the bank of 10/10ths cloud at 800ft; it was raining hard, reducing visibility to just two miles. Ten miles inland the Spitfires turned north, splitting up in the hope of finding a suitable target of opportunity. Ellis dived to attack what he thought was Bois Roubert airfield, but finding it deserted instead flew out to sea before heading inland over the Somme estuary, towards Abbeville. Failing to locate that aerodrome in the gathering gloom, 610 Squadron's CO crossed out over Cap Gris Nez and returned to base not having fired a single shot. Sergeant Page had followed a road travelling south-west from Dieppe and was fired at from the ground before also returning to Westhampnett without having found a target.

610 Squadron's Flight Lieutenant Norris crossed the mouth of the Somme, but the weather ahead was so bad that he decided not to proceed

further, and so, together with Pilot Officer Ross, patrolled the coast between Dieppe and Cap Gris Nez. Passing Le Touquet the Spitfire pair fired at a stationary trawler two miles out to sea, but otherwise had nothing to report.

Pilots were extremely vulnerable to ground fire on these low-level Rhubarbs. The Spitfire's coolant tank was situated in the nose, beneath the engine, covered not in armour plate but just ordinary airframe aluminium, and the under-wing radiator was similarly exposed. A single rifle calibre round into these assemblies was all it often took to bring a Spitfire down, so pilots were vulnerable to ground fire on these escapades. Many years later, Johnnie Johnson commented that 'We hated Rhubarbs. So many good pilots and leaders lost on these pointless sorties. Later, when I was more senior and serving as a staff officer at 11 Group HQ, I put a stop to it.'

For now, however, Rhubarbs were very much on the board and a part of the Tangmere Wing's everyday life.

<u>7 April 1941</u>
Squadron Leader Laguna's 302 Squadron departed Westhampnett to join the new Polish Fighter Wing at Northolt.

<u>10 April 1941</u>
At 0555 hrs, Tangmere was attacked by a Ju 88. Five airmen were killed and fourteen wounded. A delayed-action bomb remained outside the Watch Office, however, and No 8 Barrack Block was completely destroyed by a direct hit. Furthermore, No 5 Block was seriously damaged and a bomb passed clean through the Link Trainer Room, having ricocheted off the adjacent road.

Pat Goodenough, of 616 Squadron's ground staff:

> An interesting little story concerns the 616 Squadron Intelligence Officer, Flying Officer Gibbs. He had once lived on the Continent and every now and again took his bicycle off in the Lysander and disappeared. I said that he must have dropped the bike out over France as he always returned with it wrecked, and I had to help repair it! As a result of this favour Gibbs gave me an early chit to start my leave. While I was away there was another big raid on Tangmere: sixteen were killed and fifteen injured. Block Five suffered a direct hit and

TANGMERE WING WAR DIARY 18 MARCH – 8 AUGUST 1941

Above left: Pat Goodenough, of 616 Squadron's groundcrew.

Above right: Flying Officer Gibbs (left), with 616 Squadron's adjutant, Flying Officer Frank Walter.

Flying Officer 'Spy' Gibbs – was this the bicycle repaired by Pat Goodenough?

when I returned had to salvage my kit and sleep on the stairs of Shopwyke House. In April 1941 I attended a fitter's course at RAF Halton but did not return to 616 Squadron. I was no hero and played only a minor role.

'Bunny' Warren was a flight rigger at Merston with 145 Squadron's 'B' Flight:-

> Tangmere was often heavily bombed at night. On one occasion I had my webbing stretched across the top of my bed – it was cut in many places by shrapnel. On another occasion a few nights later, a stick of bombs landed on two sides of the billet. The blast from these threw me and others out of bed onto the middle of the barrack's floor. After this, some of us were billeted in 'Air Raid Surface Shelters', behind the flying field, before transferring to Shopwyke House, owned by Lady Paget, a well-known horse breeder.

Sergeant Jeff West's diary:

> Quite an ordinary sort of day. Had one trip of formation with Johnson after tea. Back by transport and into Chichester. Went to pictures and saw *Brother Orchid*. Good show. Had a few beers until 930 pm and went to dance in the Assembly. Caught bus back to Woodfield. Quite a bit of activity in air. Whitleys landing on drome on return from Germany. One crashed on drome and burnt out. Ten German bombers were brought down.

<u>13 April 1941</u>
616 Squadron undertook cine-gun and formation practice flights, the latter under the supervision of Wing Commander Bader.

<u>14 April 1941</u>
By this time, many senior pilots were long overdue a rest. On this day, Squadron Leader H. De C.A. 'Paddy' Woodhouse AFC took over 610 Squadron from Squadron Leader John Ellis DFC – another superb leader – who was rested as Chief Flying Instructor with 54 OTU.

<u>15 April 1941</u>
Wing Commander Bader led twelve 616 Squadron Spitfires escorting bombers returning from a raid on Brest. The sortie passed without incident, so far as the enemy was concerned, although Sergeant Bob 'Butch' Morton remembered that:

Wing Commander Bader, who always used the radio callsign 'Dogsbody', took the whole Squadron on a patrol from which we returned rather short of fuel. I was one of the last to make my approach, by which time it was dark. Our petrol gauges were never reliable, and it was no surprise that when I turned cross-wind I found that, on blipping the throttle, the engine was dead. Fortunately, my circuit, for once, was impeccable, and my glide landed me exactly beside the Chance light, whereupon my propeller, which had previously been wind-milling, just stopped dead. I trundled happily down the flarepath and turned off just before I lost my way. Walking back to dispersal, I said casually to the ground-mechanics: 'Sorry chaps, you'll have to bring it in yourselves this time!'

At this time, I had a coat of arms painted on my Mae West: argent, on a pale azure, three crowns for Hull, on a chief of the second the tail of a Spitfire diving into a cloud; the motto was 'Spotto, Squirto, Scrammo', or 'I spot, I shoot, I remove myself'. It was highly commended by Wing Commander Bader. Outside our 'A' Flight hut soon appeared

Pilots of 610 Squadron at readiness.

Squadron Leader Ken Holden (in forage cap at centre, middle row), with his new command: 610 Squadron.

Sergeants Doley and Horner of 610 Squadron inspecting the damage suffered in a flying accident by Spitfire R6599 at Acklington.

TANGMERE WING WAR DIARY 18 MARCH – 8 AUGUST 1941

a notice: 'Bader's Bus Company: Daily Trips to the Continent. Return Tickets Only!' The 'trip' turned out to usually take place twice daily, although as it turned out my season pass abruptly expired in July 1941. The 'Bus Company' bit derived from the wing's radio call sign of 'Greenline Bus'.

Above: Archery was a popular pastime to while away the hours spent on readiness – although the groundcrews made themselves scarce! Here pilots of 610 Squadron consider their results, Sergeant Peter Ward-Smith at extreme right.

Right: Sergeant Peter Ward-Smith and his 610 Squadron Spitfire at Westhampnett.

BADER'S SPITFIRE WING

<u>16 April 1942</u>

Squadron Leader Jack Leather DFC, also due for rest, handed over command of 145 Squadron to Wing Commander's great friend, the Canadian Squadron Leader Stan Turner DFC, who had previously commanded a flight of 242 Squadron. Not unnaturally, Bader was keen to import 'his' people, those known personally to him as trustworthy and competent, to key positions in the wing, and Turner's was the first such appointment. Of Turner, Johnnie Johnson later wrote that he was:

> One of the select band of adventurous young men from the old Empire who made their way to England in the mid-thirties to join the RAF and become fighter pilots. Looking as if he had been roughly hewn from granite ... somewhat casual about his dress ... difficult and something of a 'prickly pear'...

Above left: Squadron Leader Turner (right) had flown with Douglas Bader's 242 Squadron during the Battle of Britain, and was brought into the Tangmere Wing to command 145 Squadron. Turner is pictured here in Holland when a Group Captain in 1945, with Johnnie Johnson, then a Wing Commander and Fighter Command's top-scoring fighter pilot.

Above right: Sergeant Jeff West (left), the New Zealander who often flew in Dogsbody Section, kept a remarkable diary throughout the war, and is pictured reading letters from home with Sergeant Brewer, also of 616 Squadron.

tough, independent and was in there fighting when others had gone – for the simple reason that he was obstinate and would not give in.

Sergeant Frank Twitchett: 'We had a first-class CO in Stan Turner, who was a craggy Canadian who stood no nonsense from anybody but treated all his pilots, regardless of rank, with absolute fairness. I, for one, had much admiration for him.'

Truly, Squadron Leader Turner was a man in the Bader mould.

On this day, the AOC paid Tangmere another visit, arriving by air. After lunching in the Officers' Mess, 'LM' conferenced with the Station Commander, wing leader, and squadron commanders before returning to Uxbridge at 1630 hrs.

Sergeant Jeff West's diary:

> Another marvellous morning. Jim McCairns and I went to 25,000ft and then dogfighting. Jumped by 'B' Flight so I dived from 15,000ft to 2,000ft. Climbed back to 25,000ft and dog fought. Both McCairns and I lost cooling on engines. Mine particularly bad. Used a lot of engine on approach. Quite a good landing. After dinner went up No 3 – 'Nip', Ron and I. Ron had cine-gun – ballsed up exercise and argument ensued. Saw MO – stayed home. Received letters from Bruce Lightbourne and Mrs Percy.

<u>17 April 1941</u>
Between 0615 and 0745 hrs the Tangmere Wing escorted bombers to Cherbourg; the 610 Squadron diary recorded 'Escort carried out OK'. 145 Squadron reported seeing a Rotte of Me 109s shadowing the Beehive, but there was no engagement. 145 was actually the wing's longest-serving squadron in the Tangmere Sector, among the sergeant-pilots serving in which was Frank Twitchett:

> I arrived at Tangmere in December 1940, having been posted from 229 Squadron, with which I had started my period of operational service some three months before. 145 Squadron was then commanded by Squadron Leader J.R.A. Peel DFC and flying Hurricanes when I arrived. In January 1941, Squadron Leader W.J. 'Jack' Leather DFC took over, who oversaw our

Left: Sergeant Frank Twitchett of 145 Squadron.

Below: Pilots of Merston's 145 Squadron at readiness: from left, Sergeants Grant and Johnson, Pilot Officers Scott and Sabourin.

conversion to Spitfires, which he had flown with 611 Squadron during the Battle of Britain.

Between December 1940 and February 1941, our role remained almost entirely defensive, and soon after receiving Spitfire Mk Is we converted to the new Mk II. In March 1941, having fully converted to the Spitfire, we had our first success on type when a section of aircraft, of which I was a member, intercepted and destroyed a Ju 88 off Selsey Bill. We also began to do Channel sweeps, although these were largely ineffective as being purely fighter sweeps the Luftwaffe very sensibly stayed on the ground, not bothering to intercept our fighters,

Sergeant W.J. 'Johnny' Johnson of 145 Squadron aloft from Merston.

Flight Lieutenant Newling's 145 Squadron Spitfire.

which posed no threat. Wing Commander Bader arrived in March 1941, however, and by April things were really starting to happen. Shortly after Wing Commander Bader arrived, Squadron Leader Leather was posted and in April our new CO was the Canadian Squadron Leader P.S. 'Stan' Turner DFC. We carried out our first bomber escort, to Cherbourg, on 17 April 1941, and at around the same time received a new flight commander, Flight Lieutenant C.I.R. Arthur, another Canadian from Bader's former 242 Squadron.

Left: Sergeant Frank Twitchett's 'War Horse': P7990.

Below: Dave Horne (right) and Harry Patenal, both members of 145 Squadron's groundcrew.

TANGMERE WING WAR DIARY 18 MARCH – 8 AUGUST 1941

Sergeants W.J. 'Johnny' Johnson and Frank Twitchett, both of 145 Squadron, at Merston.

The crew of Frank Twitchett's Spitfire, Drew and Pattison.

BADER'S SPITFIRE WING

<u>18 April 1941</u>
Squadron Leader Woodhouse of 610 Squadron flew a solo Rhubarb, finding 'nothing worth firing at'.

<u>19 April 1941</u>
During the afternoon, 145 Squadron's new CO, Squadron Leader Stan Turner, 'visited the French coast at Cap Gris Nez. Flew along the coast at 200ft but saw no signs of enemy activity on land or sea.'

<u>21 April 1941</u>
The Tangmere Wing escorted eighteen Blenheims to Le Havre, but the bombers were unable to locate their target, flying west of it. As the Spitfires were running low on fuel they had to turn about. Sergeant Bob 'Butch' Morton:

> When our fuel was getting near danger point, Bader waggled his wings as a signal for us to set off for England. On the crossing I fear that we concentrated more on our fuel gauges than keeping lookout. Only a stream of golden rain past my canopy, and the sight of my No 2 rearing up out of control, alerted me that we were being attacked! I shouted a warning to the squadron before turning steeply in time to see two Me 109s haring back to France. There was no point in trying to catch them, so I concentrated on my No 2, a sergeant called Sellars. I saw that he had baled out and was floating above the mass of creamy foam that I later came to associate with a ditched aircraft. I circled him for a time, to provide a 'fix', then made for home before my petrol ran out. I later learned that while I had circled Sellars, so too had Flight Lieutenant Colin MacFie been protecting me. In spite of the ASR resources, and a search of the sea by the entire Squadron immediately after we had been refuelled, Sellars was never found.

Sergeant Robert Lindon Sellars had been shot down by I/JG 2's Leutnant Vogel, who claimed a Spitfire destroyed at 1012 hrs, 50km south of the Isle of Wight; the single 23-year old from Blackpool has no known grave and is remembered on the Runnymede Memorial to the missing.

TANGMERE WING WAR DIARY 18 MARCH – 8 AUGUST 1941

<u>22 April 1941</u>
Group Captain A.B. 'Woody' Woodhall OBE arrived at Tangmere, assuming command of the Station two days later and taking over as 'Boss Controller'. 'Woody' was a personal friend of both Air Vice-Marshal Leigh-Mallory and Wing Commander Bader. Of Tangmere's legless wing leader, 'Woody' wrote that he was:

> indefatigable, and, as at Duxford the year before, proved tireless in his efforts to defeat the Hun. The old team worked well together, and by now our AOC had organised 11 Group into a formidable fighting force.
>
> Douglas Bader was very apt to cut corners and ignore regulations or interpret them his own way in order to get on with the war. On one occasion when he had offended against some rule, I was given orders from a higher authority to reprove him. He was ordered to report to my office, and when he stumped in and saluted with his usual cheerful grin he noticed that I was wearing my cap and did not tell him to sit down, indicating an official interview. Douglas stood to attention and with an impish grin said, 'Woody, you're not going to be rotten to me, are you?' What could I do but laugh, then tell him to sit down? Needless to say the reproof was passed to him as a joke – but the fact that it <u>was</u> passed on proved quite effective. The administrative and operational tasks and problems increased daily, and hampered as we were by a set of peacetime rules and regulations, designed as they were in the main to prevent petty pilfering, it is not surprising that everyone trying to do his job had to cut the red tape in order to get on with the war. In this Douglas Bader and I saw eye-to-eye, and I can state that we backed each other up loyally in this matter of tape-cutting. LM, our AOC, was always on our side too, which was very comforting!

<u>24 April 1941</u>
Squadron Leader Woodhouse and Pilot Officer Tony Gaze of 610 Squadron flew a Rhubarb, crossing the French coast between Le Touquet and Dieppe. Again, Woodhouse found no action but Gaze shot-up some barges at Le Tréport, provoking a hail of green and red tracer hurled at his Spitfire,

BADER'S SPITFIRE WING

Group Captain AB 'Woody' Woodhall.

before returning safely home. Two pairs of 616 Squadron Spitfires also undertook Rhubarbs: Flying Officer Dundas and Sergeant Mabbett prowled uneventfully over Abbeville, while Flight Lieutenant MacFie and Sergeant McDevette popped over to Cherbourg. There, MacFie strafed seven I/JG 2 Me 109s on the ground at Maupertus – but his No 2 was hit by flak. Sergeant Thomas Francis McDevette vanished without trace, no doubt crashing into the sea, becoming yet another name commemorated at Runnymede.

26 April 1941
Flight Lieutenant MacFie and Flying Officer Dundas of 616 Squadron flew a high-altitude 'offensive patrol' over the French coast, landing with no action to report.

27 April 1941
145 Squadron uneventfully escorted bombers which were returning across the Channel.

Sergeant 'Thug' Mabbett, Pilot Officer Johnnie Johnson, and Sergeant McCairns at 616 Squadron's Westhampnett dispersal.

TANGMERE WING WAR DIARY 18 MARCH – 8 AUGUST 1941

Sergeant Jeff West's diary:

> Another day on readiness at 830 am. White Section, Fg Off Hugh 'Cocky' Dundas and I went on minesweeper patrol south of St Catherine's Point. Called off and vectored onto a Jerry but did not contact him. After lunch – chicken – 145 went on a bomber cover so we were again called to readiness. Went on an X Raid, 15,000ft above cloud. No action. After tea, Mabbett, Derek and I went to Chi. Mabbett called back to night fly. Pranged on landing. Went to pictures – *French Without Tears*.

29 April 1941
616 Squadron flew an identical sortie to that of 145 the previous day.

30 April 1941
Likewise 610 Squadron escorted bombers returning from France without incident.

5 May 1941
Sergeant Frank Twitchett: 'Throughout May 1941, we undertook several sorties up and down the Channel, attempting to flush out some opposition.'

Sergeant Mabbett and Pilot Officer Hepple of 616 Squadron.

145 Squadron's Pilot Officer Offenberg, a Belgian, flew a Rhubarb to Cherbourg where he engaged two He 60 floatplanes, destroying one. During the return flight he attacked two Me 109s, claiming one as a probable after seeing it dive seawards 'with smoke pouring from the engine'.

Flying Officers Roy Marples and Buck Casson of 616 Squadron intercepted and destroyed a Ju 88, as the latter recalled:

> We intercepted a reconnaissance Ju 88 at 15,000ft over Portsmouth. It dived south to just 100ft over the sea. I shot the rear gunner but was hit myself and started leaking glycol. I just managed to recross the coast at 950ft with a cockpit full of smoke. I inverted my Spitfire and baled out near Littlehampton.

Buck also remembered that 616 Squadron's officers found that their wing leader's demands extended to off-duty time:

> I had first met Bader at Coltishall on 3 September 1940, when he tried to tick some of us off for having our top buttons undone in true fighter pilot style. He was then a squadron leader,

Sergeant Mabbett (left) on readiness with an unidentified flying pilot officer and Ken Holden, then a flight lieutenant commanding 616 Squadron's 'A' Flight.

TANGMERE WING WAR DIARY 18 MARCH – 8 AUGUST 1941

Wing Commander Bader (seated at right), at readiness with 616 Squadron; from left, seated: Flight Lieutenant Denis Gillam, Pilot Officer Hepple and Squadron Leader Burton. Standing: Sergeants West and Brewer, two unknown orderlies, and Flight Lieutenant Holden.

The same group joined by Sergeant McCairns, standing between Gillam and Hepple.

Above left: Squadron Leader Burton and Wing Commander Bader, Westhampnett, 1941.

Above right: Golf was a game that the feverishly competitive and immensely enthusiastic Douglas Bader could play better than most – even without legs.

Golf was another popular past-time, the officer pilots often being summonsed to play with the Wing Leader – regardless of their own personal plans! From left: 616 Squadron's Flight Lieutenants MacFie and Holden, with Flying Officers Casson and Dundas.

commanding 242 Squadron. We were just pilot officers then, so easy prey. I came to know him briefly during early 1941, when we occasionally joined up with 242 as a 12 Group Wing, flying from Duxford or Wittering. Of course, I came to know him much better at Tangmere from March 1941 onwards. We enjoyed playing golf with Douglas at Goodwood, although this was largely at the Wing Commander's convenience, regardless of our own plans or personal commitments! We also socialised with Douglas and his wife, Thelma, at the Bayhouse, known by us pilots as the 'Baghouse'. There we carried Douglas to the pool, where he swam extremely well. He always wanted company so we often went to his digs for a drink and chat.

7 May 1941
At 0540 hrs, Pilot Officer Gaze and Sergeant Warden of 610 Squadron took off to patrol Beachy Head and escort a Lysander. At 0645 the Section was at about 400ft over the sea and travelling east when two aircraft were observed following the Spitfires, slightly higher and two miles behind. Identifying the 'bandits' as Me 109s, the Section gave chase at sea-level, pursuing the Germans back to France but observing no hits. The 109s were reported, however, to have emitted 'clouds of black smoke' – likely, as already explained, to have simply been produced by extra boost.

On this day, 145 Squadron was dispersed to Merston permanently, as a precaution against the continued night bombing, which had caused further disruption and damage. At Merston the airmen were accommodated in huts around the perimeter while the officers remained at their existing billets, 'Sycamores' and 'Sycamore Cottage'.

Sergeant Frank Twitchett:

> Merston was a landing ground with no runway or living accommodation, so we were billeted in a farmhouse on the far corner of the airfield. We had one airman who was a general potter-around, keep the place clean type of chap, and a cook to feed us. His job was to feed the eleven or twelve NCO pilots normally on the squadron strength. The conditions were such, bearing in mind that this was a private house with fairly small rooms, we lived about four to a room, so your accommodation consisted of just a bed and a very narrow steel wardrobe in which you could put some clothes. Mostly the beds were

unmade, you fell out of them in the morning, then got back into them at night! The general state of living was pretty squalid, but we coped all right. We used a local pub right on the corner of the airfield itself called the 'Walnut Tree'; this became a great favourite with all the squadron, irrespective of rank, and we tended to congregate there after getting released at night. Assuming, of course, that the pub was open and had supplies of beer, the landlord did a brisk trade.

Time off was erratic. It could be given at short-notice if the weather deteriorated, but to think in terms of a day off in a week's time was just impossible. The idea was that when you were on the airfield you were available for duty at any time. Quite often you would be called up to go on a sweep in the morning, only to find that although you were not required for the rest of the day, you were still expected to remain on the airfield and not clear off into Chichester or any of the surrounding towns. Days were generally very long, in June, of course, we were on the longest days, compounded by Double Summer Time, so that it was not unusual to come to readiness at 0400 hrs and still be on the airfield until perhaps 2200 hrs. You could be warned for a sweep in the morning, as I have said, or in the morning find that you were not required for sweeping until later in the afternoon. All this hanging about, most of which was spent asleep in chairs or even on the old camp beds which we had in our dispersal hut, was a bit wearing on the nerves to say the least. Another problem was that you could be strapped in the cockpit and ready to go on a sweep only for the sortie to be put back for one hour, or even two, and the instructions usually were to remain in the cockpit until a further signal told us to start our engines and begin taxying. You can appreciate that this caused a lot of wear and tear on the nerves, particularly as in the summertime you could be sitting there in full flying kit, out in the hot sun on the middle of the airfield.

We could apply for leave, if we were due days off, and under those circumstances we could usually expect for it to be granted. Even that was not completely secure, however – there were occasions when people were told to delay their leave by a few days, for example if we were working in conditions like a limited number of pilots, but by and large leave was granted when requested. Days off, however, again as I have said, were a different matter, largely dependent upon weather conditions preventing flying and very precious indeed.

<u>8 May 1941</u>
Wing Commander Bader continued to enthusiastically discuss tactics. On the evening of 7 May 1941, 'Dogsbody' gathered certain of his officers around him, sitting up in the Mess until late. Flying Officer Dundas:- 'We expressed our dissatisfaction with formations adopted in the past … the half pints went down again and again while we argued the toss.' Dundas suggested that four aircraft flying in line abreast, some fifty yards apart, could never be bounced from behind. Those on the right would cover the tails of the Spitfires on the left and vice versa. No enemy could therefore approach unseen, but if attacked the formation could break upwards, one pair to port, the other to starboard. This was identical, of course, to the German Schwärm. It is difficult to understand why Fighter Command took so long to imitate the enemy. The vic had rapidly been found virtually suicidal, and individual squadrons had been experimenting with their own tactical formations for some time. These generally seem to have involved some kind of line astern formation – not abreast, like the Schwärm, comprising two pairs, leader and wingman. Nursing a hangover at breakfast the following morning, Dundas regretted his inspirational suggestion: 'Not being a drinker, "DB" strode into the Mess with his buccaneering gait and was clearly in rude health. He told me that he had considered my idea and had decided to try it out. I nodded in weak agreement but was somewhat startled when he added "This morning"!'

Wing Commander Bader led his Dogsbody Section, comprising two pairs: Dundas and himself, and 610 Squadron's Squadron Leader Woodhouse and Sergeant Maine. The Section climbed to 26,500ft over mid-Channel and prowled up and down, just south of Dover – deliberately inviting trouble. Six Me 109s of Stab/JG 51 – coincidentally led by Major Werner Mölders, who had invented the Schwärm in Spain – soon appeared, tailing the Spitfires and at the same height. At what he guessed to be the optimum moment, Bader warned 'OK boys, get ready for it … BREAK!' – and broke both pairs around to reverse the situation. The Spitfires immediately whipped round, the four pilots almost blacking out, so tight was the turn. As Dundas levelled out, resuming the Section's original course, there was no sign of the enemy – but then rounds raked his machine. Thick smoke engulfed his cockpit. Dundas opened his hood and limped back to crash-land at

Above left: Sergeant West, lying on cowling, with his friend Sergeant Brewer pointing out their Wing Leader's nose-art, whilst sitting on the wing of Spitfire P7666 are Sergeant Mabbett and Pilot Officer Hepple.

Above right: An anonymous 'Chiefy', a flight sergeant responsible for a team of 616 Squadron's essential groundcrew.

From left: Squadron Leader Burton, Flying Officer Dundas, Flight Lieutenant MacFie, Wing Commander Bader, and a particularly amused Pilot Officer Johnson.

TANGMERE WING WAR DIARY 18 MARCH – 8 AUGUST 1941

In this snapshot, a visiting American pilot, Lieutenant Montgomery, is snapped outside 616 Squadron's Westhampnett dispersal with, from left: Squadron Leader Burton, Pilot Officer Johnson, Flying Officer Dundas, Wing Commander Bader and Sergeant Smith. The line-up emphasises the RAF's diverse composition at this time: Johnson and Smith being volunteer reservists; Dundas an auxiliary airman, and Bader and Burton, the Cranwellian professionals.

'A' Flight of 616 Squadron. Back row, from left: Pilot Officer Johnson, Sergeants Mabbett, Scott and McCairns; front: Flight Lieutenant Dundas, Pilot Officer Hepple and Sergeant Smith.

Above left: Flying Officer Buck Casson enjoying high summer weather.

Above right: Pilot Officer Johnson, with pipe, and Flying Officer Hugh Dundas – whose idea it was to copy the German Schwärm.

Left: When Dogsbody Section experimented with the new 'Finger Four' formation, Wing Commander mistimed the break, as a result of which Flying Officer Dundas was shot-up by Major Werner Mölders, crash-landing at Hawkinge.

Hawkinge, covered by Squadron Leader Woodhouse. During the break, tracer had also flashed past Maine, who shook off his assailant before firing at an Me 109 and hitting its fuselage. Maine was then hit by anti-aircraft fire but broke again and attacked another 109 at point blank range – which crashed into the sea. On this occasion, only one Spitfire was shot down in combat, but the Germans overclaimed; while Major Mölders filed his 60th Abschuss, Oberleutnant Horst Geyer claimed two.

After Flight Lieutenant Holden had collected Flying Officer Dundas and returned him to Westhampnett in the Station's Magister communications aircraft, Wing Commander Bader held a de-brief. Despite Dundas having been shot down, the benefits of the line abreast formation in preventing a surprise attack were evident. The fault lay with Bader, who had mis-timed the break, leading to several of the 109s remaining behind the Spitfires as they levelled out. Moreover, instead of breaking in opposite directions, the two pairs should have turned in the same direction. Once the correct timing could be achieved, all involved agreed that this new formation, the aircraft occupying similar positions to the fingers of an outstretched hand, was the future. Over the years, it has frequently been written that Wing Commander Bader was entirely responsible for the so-called 'Finger Four' – which was soon adopted not just by the Tangmere Wing but throughout Fighter Command. Pilot Officer Johnnie Johnson:

> The 'Finger Four' was really Cocky Dundas's idea. We had all seen the Germans flying in these loose formations of fighters, lean and hungry looking, with plenty of room between them, like a pack of hunting dogs. Prior to going to Tangmere, we of 616 Squadron were not flying vics but pairs. Then Bader arrived. At first, we flew in three fours, these being loose fours and in line astern, and then Dundas suggested that we should fly fours in line abreast. Consequently, after a little experimentation, we adopted this in May 1941. Bader was actually the first man to talk to us about tactics. He had the ability to dissect an air battle and learn from it. It was people like Bader and Malan, really, who dictated tactics.

It was an historic moment: Fighter Command was at last on the right track.

Also on this day, Squadron Leader Turner and Pilot Officer de Hemptinne, another Belgian, of 145 Squadron flew an uneventful Rhubarb to Cherbourg.

BADER'S SPITFIRE WING

<u>9 May 1941</u>
As a further precaution against the night raiders, 616 Squadron also moved from Tangmere to operate permanently from Westhampnett with 610. 616's airmen were accommodated in huts at the airfield while the officers remained at 'Rushman's', and the sergeants at Woodfield House, Oving.

AC1 Harold Mead, Flight Mechanic 'A', 'B' Flight, 610 Squadron:

> Having carried out the routine scheduled Daily Inspection of his aircraft, the fitter or rigger would get into the cockpit and start the engine, running to the correct revs, temperature and oil pressure and check the magneto ignition. It was surprising that sometimes a weary, over-stressed, pilot would take off on a sortie only to return immediately, complaining of 'mag drop', a weirdly unpredictable engine malfunction which so often miraculously cured itself by the time the fitter checked it over. By then it was too late to rejoin the sortie. Fighter pilots weren't super heroes like Buck Rogers, they were brave young men who did their job just as long as they could … but they were human.
>
> Usually, the fitter would hang the pilot's flying helmet over the reflector gunsight, with the oxygen and RT (Radio Telephone) plugged in ready and would place the parachute on the wingtip with the harness hanging down so that when the scramble call came, the pilot could run to his aircraft, back into the parachute harness, bring the shoulder straps down, pull the lower straps up between his legs and snap them into the Irvin quick-release lock. He would then climb up the wing root with the cumbersome parachute pack swinging and bumping up behind him, ready to serve as his cushion in the moulded metal cockpit bucket seat. While he was doing that, the fitter would start the engine, leaving it running while helping the pilot into his parachute and then into his seat harness.
>
> That was the usual general procedure but there were some exceptions. Some pilots preferred to have the parachute placed in the bucket seat, with the straps hanging clear, so they could run straight up the wing, jump into the seat and have the rigger buckle them in while they put on their helmet and plugged into the RT and oxygen. Whichever way, it was a slick, well-practised procedure that got the machines into the air in the

minimum time and with the minimum risk to personnel and aircraft.

Then it was a matter of twelve or sixteen aircraft getting off the ground and into a steeply climbing turn to make height and vector on the leader. We always had two squadrons operating from Westhampnett and to 610's credit I cannot recall a single occasion when we had a coming together of aircraft in the scrabble to get airborne. Regrettably, I cannot say the same for when we were joined by a Polish Hurricane squadron. These guys were great drinking company and as gutsy as hell but the trouble was that, in their mad enthusiasm to get up and at the Hun, their self-restraint was sometimes directly disproportionate to their blood lust. They had much to avenge and their attitude, if not always commendable, was wholly understandable. But several were the collisions and near misses they sustained ... to say nothing of their inability to maintain radio transmission discipline, which must have occasioned many other hazards.

During the day, when the squadron was on Readiness, it could be a bit boring for the fitter or rigger, just sitting in the cockpit doing nothing. Many a time it was too much of a temptation for him to start fiddling with things. Move the control column, elevators and ailerons up and down, rudder side to side, open and close the throttle, turn the firing button on and off and suddenly ... Christ almighty! Eight Brownings and a couple of 20mm cannons are blazing across the aerodrome! Not funny ... and certainly a Court Martial in the offing. But it did happen sometimes.

What I really did like was Dawn Readiness. On those occasions the crews slept in Nissen huts on the perimeter, ready to turn out at 0400 hrs. It was dark and cold, so you pulled your tunic and trousers over your pyjamas, stuck your feet in thick woollen seamen's socks and wellies, climbed into your Spit and pulled the hood shut. You did the routine cockpit check (taking a sniff from the oxygen bottle to wake yourself up) and started the engine. You pumped the primer, pressed the starter and yellow flame belched from the exhaust manifolds before turning blue. It was friendly, a world of your own, sitting there in the instruments' glow, watching as needles crept round to the right temperature and oil pressure. And all around you could see the dim shapes of the other aircraft with their ghostly blue flames just throwing the long, tapering line of their fuselages into definition as your eyes accustomed to the darkness and spires of Chichester Cathedral silhouetted against the warming of the dawn sky. And then would come a thumping on the side of your own aircraft. Sliding the hood back revealed someone from the cookhouse with a steaming mug of sweet cocoa and a hot Lyon's individual fruit pie. I don't think you can get those these days, but somehow those pies came to symbolise for me a very special time in my life – on a Spitfire squadron. Oh yes, even in a war there was a very special beauty at such times and life was very good.

12 May 1941

During the early hours, a further raid caused damage at Tangmere but no casualties. The previous night, in fact, had seen the night Blitz reach its dreadful crescendo, with a huge raid on London. By that time, considering the poor state of Britain's nocturnal defences just a few months before, great progress had been made with radar, including AI, and the new, cannon-armed, radar-equipped Beaufighters were proving most effective. What the Allies did not know, however, was that from this point onwards German units were being sent east, in preparation for Hitler's long-awaited attack on the Soviet Union – the night Blitz was largely over.

Sergeant Jeff West's diary:

> Main base again heavily bombed. Sgts' Mess gone, 219 Squadron dispersal and stick across the landing ground.

14 May 1941

Wing Commander Bader flew to and landed at Martlesham Heath, a North Weald satellite, for an unrecorded reason. Taking off, however, the 'hood fell off' his Spitfire, forcing him to return and land. Presumably a replacement was found, for Dogsbody returned to Tangmere the same day.

15 May 1941

Squadron Leader Woodhouse and Pilot Officer Hugill of 610 Squadron were 'ordered on a Rhubarb operation but did not fire'. Similarly, 616 Squadron's Squadron Leader Burton and Pilot Officer Johnson uneventfully patrolled

TANGMERE WING WAR DIARY 18 MARCH – 8 AUGUST 1941

the French coast at 4,000ft. Wing Commander Bader was also airborne, subsequently writing in his log book: 'Local snoop, squirted a Do 17.'

17 May 1941
During a Channel sweep, three Me 109s shadowed the Spitfires before attacking over the sea of Worthing; no Spitfires were lost but Flying Officer Dundas destroyed one of their assailants.

Sergeant Morton was practising dogfighting over Brighton with two new pilots:

> At about 10,000ft I put the other two into line-astern prior to beginning the exercise. At that moment I saw two aircraft approaching us, about 1,000ft above and slightly to one side. They were not Spitfires. I might have thought them 109s except they had rounded wingtips, the well-known distinguishing mark of the 109 being is square wingtips. As this pair of aircraft came abreast of us they turned onto their backs and dived vertically for the ground. This gave me sight of the engine cowlings – bright yellow! At that time everyone had heard of the yellow-nosed 109s, which we believed were from a crack unit. Forgetting all about the accepted procedure of shouting 'Tally Ho!', I simply yelled 'Come on, chaps, it's the real thing!' We gave chase! The 109s levelled out at about 1,000ft, heading back across the Channel with me in hot pursuit. Although we believed that the Spitfire 'had the legs' of a 109, I lost ground. By the time they reached the French coast I was at least 300 yards behind. Although I knew that they were out of range, I gave them a parting squirt before turning for home.
>
> That was the first time I thought about the other two Spitfire pilots. There was no sign of them. I later learned that the first had tried to follow me down, but his eardrums had perforated as he had not yet learned the art of swallowing or yawning in a steep dive. The other pilot heard my shout, but then found himself alone in the sky. Unable to locate us, he returned to base and reported the mystery.
>
> As I neared the English coast, however, I became aware that I was not alone. The 109s, or perhaps another pair, were sneaking up behind. Then began a real Biggles-style dogfight. I had first read the Biggles stories in the *Modern Boy* comic

and was greatly impressed by one of Captain W.E. Johns' footnotes. He stated that in a head-on attack it was not done for a British pilot to break away; if the German also refused to break then he should be rammed. This I thought magnificent at the time, but now knew that I did not possess courage of that magnitude! This fight began with a head-on attack. Only the previous day I had heard Wing Commander Bader say that every pilot, in his first fight, opened fire while still out of range. I determined that I would not fire until I saw smoke coming out of the enemy's gun muzzles. At the instant I did, I thumbed the firing button only to discover that the 109 was no longer there! It was not courage which had prevented me from breaking away, just my inability to think about more than one thing at a time! Fortunately for both of us my opponent was no less dim! The fight ended inconclusively shortly afterwards, how long it lasted I had no idea. For the first time it occurred to me that I had not informed the Ground Controller of the affair, so did so. 'Are you all right?' asked the Controller.

'Fine thanks', I answered. 'How are you?'

After examining my Spitfire the Flight Sergeant told me that he could only find one bullet hole. This seemed astonishing. This single bullet had whistled in all directions within the tailplane, clearing out all the internal structure so that the whole unit had to be replaced!

A week or two later, in one of our regular intelligence bulletins, we were warned to look out for the new Me 109F, which had better performance than the old Me 109E and could, in fact, outdistance a Spitfire. Apparently, it could be recognised by its rounded wingtips…!

20 May 1941
Sergeant Jeff West's diary:

Beautiful morning. Arose at 9.30 am and caught bus back to camp. On readiness until 4.30 pm. Our goods were removed from Woodfield and dumped in ghastly hut. Latrines filthy and washing facilities very poor. Kicked up quite a row with the CO. Boys somewhat appeased, so we went to Tangmere and robbed the Mess of everything we could find. Some of the

TANGMERE WING WAR DIARY 18 MARCH – 8 AUGUST 1941

chaps went into town and got inebriated. Kicked up a row on return. Ron had a day off. Letter from Thelma.

21 May 1941
Wing Commander Bader led 145 Squadron, unusually, over the Channel on a sweep covering a fighter squadron returning from France. When returning to base, Flight Lieutenant Stevens and Flying Officer Owen collided over Westhampnett at 1815 hrs, both pilots being killed. Pilot Officer Tony Gaze, of 610 Squadron, remembered that:

> One rolled over and went straight in near the airfield boundary, the other span in behind Westhampnett Mill. Douglas Bader caused the accident by bringing 145 Squadron back to us at Westhampnett, instead of their own base at Merston, and, breaking away downwards to land himself, as he was personally operating from Westhampnett. This was unannounced and unexpected. The two pilots collided trying to avoid him. Dinkie Stoop, myself and three others saw it all.

No questions appear to have been asked, and no action taken in respect of this doubly fatal flying accident.

24 May 1941
Sergeant Jeff West's diary:

> Weather still poor. No flying. Squadron put to available. In afternoon we were released. Tried to organise a party trip to Brighton. Fell through, so McCairns, Smithy, Dale and I went through to Bognor. Saw Judy Garland in *Strike Up The Band*, then went to dance at the Pavilion. Met Joyce, Dorothy and Jean. Damned good show. Stayed night in Douglas Hotel. Fire in kitchen, burning fat. Everything under control but burnt my hand – quite sore. HMS *Hood* sunk off Greenland.

27 May 1941
Sergeant Jeff West's diary:

> More unsettled weather. On readiness 8.30 pm. Weather poor and no scrambles. Went to Map Room and read reports etc.

Received letter from Thelma. News through of sinking of the *Bismarck*. Collected prints from photographer. Went to RDF Station near Arundel. Changed my flying boots – new canvas pair. On readiness 8 pm until dusk. No scrambles but I was down for some dusk flying. Used cine-gun. Took off at 9.50 pm and landed at 11.05 pm. A great night – visibility good. About seven landings and patrol over Selsey. On dawn readiness next morning.

4 June 1941
In the morning, Flying Officer Clarke of 145 Squadron flew a Rhubarb to Le Havre, where he strafed a searchlight post and destroyed a Ju 87.

During the afternoon, Wing Commander Bader, leading (as ever) with 616 Squadron, covered by 610 with 145 Squadron providing top cover, swept the French coast. Over the Channel, 'Greenline Bus' was told to 'Fly east as friends are in trouble.' Only friendly aircraft, however, were seen, so the sortie remained uneventful for all but 145 Squadron's Canadian Pilot Officer Sabourin, who baled out safely over Worthing, having run out of petrol.

On this day, Squadron Leader Woodhouse was posted to command the all-American volunteer 71 'Eagle' Squadron. Command of 610 Squadron passed to the Commander of 616 Squadron's 'A' Flight, Ken Holden – another Bader appointment.

9 June 1941
Flight Lieutenant Peter MacDonald MP, formerly adjutant of Bader's 242 Squadron and another key player in the Battle of Britain's Big Wing controversy, arrived from Manston to take up his new appointment at Tangmere as 'Flight Lieutenant Admin'. Clearly, with Group Captain Woodhall and Wing Commander Bader already ensconced, under the patronage of the AOC, Air Vice-Marshal Leigh-Mallory, this was no coincidental posting.

11 June 1941
An early morning sweep by 145 Squadron from Wissant to Berck, passing over St Ingelvert, failed to bring the enemy to battle. Later that morning, at 1130 hrs, Wing Commander Bader led another sweep by 145 Squadron, over Calais, but again the Kanaljäger failed to take the bait. These sorties with Bader leading 145 Squadron up from

Merston, however, are noteworthy as this is evidence contrary to the claims that the wing leader exclusively flew with 616 Squadron from Westhampnett.

At 1615 hrs, Squadron Leader Holden led eight 610 Squadron Spitfires up from Westhampnett, joining with four of 145 Squadron over Tangmere, and headed for Boulogne. Holden's Spitfires were top cover at 27,000ft, while 145 cruised towards France at 24,000ft. Over the French coast, however, the two squadrons lost contact. 610 Squadron then flew south, just inland, to north of Le Touquet, then north along the coast, orbiting Cap Gris Nez for ten minutes. Eventually, the Spitfires gave it up as a bad job and flew home, again without engaging the enemy.

Pilot Officer Peter Pine:

> I was posted to 145 Squadron on 5 May 1941, after abbreviated flying training courses in Canada and at Hawarden, near Chester, at which latter OTU I was introduced to and fell in love with the Spitfire.
>
> As a trainee under the Commonwealth Air Training Scheme, ours was the first course to arrive in England, our training having been drastically curtailed, firstly due to a dearth of personnel to train us, and secondly because replacement pilots were needed to replace those lost in battle. At least we could fill out the bare spots in the squadrons and hopefully gain enough experience to become useful members.
>
> 145 Squadron always flew as top cover on the sweeps and fighter escorts, while 610 and 616 Squadron saw most of the action – which was the way Wing Commander Bader wanted it. We, in Spitfire Mk IIBs, were more or less helpless against the Me 109Fs, which could operate at 35,000ft – while we floundered around at 30,000ft. Any violent manoeuvring on our part at that height almost invariably ended in our spinning out. We used to climb to 33,000ft where we would cross the French coast in a shallow dive, in an attempt to gain a modicum of extra speed.
>
> We didn't see much of Bader but I, unfortunately, ran into him at breakfast in the Mess, at which, on three or four occasions, he bawled me out, all but once unjustifiably.

I suppose I was his whipping boy. On other occasions he could be most agreeable, as at times he invited us to the Bay House. He was a good swimmer. His method of entering the pool was to propel himself out onto the end of the diving board using only his arms, and then flipping his rear end into the air with his stumps pointing skywards, and take a header into the water.

12 June 1941
On this day, another Bader import arrived when Flight Lieutenant Denis Crowley-Milling arrived from 242 Squadron, taking over 610 Squadron's 'B' Flight:

> Douglas Bader had promoted Ken Holden to command, and brought in both Flight Lieutenant Lee-Knight and, upon promotion, myself from 242 Squadron as flight commanders, having already taken Stan Turner from 242 to command 145 Squadron. From then on, we never looked back: sweeps over Northern France twice daily, escorting a few bombers, often Stirlings, to ensure a German reaction. As usual, Bader maintained a running commentary from the time we approached the French coast to the time we left on return. Also coming over the ether as we saw the French coast approaching was Stan Turner: 'Okay chaps, put your corks in!', or in other words, 'Now is the time to look out for German fighters but don't be scared!' The Germans listening on the ground to this radio chatter must have thought it an order to activate some special equipment! There were, of course, numerous encounters with the Me 109s of Adolf Galland's JG 26, based around St Omer. For us it was the first time we had taken the fight to the Germans in a big way, so we were very inspired by it all and our morale was very high.

'Crow' lost no time in flying a thirty-five minute 'Sector Recco', familiarising himself with the local area, in Spitfire Mk IIB DW-Q. Later that day, he flew that same aircraft, and DW-U, on a 'high altitude firing test'. DW-U would become Flight Lieutenant Crowley-Milling's regular Spitfire throughout his time on operations that summer.

TANGMERE WING WAR DIARY 18 MARCH – 8 AUGUST 1941

The Tangmere Wing's two Westhampnett-based Spitfire squadrons, 610 and 616, with their Wing Leader, Douglas Bader (front row, fourth left). Also pictured are Flight Lieutenant Denis Crowley-Milling (610, front row, extreme left); Squadron Leader Holden (610, third left); Group Captain Woodhall, Station Commander (front, centre); then Squadron Leader Burton, Flying Officers Casson and Marples, extreme right unidentified. Seated in second row: fourth from right: Pilot Officer Hepple, then Pilot Officer Johnson, and unknown sergeant-pilot and finally Sergeant West.

13 June 1941

At 0705 hrs, 145, 610 and 616 Squadrons provided a section of four Spitfires each for another sweep over the French coast. Crossing inland over Boulogne, the Spitfires turned left, towards the sun, and proceeded eastwards. 610 and 616 lost contact for ten minutes, so 610 came out of France over Calais and orbited off Dover before returning to Calais. There they found four aircraft above them, up-sun, which appeared to be Me 109s, although no engagement took place. Re-crossing the Channel, 610 picked up 616 again and the pair returned together to base. 145 Squadron had similarly encountered no enemy resistance.

The Spitfire, having hitherto been fitted with fabric-covered ailerons, was in the process of upgrading to metal ailerons, making the aircraft easier to control at high speeds. The conversion was being undertaken by Supermarine's engineers at Hamble airfield, near Southampton. Jeffrey Quill, the Supermarine Test Pilot, remembered that 'The word swept round Fighter Command like wildfire and in no time the air around Hamble was thick with the Spitfires of wing leaders and squadron commanders, all trying to jump the queue to get their aircraft fitted with the new metal ailerons – Douglas Bader leading the hunt!' On this day, Wing Commander Bader flew his usual Spitfire P7666, to Eastleigh airfield, inland of Southampton – from which the Spitfire had first flown on 5 March 1936 – and had the new ailerons fitted.

Sergeant Jeff West's diary:

> A fine morning. Went up for a dogfight at 18,000ft. 'Nip' broke off and did aerobatics. First 'Upward Charlie'. Then Squadron height climb. Cleaned up, changed to civvies and went on leave. Caught train to Fareham, Southampton and Salisbury.

14 June 1941

Another unopposed Wing sweep over France.

Sergeant Alan 'Smithy' Smith:

> Whenever we flew over France on fighter sweeps or escorting bombers, we were always the last to return to base. Mission completed and everyone else going home, Douglas would hang around looking for a Hun to engage so long as we had ammunition and enough fuel to get us back to base. As soon as we crossed over the English coast, Douglas would slide back

his cockpit cover and out would come his pipe, which he lit and puffed away upon contentedly. I could not help but reflect that he was virtually sitting on his petrol tank!

Pilot Officer Johnnie Johnson:

Oh yes, Bader used to light a match in the cockpit, bloody 'Swan Vestas'; he'd be there puffing away, couldn't see him for smoke sometimes! Smoking aboard His Majesty's aircraft was not only strictly forbidden it was also extremely dangerous – but in Bader's case this reckless behaviour only served to bolster the growing myth that he was indestructible. We used to veer off, to get out of the way, in case he blew up! Even his wife, Thelma, living at their billet near Bognor, the 'Bay House', with her sister Jill, came to wholeheartedly believe that the Germans would never get him. When we returned from a sweep over France, Spitfire 'DB' would swoop low over the Bay House, indicating his safe return. At night, however, Douglas slept in the Officers' Mess at Tangmere, 'Just to keep in touch'. He was very 'salty', you know, always 'effing and blinding'. Our Controller, Woodhall, would shout up and say 'Come on, Douglas, I've got WAAFs down here!', and Bader would just reply, 'Oh, it's alright, Woody, I'll just come and see 'em later and apologise'!

Even Squadron Leader Burton, according to Brickhill, was

appalled by Bader's uninhibited comments. Like Bader, he nearly always had a pipe in his mouth, and sometimes in the privacy of the pilots' room he would take it out and say 'D'you know what the Wingco called me this morning? He called me a _____!' He used to repeat these things in a voice of wonder as though they could not really have happened, then break into a puzzled laugh.

Group Captain 'Woody' Woodhall:

From June 1941 onwards, the Tangmere Wing was carrying out two or three sweeps a day over enemy occupied territory. Douglas Bader always led the wing himself. He never spared himself, and by this time was a legendary figure.

These sweeps required such accurate briefing, involving as they did such large numbers of Spitfires in addition to the bombers they were escorting, that it became necessary for Leigh-Mallory to hold a conference of Sector Commanders, wing leaders and squadron commanders at Group HQ several times a week. After the last mission of the day, on these occasions, Douglas Bader and I, and perhaps the wing's squadron commanders, would climb into our Spitfires and fly to Northolt, where we were met by car and taken to Uxbridge. These briefing conferences were most rewarding. Leigh-Mallory, with his usual courtesy, encouraged everyone to express his opinions, listened to arguments, and then laid down his plan of further action. After the conference, we visitors to 11 Group HQ would then have a quick cup of tea in the Mess, before flying back to our sectors. Shortly after landing at our aerodromes, complete and detailed instructions, implementing decisions made, for the next operation would arrive by teleprinter, headed 'Operational Order for Circus No *'.

Pilot Officer Johnnie Johnson:

Bader would come stomping into dispersal and say to Billy Burton, 'What are we doing today, then, Billy?' and Billy might respond: 'Well, the Form 'D', the Operational Order, has come through, sir, but we're not on it. The other wings are but not us.'

Bader would explode! 'Right, we'll bloody well see about that, I'll have a bloody word with Leigh-Mallory!' And then he'd call up the AOC himself, remonstrate, and, lo and behold, we'd be on ops!

<u>15 June 1941</u>
A high-altitude sweep by 'A' Flight of 616 Squadron again failed to provoke a reaction from the German fighters.

TANGMERE WING WAR DIARY 18 MARCH – 8 AUGUST 1941

17 June 1941
At 1920 hrs, the Tangmere Wing took off to participate in Circus 13, sweeping from Boulogne to Cap Gris Nez, again largely unopposed. Sergeant Beedham of 616 Squadron fired at a fleeting target but made no claim.

18 June 1941
Between 1735 and 1900 hrs, Tangmere Wing provided top cover the Circus 15, joined by the Polish 303 Squadron, which flew as 'top guard'. Five miles south of Boulogne 'a terrific flak barrage could be seen over the target area at Bois de Liques', so the Spitfires turned left to avoid it. Crossing the French coast between Boulogne and Cap Gris Nez, the wing flew over the Forêt de Guines and Marck, returning to Calais. Over Dunkirk, 610 Squadron picked up the Blenheims and escorted them back to the Thames Estuary. Sergeant Merriman of that squadron turned back with engine trouble and was attacked by an Me 109 over the Channel. Taking evasive action and turning the tables, the Spitfire pilot destroyed the 109, which crashed into the sea. At 1840 hrs, in fact, an Observer Corps post reported seeing a parachute fall into the Channel six miles off St Mary's Bay – the exact location of this combat. 145 Squadron was also engaged, over France, losing Sergeants Palmer and Turnbull.

Sergeant Frank Twitchett:

> In June 1941, the sweeps started in earnest and we often swept over Dunkirk, Calais, and Boulogne, usually escorting Blenheims. On one occasion, 18 June 1941, we even took three Stirlings. The Forêt de Licques was bombed, on which sortie we lost Sergeants Turnbull and Palmer. The average per pilot was two sweeps daily, and this, you can appreciate, became a little wearing on the nerves. We flew to such targets as Lille, Hazebrouck, Béthune, Le Touquet, St Omer, and even once to Knocke on the Belgian coast. That was particularly worrying as we escorted six Blenheims to bomb an oil tanker which had anchored off the coast and was covered by six flak ships. Four of the six Blenheims were lost and two squadrons of Me 109s attacked us. The whole operation and dogfight took place about 500ft above the sea!

19 June 1941

Tangmere Wing, with Northolt's 303 Squadron again providing top cover, should have met thirty-six bombers over base, but only two bomber squadrons arrived, the remainder having aborted. The sortie was Operation DERBY, a raid on Le Havre. The only engagement was when 616 Squadron fended off a handful of Me 109s near the target, Flight Lieutenant MacFie damaging one, probably an aircraft from JG 2's training unit which forced-landed at Octeville.

At 2040 hrs, 'A' Flight of 610 Squadron swept the French coast between Cap Gris Nez and Gravelines. Group Captain Woodhall informed Flight Lieutenant Lee-Knight of six to eight bandits south-west of Le Touquet – codename the 'Golf Course', on account of the famous course there – which the Spitfire pilots hoped to intercept over Étaples, but the enemy was not sighted.

21 June 1941

The longest day of high summer 1941.

That morning the Tangmere Wing provided Forward Support, with the Hornchurch Wing, to Circus 16, attacking the airfield at St Omer – Longuenesse, where a big fire was started in a wood. Between St Omer and the French coast, 610 Squadron was attacked by a Rotte of Me 109s; Flight Lieutenant Lee-Knight (White 1) engaged these enemy fighters in a dogfight just inland of Calais, leaving the rearmost machine 'smoking violently and apparently on fire'. He then turned north but was chased down to sea level by three more Me 109s, which opened fire as the Spitfire pilot broke hard to port. One of the Germans overshot, White 1 blasting the 109 at point blank range, sending it crashing into the sea. White 1 was then pursued by two more 109s, which he lost, but Pilot Officer Gaze (White 2) was bounced by a Schwärm of 109s over Dunkirk. Making a head-on attack, White 2 was unable to see the results of his fire because his windscreen became smothered in oil, probably from a damaged 109.

Sergeant Macbeth became separated from 145 Squadron over St Omer – codename the 'Big Wood' – and came under attack from a 109, which he managed to evade and fire a fleeting burst at. Oberfeldwebel Luders of 6/JG 26 was attacked by Flying Officer Machacek of 145 Squadron, and Squadron Leader Burton of 616; the latter reported that:

> Just after take-off my hood came adrift and I landed, had it fixed in about ten minutes and endeavoured to catch up the wing. Climbed to 20,000ft over Dungeness, could see no

sign of wing so dived and patrolled speedboat with two other Spitfires, about ten miles east of Dover. About 1220 hrs our fighters started to come in and I suddenly noticed two Me 109s crossing the coast NE of Dover. I then saw one Spitfire attacking. I joined in and we cut off one Me 109; the other one quickly disappeared. We dived and zoomed for several minutes overland between Dover and Manston, alternately engaging E/A with quarter and beam attacks. Finally, E/A opened hood and baled out. His machine crashed into a railway embankment and blew up. Pilot landed safely and was made prisoner by a civilian. I personally cannot be sure which Spitfire pilot was responsible for destroying the E/A. It appeared that he was hardly damaged at all when he baled out. The other Spitfire attacking was of 145 Squadron, SO-D.

145 Squadron's Sergeant Twitchett, however, was attacked over the Channel by II/JG 26's Oberleutnant Matzke:

The running battle started over St Omer, with several squadrons of Me 109s attacking us while we were at about 25,000ft. Obviously, the whole thing then broke up into a series of individual combats. Once you realise that you are separated from your squadron, the thing to do is get the hell out of it, so I followed this normal pattern and headed for ground-level and home. By the time I reached mid-Channel at about 500ft, I foolishly lowered my guard slightly. The next thing I became aware of was an enormous BANG! The cockpit filled with cordite fumes and the Spitfire lurched wildly sideways. My immediate reaction was to throw the aircraft into a violent left-hand turn and look in my rear-view mirror. There I saw the unmistakable shape of an Me 109. To use the famous expression, I had really been caught with my trousers down. I subsequently learned that the German pilots were well briefed on our defensive tactics, so when I broke left my assailant was prepared for this. We circled round for several minutes, during which my petrol supply began getting very low, and finally I lost the 109 in the haze.

I then set course for England and worked my way along the south coast towards Merston, where I became aware of blood coming from my battledress jacket, and my knee. I damage-checked my aircraft, saw damage to the right-hand wing, and when I pushed the rudder bar, the rudder went over to 'full' with hardly any effort! Luckily the engine was still running perfectly and I was still flying. I landed safely, and was taken to the Station Sick Quarters, from where I went to St Richard's Hospital in Chichester. There I had stitches put in my knee and told I would be out of action for a few days.

It was a lucky escape.

During the afternoon, between 1550 hrs and 1710 hrs, Wing Commander Bader led the wing on Circus 17, a raid on the enemy airfield at Desvres. Jafü 2 scrambled I/JG 26 and a Gruppe of JG 2.

Wing Commander Bader:

> I was leading the Tangmere Wing, which was milling around in and off the coast around Desvres. Saw the bombers and escort go out near Boulogne, followed by AA bursts. We stayed around, above and behind the bombers and escort when I noticed two Me 109s in line astern, about to turn in behind my Section of four. I told them to break left and twisted round quickly (metal ailerons) and fired a very close deflection burst at the first Me 109E at about fifty yards range, about ½ to 1 second. My bullets appeared to hit him as his glass hood dispersed in pieces and the aeroplane pulled up vertically, stalled and spun right-handed. I foolishly followed him down with my eyes and nearly collided with a cannon Spitfire of another squadron in the wing and then re-formed my Section. I claim this as destroyed (a) because I <u>know</u> it was and (b) Flying Officer Marples, 616 Squadron, saw an Me 109 spinning down at the time and place, and Squadron Leader Turner of 145 Squadron saw a pilot bale out of a 109 at the time and place as also did one of his pilots, (c) Flying Officer Machacek of 145 Squadron saw an Me 109 dive into the sea right alongside another 109 which had been shot down by one of 145 Squadron, same time and place, and (d) no one claims the second 109, which I am sure was mine.

The wing leader was credited with the Me 109 destroyed.

TANGMERE WING WAR DIARY 18 MARCH – 8 AUGUST 1941

Above left: Sergeant Frank Twitchett – who had a lucky escape when shot-up on 21 June 1941.

Above right: Dave Horne pokes his head through the damaged rudder of Sergeant Twitchett's Spitfire, P8341.

616 Squadron, however, lost Pilot Officer Edward Brown – shot down by none other than Oberstleutnant Adolf Galland, JG 26's famous Kommodore. The German ace, however, also committed the cardinal sin of hanging around hoping to see the Spitfire crash – and was fired upon by a Spitfire. Galland's fuselage was holed, his radiator badly hit, and the pilot peppered in the head and arm by shrapnel. Then Galland's petrol tank blew up, at which point 'Dolfo' was over the side in short order, making a safe parachute descent. It is claimed that the Spitfire pilot responsible was 145 Squadron's Sergeant R.J.C. Grant, a New Zealander:

> I was coming home from Boulogne when I was about halfway across when a 109 suddenly loomed out of the haze in front of me at 2,000ft. I throttled back and gave him a three second burst with machine-guns and cannon, closing to fifty yards. Black smoke burst from the cockpit and he rolled over slowly

to the left and dived into the sea. I was rather excited and circled round watching him go in, but, luckily, he was alone, and I was not attacked. He was right in front of me and I made a quarter attack. The E/A had square wingtips, one black and one white wing on under-surface.

Galland, however, was flying an Me 109F-2, not a Me 109E.

Pilot Officer Brown was the first officer pilot lost by 616 Squadron in 1941, which considered this 'a great loss ... as he was liked by both officers and men'. Although it was hoped that Brown was a prisoner, it was not to be. No trace of him has ever been found, and his name is also commemorated at Runnymede.

While the Tangmere Wing orbited the target area at 20,000ft, twenty Me 109s were seen over Hardelot, 610 Squadron breaking away to engage a Schwärm approaching from the rear. In the ensuing combat, Pilot Officer Scott shot down a 109, also attacked by Flight Lieutenant Crowley-Milling, which crashed into the sea seven miles off Le Touquet (confirmed by Pilot Officer Hugill).

Oberstleutnant Galland also had a lucky escape on 21 June 1941, when shot-up by 145 Squadron's Sergeant Grant.

TANGMERE WING WAR DIARY 18 MARCH – 8 AUGUST 1941

On the return flight, 145 Squadron's Flight Lieutenant Newling was shot-up and forced-landed at Dungeness – concluding what had been a busy day for both sides.

Sergeant Jeff West's diary:

> A very clear day. On dawn readiness – a panic re missing gear. Scramble 17,000ft St Catherine's. Newspaper from home. Rotten dinner. On sweep with Wing Commander Bader. Missed out because Plt Off Hepple, CO and Wing Commander Jenks squirted. In afternoon had another Wing sweep over France. I went as Red 2. Flight Lieutenant Gibbs had shells in machine. I got in 450 odd rounds at two 109s on his tail. Think I hit both – one a probable.

<u>22 June 1941</u>

On this afternoon, Circus 18 went ahead, an attack by eighteen Blenheims on Hazebrouck. The Tangmere Wing swept over St Omer to Dunkirk, watching the Beehive cross inland over the French coast. Jafü 2 reacted sharply, scrambling five Gruppen at 1544 hrs. Sixteen minutes later, all of these German units were engaged, a confused combat developing from 18,000ft to ground level. 610 Squadron's CO, Squadron Leader Ken Holden, destroyed a 109 which crashed south of St Omer, and strafed a sandbagged machine-gun emplacement as he crossed out over the French coast. As the Spitfire hurtled overhead at 500ft, other ground posts and ships opened up, but fortunately their aim was poor. Over France, Pilot Officer Horner, also of 610 Squadron, saw an Me 109 about to attack a Spitfire, so hurried to assist. The 109 pilot broke off his attack even before Horner set the enemy aircraft on fire with a long burst. When attacked, 610 Squadron broke left, at which point Sergeant Raine became separated. Diving to ground level, as per standing orders, Raine encountered an enemy airfield, which he strafed before successfully engaging a 109 which crashed in the Merville-Bethune area, somersaulting onto its back in a 'terrific cloud of smoke'. 145 Squadron's Sergeant Larry Robillard, a Canadian, was attacked by three 109s, one of which he destroyed, the German aircraft exploding in mid-air. Meanwhile, over the French coast, 616 Squadron's Flying Officer Casson and Sergeant Beedham shared the destruction of another 109, and north-west of Hazebrouck Flying Officer Marples got another.

As the 616 Squadron diary recorded, 'Altogether it was a very successful operation in which the Tangmere Wing destroyed six enemy

Soldat Frank Kamp, who considered the invasion of Russia disastrous, and where he later fought.

aircraft for no loss to themselves.' In total, Fighter Command claimed a staggering thirty-one German aircraft destroyed, six probables and another six damaged, offset against just two Spitfires lost, with one pilot killed, and another damaged. This was an impressive victory – were the figures accurate, which they certainly were not. Indeed, Luftwaffe historian Don Caldwell rightly wrote that 'Fighter Command's victory claims had lost all touch with reality.' The 'reality' of this day's fighting, in fact, was that JG 26 only lost one aircraft, the pilot being killed, claiming four Spitfires destroyed in response; JG 2 lost two aircraft and pilots, against two Blenheims and five Spitfires claimed destroyed. So, although the Germans also over-claimed, the accuracy was still somewhat closer to 'reality' than Fighter Command's claims. The reasons for these inflated figures, however, has already been explained.

Nonetheless, it was this day, above all others, that the Non-stop Offensive achieved unquestionable strategic justification: Hitler unleashed Operation BARBAROSSA and invaded Russia, achieving complete surprise against Germany's former ally. At the time, German soldat Frank Kamp was an engineer serving in Infantrie Pioneer Ersatz Kompanie 211, based in Münster:

> On Sunday 22 June 1941, a Sondermeldung [special announcement] was broadcast over the radio, this making Operation BARBAROSSA public knowledge. I simply could not believe it, although I understood to some extent Hitler's thinking. Now we had a war on two fronts. I talked to a Kamerad and he agreed that this development was quite incredible and to our great disadvantage. Gone were any hopes of an early end to the war, replaced now by the prospect of a long and drawn-out fight to the death with our ideological enemy.

Soon, the Soviet dictator Joseph Stalin would be pressurising the Western Allies to open the 'Second Front' and invade enemy occupied Europe – but that would take time, and at this stage America had still yet to enter the war. In 1941, all Britain could do was keep fighting and support the Soviets through the provision of materiel. Militarily, it was hoped that the RAF effort would force the Germans to reinforce the Channel coast with units from Russia, or at least pin down those serving there, thereby reducing the pressure on Stalin's Red Army. Fighter Command's losses, however, were already becoming an issue, regarding which Air Vice-Marshal Leigh-Mallory wrote to Air Marshal Douglas at this time, expressing doubts that the required objective was being, or would be, achieved. Douglas subsequently wrote to Portal, the CAS, requesting a review of the whole daylight offensive strategy. According to Douglas, Portal's response was clear, emphasising that 'the value of our offensive operations was in helping the Russians'. Consequently, as Douglas later wrote, 'We immediately stepped up our day offensive, with more bombers escorted by fighters operating within their maximum range.'

More than ever before, the Non-stop Offensive had become an increasingly political expedient.

<u>23 June 1941</u>
In the morning, a Circus was flown to the chemical factory at Choques, the Tangmere Wing crossing into France over Le Touquet and sweeping south of St Omer. There was no contact with the enemy for Wing Commander Bader and his pilots.

That evening, Circus 20 was mounted against the airfield at Mardyk. The Tangmere Wing swept around Calais and were told that bandits were mid-Channel. Climbing into the sun, the wing swept the Dover Straits, being informed of an engagement in progress over Dover. Although Wing Commander Bader led the wing east of Dover, and orbited, nothing was seen, so again there was no contact.

616 Squadron's Sergeant Beedham found himself out of petrol and baled out into the sea off Brighton. The Squadron's diary recorded sternly that 'It is thought that he could have easily made a forced-landing on the Downs.'

It was not all action 'high in the sunlit silence', though, as Group Captain Woodhall recalled:

> On the odd occasions when, in the evening, weather conditions were such that in air force parlance 'the birds were walking' –

that is low cloud or fog making the enemy's night bombing either impossible or improbable, we would declare a 'Thrash' in the Mess. We had an excellent amateur dance band on the Station, and when required they were delighted to demonstrate their talents for our benefit. On one of these 'Thrashes' (on these occasions there were no ladies present) it was just a party that developed because the weather justified a hangover the next day. After a few beers I was persuaded to produce my piano-accordion, and a sing-song started. Douglas Bader loved a sing-song and made a very able chorus master, beating the tune with one hand and resting the other on my shoulder. He would roar out the old flying songs, and songs like *Rolling Round the Mountain*, *Little Angeline*, and *My Brother Sylvester*, that he had learned from the Canadians of 242 Squadron.

Then the inevitable high-spirited games started. I usually got mixed up in a 'scrum down' that developed, and of course

Group Captain Woodhall, enjoying a 'Thrash'.

Bader enthusiastically joined in. I was somewhere at the bottom of a laughing, struggling, heap of pilots when something very hard and painful hit my right elbow. It was one of Douglas's tin legs. My arm was less painful after another drink or two, but next morning I was very stiff and sore, and our Medical Officer (MO), Squadron Leader Simpson, diagnosed it as an impact fracture and put my arm in a sling. That day, 'LM' came to visit us and I hurriedly discarded the sling, and hoped that the AOC would not comment if I saluted left-handed. When 'DB' and I met the AOC, I forgot my injured arm and instinctively tried to salute with it – with miserable and painful results. Douglas Bader, with an unnecessary chuckle I thought, explained that it was entirely his fault for falling on me, and of course LM thought it was equally funny – but told me to put it in the sling again. With a twinkle in his eye, he said 'You mustn't be rough with your Station Commander, Douglas, he's older than you are!'

24 June 1941
On this day, the Tangmere Wing operated from Redhill, joining with Wing Commander 'Sailor' Malan's Biggin Hill Wing over North Foreland, the two Wings crossing into France over Gravelines and heading towards Lille. Ten Me 109s were seen flying west at 19,000ft, but were too far ahead for the Spitfires to intercept. 'Heavy and accurate flak' was experienced in the St Omer area. In his log book, Squadron Leader Burton wrote 'Odd squirt here and there at 109s which disappear downwards at fantastic speeds. Majority appear to be 109Fs.'

Squadron Leader Burton's wife, Jean (left), and friend awaiting the Wing's return from a sweep.

BADER'S SPITFIRE WING

Squadron Leader Burton's young wife, Jean (the now late Mrs Jean Allom), reflected upon those heady days of high summer:

> Now, looking back over half a century later [1995], I realise that there is always the temptation to view the events of summer through rose-tinted spectacles, but even allowing for this and the undisputed effect of time on one's memory, I cannot reflect upon the summer of 1941 as anything but a succession of beautiful English sunny days, such as one would long for in peacetime.
>
> However, in wartime, from the RAF wife's point of view, it would prove to be the reverse. After the gallant defensive fighting of the previous summer, 1941 was the start of Fighter Command taking the war to the enemy, so those sweeps over France and occupied territories were mostly conducted from airfields in southern England, including Tangmere. Thus, nearly every day the wonderful weather presented yet another chance of risk to life or limb for my husband, so for me bad weather, a day without flying, was always something to be thankful for.
>
> Wing Commander Douglas Bader chose to lead the Tangmere Wing and fly with 616, Billy's Squadron. They were great friends despite the gap in age and seniority, but no doubt their mutual Cranwell background played a part in this. On 9 May 1941, 616 Squadron moved to Westhampnett. I had spent a very cold and snowy winter up at Kirton, so I was delighted to be back in warmer climes and to find lodgings in a large country house in Lavant; from the bottom of the garden, I had a ringside seat of the squadron taking off and landing. I could thus approximately gauge the time 616 would return from a sweep and station myself in the garden anxiously and hopefully awaiting the safe return of Billy's Spitfire, QJ-K. Although this was to prove a somewhat stressful occupation, the relief when I saw those familiar aircraft letters on landing was well worth it.
>
> I was, of course, liable to be called up for war work, but as luck would have it I was invited to drive a mobile canteen in the Goodwood area. The canteen catered for the needs of the many army units in the area, largely ack-ack posts, and Westhampnett airfield, which of course meant visiting 616 Squadron, which I would otherwise have been unable to do!

TANGMERE WING WAR DIARY 18 MARCH – 8 AUGUST 1941

I had already met Douglas Bader and his wife, Thelma, the previous summer in Norfolk, and during the summer of 1941 got to know then really well, largely due to their generous open-house entertaining at the Bay House, Aldwick, in the evenings, which Billy and I, together with other members of

Wing Commander and Thelma Bader with Flying Officer Dundas and friend.

High tea at the Officers' Mess, Shopwyke House: Flying Officer Dundas, Squadron Leader Burton, Wing Commander Bader and Lady Diana Wortley.

The same group, Lady Wortley served as a despatch rider during the war.

the wing, were often invited. It was a friendship which lasted until the Baders' deaths, and one I valued greatly.

Owing to the demanding routine of operational flying day after day, organised social events were a rarity. Only one such evening stands out in my memory, a dance held at Shopwyke House, the Officers' Mess, when hospitality was of a pre-war standard. I recall thinking that as the band played *We'll Gather Lilacs* that the atmosphere was reminiscent of the famous ball in Brussels on the eve of Waterloo; behind all the glitter, the reality of war was uncomfortably close as the wing would soon be in action again.

The rest of the summer passed swiftly by, Billy with little respite from ops, me driving the mobile canteen and snatching what little time we could together.

25 June 1941
As the 616 Squadron diary records, this would be a 'busy day for the pilots in which two wing sweeps were made'. Both operations were Circuses involving two squadrons of Blenheims supported by sixteen Spitfire squadrons. Circus 22 was first, an attack on the Hazebrouck marshalling yards, the Tangmere Wing providing cover between 1200 hrs and 1300 hrs. In his diary, the New Zealander Sergeant Jeff West of 616 Squadron

TANGMERE WING WAR DIARY 18 MARCH – 8 AUGUST 1941

wrote: 'Another lovely day. Went on another sweep in the morning. Flew No 2 to Wing Commander Bader. We squirted an Me. DB saw the pilot bale out and we shared one confirmed – half each.'

Sergeant West's combat report elaborates:

> I was flying as Dogsbody 2 in Wing Commander Bader's Section, taking part with 145 and 610 Squadrons in a Wing operation over France. We took off at 1158 hrs from Westhampnett and climbed up over Dungeness to 20,500ft, then on until we were just north of Gravelines, crossing coast over the latter.
>
> When at about 18,000ft, we came across four to six Me 109E, and Wing Commander Bader, turning to port, got in a good burst at one which was climbing rapidly. I was on the inside of the turn and put in a two second burst at the same E/A, which was by this time almost on the stall and turning over on its back. The Wing Commander broke to starboard and I broke to port, losing sight of the E/A. The Wing Commander followed it down and saw the pilot bale out, about five miles off Gravelines, into the sea.
>
> I rejoined the Wing Commander later and returned home at 1335 hrs.

It is perhaps surprising that so experienced a pilot, and such a valuable leader, as Wing Commander Bader saw fit to follow the enemy aircraft down, in order to witness its fate. A few days previously, Oberstleutnant Galland had only narrowly escaped violent death after foolhardily doing a similar thing. Unfortunately there are no enemy losses correlating to this claim. 9/JG 26 lost a pilot off Dunkirk in an Me 109F; three II/JG 26 Me 109Es crash-landed in France with combat damage, but none of these pilots baled out, which Wing Commander Bader reported seeing. JG 2 lost two Me 109Fs over the sea, both pilots posted missing, but no Me 109Es. However, as we have seen, aircraft identification in the heat of battle was often very confused, so it is possible that Bader and West actually attacked a 109F. Also in this action, 616 Squadron's Flight Lieutenant Gibbs and Sergeant Brewer each claimed a probable, and both Flying Officer Dundas and Flying Officer Marples a damaged.

Over Gravelines, having been warned of thirty Me 109s approaching from the south-east, 610 Squadron also contacted the enemy, Pilot Officer

Scott claiming a 109 destroyed which was seen to crash in France. Flight Lieutenant Crowley-Milling attacked two 109s, leaving one streaming 'thick black smoke coming from underneath and just in front of the pilot's seat'. Sergeant Davies, however, was shot-up, and forced-landed at Manston, wounded.

At 1545 hrs, the Tangmere Wing was airborne again, on Circus 23, escorting bombers to St Omer-Wizernes, crossing the French coast at 23,000ft over Le Touquet. Some fifteen miles inland, twelve Me 109s were sighted approaching from the east, in 'rough formation'. Wing Commander Max Aitken, flying with 610 Squadron, attacked a 109 and sent it crashing into some trees beyond Le Touquet. Sergeant Raine, also of 610, inconclusively engaged a 109E which escaped in cloud, but the Spitfire pilot caught the German as he emerged, shooting off a large section of the enemy fighter's port wing, leaving it wreathed in smoke. Hedge-hopping back to the coast, Raine shot over an airfield near Calais at just 30ft, machine-gunning a 109 and hitting several ground staff as he went. Chased out by a 109, Raine luckily escaped with just a single bullet hole through an elevator. 610 Squadron's CO, Squadron Leader Holden was also in action, leaving a 109 streaming coolant over France. Similarly, 145 Squadron's commander, Squadron Leader Turner, engaged a 109E which was last seen diving, pouring smoke and glycol. Sergeant Grant and Flight Lieutenant Arthur each claimed Me 109s destroyed, while Sergeant Camplin damaged another before he and Flying Officer Scott fired at flak ships.

For 616 Squadron, however, this operation was not a success. Having been bounced over the French coast on the return flight, both Sergeants Brewer and Jenks were missing. Sergeant Bob 'Butch' Morton was also attacked over France:

> I was flying as No 2 to Flying Officer Roy Marples when jumped from behind by a pair of 109s. There was the usual display of golden rain, accompanied by sundry bangs as cannon shells exploded inside my machine. Instinctively, I rolled onto my back and went vertically down. The first thing I noticed was – nothing; the cockpit was so full of smoke that I couldn't even see the instruments. We had recently been advised that if smoke came into the cockpit we should unfasten our Sutton harness and unplug both our radio and oxygen leads ready to bale out and before opening the canopy, as the extra draught would suck in the flames causing the smoke. I deliberately – and

foolishly – ignored this sound advice; my immediate desire was to see. I put up a hand to open the canopy but it was jammed. At very high speeds – and I was certainly moving – the aerofoil shape of the canopy tended to hold it in the closed position. At last, using both hands and all my strength, I pulled it back. The smoke ended as if by magic, and as I pulled out of the dive, I surveyed the damage. A couple of machine-gun panels were missing from my starboard wing, indicating that a shell had exploded inside it, and there was a bullet-hole in the engine cowling. Although that was the only visible damage, the engine sounded like a cement mixer! I quickly throttled back and surveyed the instruments. The radiator temperature was jammed against the upper stop, as was the oil temperature indicator. The oil pressure needle had dropped below the scale. Obviously damage to the radiator had caused loss of all glycol coolant, accounting for the white smoke.

My only hope was to hold a northerly course towards the Channel. Ditching there I would at least have a chance of being picked up by our ASR. I chose coarse pitch for the propeller, to nurse the engine, which sounded worse every minute, and willed it to keep turning over until I had crossed the French coast. Then came what I had dreaded: a lone 109 coming up from behind. Reluctantly I went into the defensive circle. While this was held neither pilot could gain the advantage. The first to break away, however, would have the other on his tail, and my time was rapidly running out. Suddenly, I discovered that my opponent had broken away and was zooming inland. I have often wondered whether this was one of the last acts of chivalry in modern warfare. My Spitfire was obviously quite damaged and by then was pouring black smoke from its exhausts. It would have taken little effort to shoot me down, thus adding an easy kill to the German's score. Instead, like a true aerial knight, he gave me a sporting chance to reach the Channel.

Neither of us had allowed for the magnificent Rolls-Royce Merlin engine in our estimation of my chances of survival. Against all reason, the engine, the moving parts of which must have been near red-heat, kept going, not just to the Channel, but across to Hawkinge! My circuit attracted all eyes, so fortunately I made a copy-book approach, although

> I was unaware that my right tyre had been burst by the cannon shell in my right wing. My landing, therefore, was a series of ungainly hops, with a tight little circle at the end of it!

Wing Commander Bader reported that over Boulogne, he

> attacked four Me 109Fs, with my No 2, which were climbing in a slightly left-hand turn. I gave a short burst at one from close range, from inside the turn, and saw white, black and orange coloured smoke envelope the aircraft, which went in an increasingly steep dive which finished up beyond the vertical.

In total, Fighter Command claimed five Me 109s destroyed on Circus 23, although only a II/JG 26 was shot-up and force-landed, while JG 2 lost a single aircraft and pilot. Four Spitfires, however, were lost, and a Blenheim destroyed by flak.

26 June 1941

Again, the Tangmere Wing operated from Redhill, participating in Circus 24. Crossing the French coast over Gravelines, Wing Commander Bader was warned of twenty-four plus Me 109s to the south-east – which were seen ahead of the wing and in their usual loose formations. The Me 109s then swung behind and climbed to attack 610 Squadron from the rear. Pilot Officer Tony Gaze, however, promptly sent one of his Squadron's assailants into the sea, just off the French coast. Going down to sea level, Gaze saw the downed enemy pilot inflating his yellow dinghy. Squadron Leader Holden had shot pieces off another 109 before losing control of his Spitfire; he then noticed a parachute had opened 5,000ft below, but was unable to say whether this was the enemy pilot he had attacked. Flight Lieutenant Lee-Knight was 'chased a long way out to sea by four to six enemy aircraft', at which he managed, by turning, to fire several quick bursts, damaging one, which began 'smoking badly'. 145 Squadron's Sergeant Johnson claimed a Me 109F destroyed near Dunkirk – but Sergeant Macbeth was missing.

616 Squadron was also engaged, Pilot Officer Johnson, Dogsbody 4 in the wing Leader's Section, having previously shared a Do 17 with Flying Officer Dundas the previous winter, made his first full kill:

> I became detached from Wing Commander Bader's Section at 15,000ft, through watching three Me 109s immediately above

> me. I saw them dive away to port and almost immediately afterwards saw an Me 109E coming in from my starboard side, which flew across me about 150 yards away, turning slightly to port. I immediately turned towards the E/A and opened fire, closing to 100 yards. After two one second bursts, the E/A jettisoned hood, rolled over and the pilot baled out, his parachute opening almost immediately. I then broke away as there were other E/A about. I estimated I was over Gravelines when I was in combat…. I then joined up with Flying Officer Scott of 145 Squadron and landed at Hawkinge for refuelling.

Johnnie's victory had been witnessed by several pilots of 145 Squadron; he had fired 278 machine-gun rounds. His victim was probably one of the five Me 109Fs lost that day by JG 2.

Flying Officer Casson damaged another Me 109 – but Sergeant Morton found himself in trouble again:

> It grieves me to have to report an incident worthy of the notorious 'Pilot Officer Prune', who at the time had yet to appear in the pages of our training publication *Tee-Em*. While returning alone across the Channel from the morning sweep, I kept the sun over my right shoulder, saving continuous study of my compass. In the afternoon we carried out another sweep. Again, I became separated from my companions, though no action came my way, and again I set out for home – with the sun again over my right shoulder! Consequently, it seemed to take longer to reach the eastern end of the Isle of Wight. What in fact I eventually reached was the Naze, near Clacton, but this, like my intended point, had a sunken ship with masts and a funnel showing above water. I was satisfied, so struck inland for the aerodrome having not looked at my compass.
>
> When my fuel began to run low, I selected a suitable field for a precautionary landing. It looked like a grass field. In fact, it was ploughed and full of growing wheat. The first touch sheared off my undercarriage legs. The Spitfire dug its nose into the ground, rotated laterally through 180°, smashed down travelling tail first, reared up on its tail and turned through another 90° before coming to rest. Sometime during this performance, the fuselage snapped in half. As a few hundred

(or perhaps just a dozen!) soldiers came running up, I turned my attention to the panel over the radio set in the fuselage, mainly to hide my red face.

'Are you all right?' asked one of the soldiers.

'No!' I replied savagely, 'I've swallowed my chewing gum!'

As the 616 Squadron diary noted, Bob had 'mistaken the northern part of the Thames Estuary for the south coast near the Isle of Wight'. His Spitfire was a write-off – but fortunately the pilot walked away.

27 June 1941
Three 'Rodeo' fighter sweeps were flown by 11 and 12 Group, a 'Roadstead' targeting shipping off Dunkirk, and an evening Circus, No 25, to steel works at Lille. Between 1300 hrs and 1430 hrs, 610 and 616 Squadrons flew an uneventful Rodeo, sweeping some thirty to forty miles into France without sighting the enemy. That evening, between 2055 hrs and 2220 hrs, the whole Tangmere Wing participated in the Circus operation, again sweeping forty miles into enemy occupied territory. Flak was reportedly 'very accurate over Boulogne' and 145 Squadron lost the wing's other Spitfires in the haze. Formating on a dozen fighters believed to be 616 Squadron, Squadron Leader Turner's men were shocked to discover that their new companions were, in fact, Me 109s! Both formations broke, the Germans disappearing into the sun, although Flight Lieutenant Newling sent one hurtling earthwards 'shrouded in black smoke'.

On this day's fighting, II/JG 26 lost a pilot killed while another crash-landed, Galland's pilots claiming four Spitfires in response, while JG 2 reported the destruction of a Blenheim and three Spitfires for no loss. Fighter Command claimed the five Me 109s destroyed, three probables and six damaged. The German claims were remarkably accurate, however: eight Spitfires were lost, and one of those, flown by the highest-ranking RAF casualty of the day, Wing Commander Piotr Laguna, the Polish Northolt wing leader, was not lost in aerial combat but hit by flak during a low-level attack on the airfield at Coquelles, near Calais. Wing Commander Sailor Malan's Biggin Hill Wing also suffered a grievous loss that day, when Squadron Leader John Mungo-Park DFC, Malan's successor in command of the famous 74 'Tiger' Squadron, was among those who failed to return. These were experienced leaders, the loss of which Fighter Command could ill-afford. Sadly, there would be many more in the weeks ahead.

TANGMERE WING WAR DIARY 18 MARCH – 8 AUGUST 1941

Sergeant Jeff West's diary:

> A clear morning. Breakfast was bloody awful. Payday £6-10-0. Sergeant Mabbett collected on my authority. Went to landing ground at Beachy Head – bloody awful. Flew in front with Wg Cdr and Fg Off Dundas. Went on another sweep over France but no action.

<u>28 June 1941</u>

Between 0745 hrs and 0940 hrs the Tangmere Wing was up on Circus 26, a raid on Comines power station. The bombers were seen withdrawing over Dunkirk and Squadron Leader Holden reported two Me 109Fs streaking inland, 5,000ft below; he gave chase, but the enemy fighters dived away, inland, at the usual high speed. The only other bandits seen were 'a long way off', although Flying Officer Machacek became separated from 145 Squadron and claimed a 109 probably destroyed over Cassel.

Fighter Command's only casualties were Poles from the Northolt Wing, one of which was killed, another captured, while the third was rescued from the Channel. Again, German claims were 100 per cent accurate, JG 26 claiming two Spitfires, while 1(F)123, a reconnaissance unit, claimed a third. JG was not engaged. RAF claims were light, six Me 109s destroyed in addition to Machacek's probable. For once, these were very close to the actual mark: JG 26 lost four Me 109s in combat. In addition, the Kanaljäger suffered a deeply-felt loss: Hauptmann Gustav 'Micky' Sprick, Staffelkapitän of 8/JG 26, whose Me 109F-2 went straight in after its right wing collapsed during a routine split-S manoeuvre. The popular ace went to his grave near St Omer, his final score thirty-one victories achieved in 192 combat flights. After this, tests were carried out on the 109s, which identified weak areas in the wing construction, requiring stiffeners to be fitted at the repair depot in Antwerp.

Sergeant Jeff West's diary:

> Not as good a morning but again we went on a sweep over France – Lille. Hundreds of planes and this time saw the bombers and escorted them back to Dover. Flew home with Flt Cdr and Wg Cdr in tight formation. Rather fun. Released in afternoon so we went to Brighton with crew. Met two chaps and did pub crawl. Brighton's a great place. Home quite late in transport. Changed library book and had a haircut.

30 June 1941

Between 1740 hrs and 1935 hrs, the Tangmere Wing participated in Circus 27. Sweeping over Le Touquet, fifty plus bandits were reported to the east. Sighted by 610 Squadron, flying in pairs, the Germans were twenty miles away, so the wing proceeded to St Omer, which the Spitfires orbited for some thirty minutes. Over the Channel, another pair of 109s was seen but not engaged. 145 Squadron, however, found trouble over Le Touquet, Flying Officer St Pierre and Sergeant Robillard sharing in the destruction of a 109, while the latter also strafed a flak position near Boulogne. 616 Squadron's Sergeant McCairns was fired upon, his cockpit being damaged, but fortunately he was uninjured and returned safely to Westhampnett.

On this day there was a change in 616 Squadron, when Buck Casson was promoted to Flight Lieutenant and took command of 'A' Flight.

1 July 1941

At 1739 hrs, the Tangmere Wing took off on a sweep, orbiting Béthune for twenty-five minutes. Again, there was no opposition to speak of, although 145 Squadron's Sergeant Smith fired an inconclusive burst at a 109.

On this day, 616 Squadron's Sergeant Alan Smith recorded in his log book having flown Spitfire P7754 to and from Hamble, having metal ailerons fitted there.

On this day, the black-painted Hurricanes of 1 Squadron arrived at Tangmere. 'Pop' Elvidge was a member of the squadron's groundcrew:

> We arrived in the blackout and were given the camp cinema as sleeping quarters. The next day I realised why: Other Ranks' quarters had been bombed, together with several hangars. The routine from then on was twenty-four hours at Tangmere, twenty-four at Goodwood racecourse, sleeping in the open stands. The Squadron was on night intruder operations, but in the day-time we would assist with the refuelling and rearming of the Polish Wing from Northolt which used our airfield for sweeps over the Channel. All we groundcrew knew of the intruder operations was the friendly rivalry which existed between the two flights, their respective commanders being Flight Lieutenants Karel Kuttlewascher, a Czechoslovakian, and Jimmy Maclachlan. The latter, I understood, was formerly a pilot of Malta's famous Gladiator defenders, *Faith*, *Hope* and *Charity*, and in one particular combat had an arm blown off by a cannon shell. The

cockpit of his Hurricane Mk IIC had been specially adapted to accommodate his artificial arm. As indicated, little was known of their actual nocturnal operations, our best source of information being our riggers, who used to record on the aircraft their sorties: red swastikas for aircraft destroyed, little red steam trains for locomotives. The Squadron was also experimenting with a Turbinlite Havoc, which had radar and a nose-mounted searchlight. This idea was abandoned, however, as the light's batteries were found to be of insufficient duration.

I remember once that the 'All-Clear' had sounded following a raid on Portsmouth, when our Ops phone rang, informing us that an unidentified plot remained on the board. A Flying Officer Parsons scrambled to investigate, a relatively inexperienced pilot. He returned sometime later having destroyed a bandit, but the Ops phone rang again: a Bomber Command Stirling had been shot down over Midhurst. Our celebrations stopped immediately, for this was Parsons' victim, although at least the crew baled out safely.

On a lighter note, the Station Band was that of the famous bandmaster 'Snake-hips Johnson', who had been bombed out of the Café de Paris in London, after which he and his band joined the RAF.

Tangmere was certainly a busy sector in 1941. Also based at Tangmere itself were the Beaufighters of 219 Squadron, an AA cooperation unit, and an ASR flight. Alan Baldwin, of Station Sick Quarters, remembered that:

A Lysander squadron was also based at Tangmere. Their purpose was a closely guarded secret and they operated mainly at night. On one or two occasions, presumably because it was thought medical assistance might be needed by an incoming flight, I went with the MO to the landing ground, which seemed to be in a far corner of the airfield. Our help was not needed, and we were not allowed near enough to the plane to see what was happening, although on one occasion I was aware that the passenger was a civilian – at any rate in civilian clothes. The planes took-off and landed by the light of the moon or with the help of torches. It was not until long afterwards that I learned the reason for those flights.

'Pop' Elvidge adds:

> I also remember the comings and goings of a Lysander which appeared at our dispersal from time to time. We would see an RAF pilot and what appeared to be civilians board the aircraft. We had our suspicions, but it was not until after the war that these were confirmed when the story of Special Operations Executive (SOE) was told.

This clandestine unit was 1455 Special Flight, which ferried secret agents to and from rendezvous in enemy occupied France, by the light of the moon. As 'Pop' said, 'A highly dangerous way to earn a living, and no respect is too high for these brave men and women, who operated behind enemy lines, certain of torture and death if captured.'

<u>2 July 1941</u>

The relentless pressure of daily offensive operations continued. Between 1145 hrs and 1350 hrs the Tangmere Wing escorted bombers on Circus 29, to Lille. Near the target all three gruppen of JG 26 pounced on the Beehive. 610 Squadron's Sergeant Mains claimed a 109 destroyed in the ensuing combat, while Pilot Officer Gaze damaged another. 145 Squadron, however, lost Sergeant Larry Robillard, who was shot down at Cauchy-en-la-Tour; the Canadian evaded capture with the help of brave local people and the French Resistance, eventually returning to England via mainland Spain and Gibraltar. 616 Squadron's Sergeant Alan Smith, flying as Dogsbody 2, machine-gunned some workshops and German soldiers on a beach, and claimed a 109 destroyed and damaged another. Pilot Officer 'Nip' Hepple unquestionably destroyed an Me 109F, the pilot of which was seen to bale out. Wing Commander Bader also claimed a German fighter destroyed and another damaged, his subsequent combat report making interesting reading:

> I was leading 616 Squadron's first section. Sighted approximately fifteen Me 109Fs a few miles SW of Lille, so turned south and attacked them. They were in a sort of four formation, climbing eastwards. They made no attempt to do anything but climb in formation so I turned the squadron behind them and attacked from about 2,000ft above and behind. I attacked an Me 109F from quarter astern to astern, and saw his hood come off – he probably jettisoned it – and

the pilot started to climb out. Did not see him actually bale out as I nearly collided with another Me 109 that was passing on my right in the middle of a half-roll. Half-rolled with him and dived down on his tail, firing at him with the result that glycol and oil came out of his machine. I left him at about 12,000ft, as he appeared determined to continue diving, and pulled up again to 18,000ft. My Air Speed Indicator (ASI) showed rather more than 400 mph when I pulled out. Found the fight had taken me west a bit so picked up two 610 Squadron Spitfires and flew out at Boulogne, round Gris-Nez and up to Gravelines where we crossed the coast again and found an Me 109E at 8,000ft, and at which I fired from about 300 yards. No damage, but this one is claimed as 'Frightened'! The first 109 is claimed as destroyed since, although I did not actually see the pilot leave the aircraft, I saw him preparing to do so, and several pilots of 616 Squadron saw two parachutes going down, the pilot of one of which was shot down by Pilot Officer Hepple. The second 109 was seen by Pilot Officer Hepple and is claimed as damaged.

During this day's fighting, JG 26 claimed two Blenheims and three RAF fighters, while JG 2 claimed five more; Fighter Command lost eight Spitfires, with two more damaged. JG 26 lost just one Me 109F, the Staffelkapitän of 2/JG 26, Oberleutnant Martin Rysavy, who was killed in a 'friendly fire' incident when hit by German flak. JG 2 lost three aircraft, all pilots safe. Once more, however, Fighter Command's claims had lost touch with reality, recording the destruction of twenty-three Me 109s, four probables and seven damaged.

On this day, Wing Commander Bader was awarded a Bar to his existing DSO; the citation read:

> This officer has led his wing on a series of consistently successful sorties over enemy territory during the past three months. His high qualities of leadership and courage have been an inspiration to all. Wing Commander Bader has destroyed fifteen enemy aircraft.

This was cause for celebration, and doubtless another boisterous 'Thrash' ensued that evening.

BADER'S SPITFIRE WING

Pilot Officer Johnnie Johnson:

It was awe-inspiring, really, we were pilot officers and so on and Bader was older, Wing Commander DSO DFC, legendary, but he treated us all as equals; he was a great leader, inspiring confidence and putting steel into a man. Extraordinary.

Flight Lieutenant Archie Winskill:

On arrival at Tangmere as a young flight lieutenant I found Bader a very charismatic leader and a truly impressive individual. A wing briefing went something like this: Wing Commander Bader would waddle into the briefing marquee in his usual peg-legged style, halt in front of the thirty-five pilots present, stare at us for a few seconds, take his pipe out and in a loud, confident, voice say 'Okay, chaps, St Omer today – return tickets only! Press tits at 1300 hrs.' Then he would waddle out. We would have followed him to the ends of the earth!

Flight Lieutenant Archie Winskill of 41 Squadron.

TANGMERE WING WAR DIARY 18 MARCH – 8 AUGUST 1941

Not all members of the Tangmere Wing, however, agreed; Sergeant Frank Twitchett:

> While we had a first-class CO in Squadron Leader Turner, I cannot say the same in respect of Wing Commander Bader as wing leader. Obviously, we admired the man tremendously but he did create division and problems through persistently basing himself at Westhampnett and flying solely with 616 Squadron. We very rarely saw him at all. In fact, despite having been with 145 Squadron for its entire tour at Tangmere in 1941, I can only recall having seen him twice.

George Reid, 616 Squadron groundcrew:

> When Wing Commander Bader arrived at Tangmere, he was already a legend, there being quite a myth being built up around him. While with 616 Squadron I came into direct contact with him and learned to both fear and dislike the fellow. He had a filthy mouth and lacked patience. He was a show-off and the most pompous chap I have ever met. My last recollection of Wing Commander Bader was when his Spitfire's wheels would not lock-up correctly. There was a sweep to be flown at 1500 hrs and by this time it was already 1400 hrs. He came over in his car, stomped up to the Flight Sergeant 'Chiefy' and myself, and raged, turning on high-powered filth from the mouth, and thumped his car bonnet with a stick. I actually thought that he would strike Chiefy with that cane. I dived back under the Spitfire and fortunately off he went! In the

Harold Clowes, Tangmere's Link Trainer Instructor.

end he settled for a new Spitfire just delivered by a female Air Transport Auxiliary ferry pilot.

Sergeant Harold Clowes, Tangmere's Link instructor, adds that 'I never actually met Wing Commander Bader but once I heard him cursing the groundcrew in a nearby hangar.'

Clearly, there were two sides to this legendary figure.

3 July 1941

1000 hrs saw the Tangmere Wing airborne on Circus 30, closely escorting six Blenheims to Hazebrouck. I and III/JG 26, and elements of JG 2, intercepted the Beehive over the target. Flight Lieutenant Lee-Knight of 610 Squadron destroyed an Me 109 which crashed south-west of Lille. Attacked by more 109s, Lee-Knight sent another 'diving vertically down, smoking violently'. By then, the Spitfire pilot was at ground level, machine-gunning a searchlight post near Cap Gris Nez. 610's Sergeant Merriman, and 616's Sergeant Bowen, attacked and shared as a probable an unfortunate Hs 126 communications aircraft. As he broke away, however, Merriman's port wingtip struck the Henschel's wing strut and port tailplane, although without overly negative consequences for the Spitfire.

Next up, between 1510 hrs and 1700 hrs, was Circus 31, a raid by six Blenheims on the Hazebrouck marshalling yards. The Tangmere Wing orbited St Omer, but only Sergeant Beedham recorded a success, claiming a 109 probable. In his log book, Flight Lieutenant Crowley-Milling recorded having seen '20 Me 109s – tried to engage but they dived away'.

On this day, Fighter Command lost six Spitfires, three pilots killed, three captured, while one evaded. Both JG 2 and JG 26 lost a pilot killed, while one of JG 2 baled out and another forced-landed. Fighter Command, however, claimed twelve destroyed, seven probables and six damaged. Nonetheless, JG 2's fatal casualty was significant: Hauptmann Wilhelm Balthasar, the Kommodore, who was shot down near Aire. Only the previous day, Balthasar had been awarded the Eichenlaub (Oak Leaves) to his Ritterkreuz, for forty aerial victories; he was buried next to his father, a casualty of the First World War.

4 July 1941

Circus 32 targeted the chemical plant at Chocques, the Tangmere Wing orbiting St Omer. Pilot Officer Johnson and Sergeant Morton, both of

616 Squadron, each damaged a 109. Wing Commander Bader reported that he had:

> Intercepted one Me 109F some miles south of Gravelines at 14,000ft, while with a section of four. Turned on to its tail and opened fire with a short, one second burst at about 150 yards. I found it very easy to keep inside him during the turn and closed quite quickly. I gave him three more short bursts, the final one at about twenty yards range; as he slowed down very suddenly, I nearly collided with him. I did not see the result except one puff of smoke half way through. Squadron Leader Burton in my Section watched the complete combat and saw the Me 109's airscrew slow right down to ticking over speed. As I broke away the 109 did not half-roll and dive but just sort of fell away in a sloppy fashion, quite slowly, as though the pilot had been hit. Having broken away I did not again see the 109 I attacked, since I was trying to collect my Section together. I am, however, satisfied that I was hitting him and so is Squadron Leader Burton, from whose evidence this report is written.

The day's after-action balance sheet on this occasion favoured Fighter Command, with three Spitfires failing to return while the Hornchurch wing leader, Group Captain Harry Broadhurst, was wounded. JG 26 lost two aircraft and JG 2 three. Fighter Command, however, claimed a staggering seventeen Me 109s destroyed, five probables and fourteen damaged. It is interesting to note that between 14 June – 4 July 1941, JG 2 and JG 26 lost forty-eight aircraft, with thirty-two pilots killed. Fighter Command had lost eighty aircraft and sixty-two pilots – a ratio of 2:1 in favour of the Kanaljägern. Nonetheless, as the CAS had already made clear to Air Marshal Douglas, the offensive was too important politically to be downscaled; the pressure was maintained, regardless of losses. According to Fighter Command's victory claims, though, there was no problem: 214 German fighters had been claimed destroyed, eighty-four probables and ninety-five damaged. As Luftwaffe historian Don Caldwell rightly commented 'The RAF commanders had to know that their pilots' claims, amounting to 167 per cent of German strength in the theatre, were absurdly high.'

Sergeant Jeff West's diary:

Fg Off Cocky Dundas went to test 'G' and taxied into 'K'. After tea we were called to readiness. Johnnie and I did an hour's convoy patrol. 11 Group got 14 destroyed – Wg Cdr Malan four alone. Lost four fighters. Went down to Royal Oak. Letters from Mollie, Mattie and cable from Phil.

5 July 1941

That afternoon saw the Tangmere Wing orbiting Lille on Circus 33, watching three Stirlings accurately bomb the Lille-Fives steel works. The wing then weaved behind the bombers, shepherding them out of France over Gravelines. 610 Squadron's Flight Lieutenant Lee-Knight escorted a Spitfire out of France which had a 'dead propeller', but approaching Margate the pilot baled out. Lee-Knight broadcast a fix on the downed airman's position, some ten to fifteen miles east-south-east of Manston, covering and guiding a Lysander to that location, which was then able to direct ASR operations. Thanks to Lee-Knight, the Polish pilot, Sergeant Kryzyzagórski, was rescued safely. Over the target area, 610 Squadron's Sergeant Mains destroyed an Me 109E, the pilot of which baled out, but then the Spitfire pilot noted with some alarm that his oil temperature was 97°, forcing him to retire and land at Hawkinge. 616 Squadron, however, suffered a significant loss: Flight Lieutenant Colin MacFie, the commander of 'B' Flight, was shot down over France and captured; the ORB recorded that 'We are all very sad at his loss as he had been with the squadron since the beginning of September 1940, and had endeared himself to everyone despite his taciturnity.' Fortunately, however, news was later reported that MacFie was a prisoner.

By now, Fighter Command was receiving a new Spitfire – the Mk V. The new Merlin 45 engine produced a top speed of 359 mph at 25,000ft, an altitude attainable in eight-and-a-half minutes, and in just under fifteen minutes the Mk V could reach its maximum ceiling of 35,000ft. The Mk VA was purely machine-gun armed, and favoured by Wing Commander Bader, while the VB, like the Mk IIB, had two machine-guns and a 20mm cannon in each wing. The important difference between both cannon-armed variants was that the VB's extra power, addressing the fact that the Mk IIB was under-powered. Whereas the Me 109F had the edge over the Spitfire Mk II, the Mk V redressed the balance.

6 July 1941

In the morning, eleven Spitfires of 145 Squadron patrolled the Channel uneventfully, except for an aborted attack by a lone Me 109F.

TANGMERE WING WAR DIARY 18 MARCH – 8 AUGUST 1941

Between 1330 hrs and 1530 hrs, Wing Commander Bader led the Tangmere Wing on Circus 35, providing Target Support to six Stirlings bombing Lille. 'Dogsbody' subsequently reported that:

> During the withdrawal from Lille to Gravelines we were pestered by Me 109s starting to attack and then half-rolling and diving away when we made to engage. Of an initial three bursts I fired at three Me 109Es, I claim three as frightened (Pilot Officer Johnson subsequently destroyed number three). Finally, two Me 109s positioned themselves to attack from starboard quarter behind when my Section was flying above and behind the bombers south of Dunkirk. These two were flying in line-astern and I broke my Section round on to them when they were quite close (250 yards away). They both did a steeply banked turn, still in line-astern, and exposed their complete underside (plan view) to us. I gave one a short burst (no deflection) full in the stomach from 100 – 150 yards and it fell out of the sky in a shallow dive, steepening up with white and black smoke pouring from it, and finally flames as well. The pilot did not bale out while I was watching. This is confirmed by Pilot Officer Johnson and Sergeant Smith in my Section, and is claimed as destroyed.

In the running battle that developed as the Beehive withdrew, following bombing described as 'extremely impressive', the Tangmere Wing claimed four Me 109s destroyed. The enemy fighters were reported as having 'adopted their usual tactics of trying to get a surprise attack and rushing away when Spitfires turned on them'. In the cut and thrust over France, two 145 Squadron pilots reported having been 'actually shot at by a Spitfire over the target area'. Such incidents of so-called 'friendly fire', in the speed and confusion of what was a high energy and volatile scenario, were common. Pilot Officer Arthur fired at a 109, but having only thumbed the machine-gun trigger, given the range there was little effect. Sadly, Flight Lieutenant Michael Newling DFC, a stalwart and long-standing flight commander in 145 Squadron, failed to return; he remains missing to this day and is commemorated on the Runnymede Memorial.

Sergeant James Atterby McCairns, of 616 Squadron's 'A' Flight, was shot down by an Me 109 during the fighting withdrawal, crash-landing Spitfire P8500, YQ-D, on the French coast near Gravelines. Captured by the

Germans, with help from the Belgian Resistance's 'Comet' organisation, 'Mac' escaped, making a home run over the Pyrenees and returning to England via Gibraltar. Upon return, he was commissioned and, determined to directly and personally support the resistance movement, became a Lysander pilot with 161 Squadron, flying SOE agents in and out of enemy occupied France. Later, he returned to fighters, flying Tempests, but was killed in a flying accident after the war, in 1948, while once more serving with 616 Squadron.

7 July 1941
Three Circus operations were flown today, the first, to Hazebrouck, involving eleven Spitfire squadrons, as Sergeant David Cox, of 19 Squadron, remembered: 'We escorted ONE Stirling, which was surrounded by about 200 Spitfires!'

Circus 37 went ahead next, four Stirlings attacking the Potez factory at Albert. Wing Commander Bader led the Tangmere Wing between 0940 hrs and 1130 hrs, observing bombs exploding in the target area and sighting 'the odd Me 109', but there was no contact. A flotilla of E-Boats was strafed by the Spitfires off Le Touquet, but with no noticeable result, and an aircraft was seen to crash in the sea off Berck. Aircraft wreckage, and patches of oil, were also noted in the Channel, and another aircraft was thought to have crashed into the water off Le Touquet.

Next up was Circus 38, Bader's Tangmere Spitfires operating from Redhill between 1430 hrs and 1620 hrs. Bombs were reported exactly on target at Choques, but there was little opposition, although 145 Squadron's Sergeant Silvester was badly shot-up and slightly wounded, crash-landing at Hawkinge.

On this day, Hugh 'Cocky' Dundas was promoted to flight lieutenant, taking command of 616 Squadron's 'A' Flight.

8 July 1941
The first Circus, 38, was flown at dawn, Wing Commander Bader leading his wing between 0540 hrs and 0720 hrs on another Target Support commitment. Four Stirlings split into two pairs to attack targets near Lens, the 'main target being left in flames and the second with large volumes of smoke issuing from it'. On the return flight, one of the bombers was hit by flak near St Omer and exploded, scattering wreckage on buildings below. Only two of the crew baled out, and as 616 Squadron recorded, 'it was not a very pleasant sight to watch'. This was Stirling N6034 of Oakington's 7 Squadron; Sergeants

TANGMERE WING WAR DIARY 18 MARCH – 8 AUGUST 1941

Edwards and Chappell were captured, their five crew-mates killed. While the wing returned to the French coast, a Spitfire was seen 'spinning down very fast with glycol fumes pouring from it'. Although some Me 109s shadowed the wing at a safe distance, there was no contact.

At 1155 hrs, Sergeants 'Peter' Merriman and Joe Doley of 610 Squadron were scrambled from Westhampnett. After being given several vectors by the controller, the Spitfire pilots sighted a Rotte of Me 109s at 15,000ft, flying towards Portsmouth. The Spitfires intercepted the bandits, one of which Merriman shot down into the Solent. While returning to base, the euphoric Tangmere Wing pilot encountered another Me 109F, which he attacked and left 'trailing smoke and diving towards the sea'.

Between 1435 hrs and 1640 hrs, Wing Commander Bader and the Tangmere Wing flew Circus 40, a raid on Lille. Again providing Target Support, while orbiting the target, Bader's Spitfires were 'embarrassed by another wing' which was flying at the same height, 22,000ft. As the Beehive re-crossed the French coast over Gravelines, several Me 109s were seen, one of which attacked Flight Lieutenant Lee-Knight of 610 Squadron, who turned the tables and claimed a probable. Pilot Officer F.G. Horner, however, was shot down and captured – probably the Spitfire reported spinning down slowly north of Lille, with a parachute floating down nearby. Another aircraft was seen in flames near Dunkirk, and three 109s near Lille 'camouflaged grey with black crosses'. Three new Spitfire Mk VAs of 145 Squadron returned to base with technical issues before reaching the French coast, but the nine remaining aircraft became separated from the wing while later taking evasive action. Two of their number failed to return:

The Spitfire Mk VB of 610 Squadron's Flight Lieutenant Denis Crowley-Milling, pictured at Ludham.

Flight Lieutenant Crowley-Milling's groundcrew.

Pilot Officer Peter Pine, a Canadian, was shot down and baled out over Courtrai, becoming a prisoner, and the Czech Flying Officer J. Machacek, believed shot down over Moere, Belgium, remains missing.

In total, fifteen Spitfires were shot down this day; five pilots were killed, three wounded, and four captured. One crash-landed in England, and another was rescued from the sea. JG 26 claimed eleven Spitfires, JG 2 eight. JG 26 lost two Me 109s, the wing of one failing in combat near St Omer, both pilots killed, while JG 2 lost one aircraft and pilot. Fighter Command, however, claimed the destruction of twenty-two Me 109s, seven probables and nine damaged. Again, these claims were simply unrealistic.

9 July 1941
The day's main commitment was Circus 41, a raid on Béthune by three Stirlings. The Tangmere Wing, as ever led by Wing Commander Bader, took off at 1305 hrs, providing Close Escort, crossing out over Rye and making landfall at Hardelot. Me 109s then approached 'in pairs and larger formations but not close enough to attack effectively, adopting instead their tactic of trying to lure the Spitfires away'. 145 Squadron's Squadron Leader Turner managed an inconclusive burst at a fleeting 109, but Sergeant James McFarlane, who made a solo attack, was last seen ablaze and diving towards France; he remains missing, and is also remembered at Runnymede.

616 Squadron was also engaged, Wing Commander Bader later officially claiming one Me 109 probable, one damaged, and one 'frightened':

> Just after crossing the French coast [with the bombers] at 18,000ft, I saw an Me 109 behind and above me, diving very steeply, obviously intending to get down below and behind bombers and attack from underneath and then zoom away. I instructed my Section I was diving down, and dived straight through and under the Escort Wing converging on this Me 109 who had not seen me. He saw me as he was starting his zoom and turned right-handed, i.e. into me, and dived away. I was very close by then and aileroned behind him and gave him one to two second burst from 100 – 150 yards straight behind him. Glycol and heavy black smoke streamed out of his aeroplane and he continued diving. I pulled out at approximately 10,000ft and watched him continue downwards. When he was about 2,000ft I lost him and then saw a large flash on the ground where he should have hit. I am sure it was him but am claiming a probable only because when flying out over the same terrain I noticed sun flashes on glass in various directions, and as I did not actually see the 109 right into the ground these sun flashes must be recorded. Just after leaving the target area my Section was attacked from above and behind, and we turned into the attackers, Me 109Fs, who started half-rolling. I got a good squirt at one and glycol stream started. Did not follow him down and claim a damaged. Several others were frightened and I claim one badly frightened who did the quickest half-roll and dive I've ever seen when I fired at him.

Dogsbody 2, Sergeant Smith, claimed a 109 damaged, but Squadron Leader Edward P. 'Gibbo' Gibbs and Sergeant Bob 'Butch' Morton were both missing.

When posted to 616 Squadron, Gibbs, according to Pilot Officer Johnnie Johnson, was 'somewhat elderly, pedantic and heavily moustachioed' and lacked combat experience – which was not the case; on 21 May 1941, Gibbs had already damaged a 109 over St Omer, while flying Hurricanes with 56 Squadron. Nonetheless, according to Johnnie, the newcomer was, 'an aerobatic pilot of exceptional ability'. One day during that summer of summers, Wing Commander Bader had 'given the troops his usual breezy performance' of aerobatics over the airfield, but was unable to complete a roll off the top of two 'upward Charlies'. Discussing this with Squadron Leaders Burton and Holden, Bader opined that the Spitfire had not the power to pull off this ambitious manoeuvre. Suddenly, the roar of a Spitfire shattered the peace, the pilot raising the undercarriage immediately she became airborne. This was, of course, how the wing leader took off, but Bader was unimpressed, commenting that such demonstrations were 'bad flying discipline'. The 616 Squadron pilots gathered outside dispersal watched the Spitfire begin an aerobatic sequence, counting the rolls: one, two.... 'He'll never do the roll off,' said Bader, ... '*Three*!', the audience chorused. Johnnie wrote that:

> Very slowly but with perfect timing the Spitfire half-rolled off the top of the loop and resumed level flight. The whole manoeuvre was carried out with exquisite skill, and to demonstrate that it was no fluke, the pilot repeated the performance and then side-slipped his Spitfire to a perfect three-point landing.

And so, much to Wing Commander Bader's displeasure, Gibbs 'became the aerobatic king of Tangmere'. On that fateful day over France, 9 July 1941, it was that rare skill that saved his life; having destroyed a 109 near Mazingarbe, Gibbs was attacked himself. Flying inverted, very close to the ground, Gibbs deceived his pursuing enemies into believing he was finished; at the last minute, Tangmere's 'aerobatic king' righted his Spitfire, lowered the undercarriage and made a perfect landing in a French field.

Squadron Leader Burton's wife, Jean, recalled that:

> Most of 616 Squadron's pilots were young bachelors, and few of those who were married had their wives with them. It was a strange feeling at the tender age of 21 to be the CO's wife, as before the war officers were rarely allowed to marry or be eligible for a Marriage Allowance either before the age of 30 or attaining the rank of squadron leader. However, during that summer hardly any of the normal duties of a CO's wife fell on my youthful shoulders. The sole occasion was when one of the older 616 Squadron pilots, Squadron Leader Gibbs, did not return from operations. His wife was one of the few at Tangmere and so, feeling extremely nervous, I was despatched by Billy to offer such words of support and comfort as I was

able. All I can recall is that the wife in question was naturally very upset and overwrought, and I fear that I was probably not of much help. I was pleased to later discover that her husband had actually safely landed in France and cleverly evaded capture, making his way back to England via the escape route through Spain.

Clearly, Gibbs was, without doubt, an exceptional airman.
Sergeant Bob Morton:

On 8 July 1941, our first Spitfire Mk VB was delivered, with two cannon instead of eight machine-guns. To my delight the CO asked me to take it out over the sea and test the cannon. Why I was chosen was a mystery; none of our officers, except Wing Commander Bader, had ever used cannon and all would have liked the chance. I went straight down to the hangar and sought out the Flight Sergeant. 'I know what you've come for,' he said. 'We're having a bit of trouble lining up the cannon. Can you come back after lunch?' I said that I would, but during lunch an afternoon sweep was ordered. I flew with my heart in my mouth, fearful that someone else would be testing the new Spitfire. Immediately we landed I went straight to the hangar but the work was still not finished, nor was it after tea, when I was asked to return in the morning. Again a sweep intervened, and after lunch another. On that occasion I flew as No 2 to a new pilot, Flying Officer Gill. As soon as we got over France he commenced imitating the Blackpool Big

Squadron Leader E.P. Gibbs, Tangmere's 'Aerobatic King' who was shot down and captured on 9 July 1941.

Dipper. My maps kept being flung from their storage pocket, and it was all I could do to remain in contact with him. Looking behind was out of the question. The result was inevitable: again the golden rain, again the explosions within my Spitfire.

This time, as I levelled out, the whole aircraft was vibrating. I discovered later that a shell inside my port tailplane had opened it up like a baked potato. As before, I made for the coast, but this time the engine stopped completely, one propeller blade sticking up in front of me in silent immobility. I tried to call up the other aircraft, as MacFie had done a few days before, when he too was shot down, but I knew that nothing was getting through. I also knew that I had five engine starter cartridges left. With great concentration, I went through the whole starting procedure with each one. Each time the propeller kicked over but stopped again. I looked at my altimeter; all prisoners of war begin to go 'round the bend' eventually, but I started early: the altimeter read 3,000ft, the minimum safe height for baling out being 300ft. For some reason I decided that it was already too late. However, the aircraft was still under control and I had no sure knowledge that my parachute was undamaged following the cannon shells exploding within the fuselage. Fortunately there was a huge expanse of ripening wheat below, near St Omer, with a large house in the middle of it. I steered away from the house, not wishing to give the occupants the danger of sheltering me or the embarrassment of refusing, and landed gently with wheels up. Some German soldiers then captured me and took me to St Omer in a lorry which only had one tyre.

I never returned to Tangmere, but I would like to think that if ever I do, I shall find a new Spitfire Mk VB awaiting my test flight.

As it happened, in Sergeant Morton's enforced absence, his CO, Squadron Leader Burton, test-flew the new Spitfire, recording in his log book, 'Cannon firing, P8707. Nearly hit a boatload of fishermen!'

On this day, eight Spitfires in total were lost, three pilots killed, three captured, one evaded and another, the Kenley wing leader, Wing Commander Johnny Peel DFC, rescued from the sea. Additionally, another Spitfire was shot-up, the pilot wounded, although he returned to base. JG 26 claimed five Spitfires, but on this occasion JG 2's claims were inflated: a Hurricane plus twelve Spitfires throughout the day. Just one JG 26 pilot forced-landed with combat damage, and JG 2 lost a pilot killed near St Pol. Fighter Command claimed sixteen Me 109s destroyed, four probables and eight damaged.

10 July 1941
At 1135 hrs, Wing Commander Bader led the Tangmere Wing off on Circus 42, escorting three Stirlings to Chocques. Over the target, 616 Squadron contacted Me 109s, and 145 Squadron investigated a formation approaching through the haze, which transpired to be Spitfires, before losing the wing in the reduced visibility. Six 145 Squadron Spitfires aborted soon after crossing the French coast, and two more turned back at St Omer, probably having become separated in the haze. One of 610 Squadron returned to Westhampnett after just ten minutes with an unserviceable Air Speed Indicator (ASI). As the wing withdrew, 610 was attacked, losing Sergeant H.C.D. Blackman, who was killed, and both Sergeants J.E. Anderson and Peter Ward-Smith, both of whom were captured; the latter recalled that 'I felt a pain in my leg and the aircraft became uncontrollable. Realising that I could not get home, I baled out: the parachute worked perfectly.'
  Wing Commander Bader:

> Was operating in a four over the Béthune area at 24,000ft when we saw five Me 109s below us in a wide, loose, vic. We attacked, diving from above, and I opened fire at 200 yards closing to 100, knocking pieces off it round the cockpit and pulling up over the top. I saw flashes as some of my bullets struck (presumably De Wilde). Was unable after pulling up to see it again, but saw and attacked without result three of the same five (so it is to be supposed that two were hit), immediately after turning. My own aeroplane shielded my view immediately after the attack and I claim this one as probable only, because of the incendiary strikes and pieces coming off the cockpit.
>
> Was flying with section of four northwards over 10/10ths between Calais-Dover. Sighted three Me 109Es below, flying south-west over the cloud. Turned and dived to catch them up, which we did just over Calais. The three 109s were in line abreast and so were my Section, with one lagging behind.

I closed in to 150 yards behind and under the left-hand one, firing a two-second burst into its belly beneath the cockpit. Pieces flew off the 109 exactly under the cockpit and there was a flash of flame and black smoke, and then the whole aeroplane went up in flames. This was seen by Sergeant West and Pilot Officer Hepple of my Section. Time approximately 1250 hrs, height 7,000ft, position either south of Calais or over Calais.

JG 26 lost three aircraft: one pilot was killed and another wounded, while Hauptmann Rolf Pingel, Kommandeur of I/JG 26, had pursued a Stirling back to England, damaging it, but was himself shot-up by the rear-gunner; attacked by a Polish Spitfire pilot, the Ritterkreuzträger was forced to land at St Margaret's Bay, Dover. Captured, Pingel had inadvertently presented the RAF with the first opportunity to examine and evaluate a virtually undamaged Me 109F. In response, JG 26 claimed three Spitfires, JG 2 ten without loss. Fighter Command actually lost ten Spitfires in total, with another damaged; fifteen Me 109s were claimed destroyed, three probables and four damaged.

Sergeant Jeff West's diary:

> Another fine morning. Mardon back from leave. Went on sweep with Wg Cdr, No 2 again. 2 combats. 2 squadrons of only 8 aircraft. Slow machine. Claim 1 probable over Calais. On 30 mins all evening. Went down to the local Royal Oak from 7 pm until closing time with Sgt Terry, Ian's brother. Got quite full. Received letters from Phil, Jane and Mum. Posted letter to Mum.

<u>11 July 1941</u>
Between 0640 hrs and 0840 hrs, 610 Squadron uneventfully swept the Channel. The day's next sortie was the main effort, Circus 43, a raid by three Stirlings on a U-Boat repair facility at Le Trait, west of Rouen, while three fighter wings flew a diversionary sweep over Lille. On this sortie, unusually, Tangmere's Station Commander, Group Captain Woodhall, flew with 610 Squadron, and Biggin Hill's Station Commander, Group Captain Dickie Barwell, accompanied Wing Commander Sailor Malan's Wing. Equally untypical was that on this occasion it was not Wing Commander Bader at the Tangmere Wing's head, but the capable Squadron Leader Billy Burton of 616 Squadron. Over France, 610 Squadron contacted

Me 109s, Sergeant Merriman claiming a probable and Pilot Officer Gray one damaged, but Flight Lieutenant Crowley-Milling was forced to return to base with an unserviceable ASI. 616 Squadron's Sergeant Alan Smith, however, experienced oxygen supply problems, so sensibly dived, strafing a German airfield, destroying two Ju 87s on the ground, having a 'squirt' at a hut and an E-Boat as his Spitfire flashed overhead at 'zero feet'.

Wing Commander Bader was again at the helm for Circus 44, between 1450 hrs – 1640 hrs, this sweep intending to catch the enemy refuelling after the earlier fighting. Although eight Me 109s were seen over France, there was no contact.

During the day, JG 26 suffered no loss, while JG 2 suffered a pilot killed over Calais. Fighter Command claimed eight 109s destroyed, six probables and six damaged. In total, five Spitfires were lost, one pilot being killed, three captured and one who evaded.

12 July 1941
The pace of operations remained intense. On this day, Wing Commander Bader led the wing on Circus 46, a two Stirling raid on the ship lift at St Omer:

> When orbiting the wood at Bois de Dieppe, about to proceed to St Omer at 26,000ft, we saw approximately twelve to fifteen Me 109Fs climbing in line-astern from Dunkirk, turning west and south. I told my Section we would attack and told the two top squadrons to stay up as I thought I had seen more Me 109s above. We turned so that the enemy – who were very close and climbing across our bows – were down-sun, and I fired a very close deflection shot at the second last one at 100 – 150 yards range. I saw De Wilde flashes in front of his cockpit but no immediate result as I passed him and turned across him and fired a head-on burst at the last Me 109 who had lagged a bit. A panel or some piece of his machine fell away and he put his nose down; as I passed over him I lost him. I then turned round 180° to the same direction as the 109s had been going but could not see them. I called my section together and, after a little, made contact with them. I then saw the Beehive and bombers flying over the St Omer wood travelling south-east just below with a squadron of Spitfires above. I saw two Me 109Fs above the Spitfires and dived down to attack. These two

flew away south more or less level and I closed up quickly on one which I shot from 100 yards dead astern and produced black smoke and glycol.

The second one was banking to the left when I attacked the first and he dived a little after the first. I got behind him with a good burst, followed him through 10/10ths cloud (about 100ft thick) and gave him one more burst which set him on fire with a short quick flame under the cockpit, then black smoke, then the whole machine caught fire around the fuselage. The pilot did not bale out. I pulled away at 9,000ft and I reckon this aeroplane crashed between St Omer and Bethune. I went up to 14,000ft and called my Section together, they were both above the cloud in the same area, and we had no more combat. I believe they had a fight at the same time. Of the four Me 109Fs one was definitely destroyed and the other three are considered damaged. The one which disappeared through the cloud layer emitting black and white smoke I consider was more likely a probable.

The Wing Commander claimed one 109 destroyed over St Omer, and three more damaged south of Dunkirk. 616 Squadron's Pilot Officer Hepple added a damaged 109 to the score, and Sergeant Smith a probable. These were the day's only claims by the Tangmere Wing. 2/JG 26's Unteroffizier Gottfried Dietze was shot-up and crash-landed at St Omer – it was his first taste of combat – and the unit's Staffelkapitän of just ten days, Oberleutnant Horst Ulenberg, was shot down and killed over Coquelles. III/JG 2's Unteroffizier Erich Frohner was shot down and severely wounded near Hazebrouck. Although these represented the enemy's only casualties in the day's fighting, Fighter Command claimed six 109s destroyed, two probables and nine damaged.

14 July 1941
Pilot Officer Johnnie Johnson:

> My job as one of two wingmen in Dogsbody Section was to protect the remainder of the Section from a flank or stern attack. Sergeant Alan Smith was the other wingman and did likewise from his position on the port side. My head, therefore, was usually turned to the left or strained right

round so that I could watch our vulnerable rear. We had little idea of what lay ahead, but knew from radio chatter and our own manoeuvres when Bader was wading into a gaggle of 109s. We had to watch our leader, and resist the natural instinct to personally break formation to chase a 109. The Squadron's total of kills and the scores of certain individual pilots increased. A combination of my role as a wingman and the fact that it seemed as if there just wasn't time to single out an opponent from the maelstrom of fighters as we jockeyed and vied for an opening, meant that I was slow to score. It was an acutely frustrating time.

On 14 July 1941, the Tangmere Wing flew on Circus 48 to St Omer. A section of 610 Squadron Spitfires were attacked over St Omer, without loss; in his log book, Flight Lieutenant Crowley-Milling wrote 'Did a head-on attack on four Me 109s – no results!'

145 Squadron was also in contact, the CO of which, Squadron Leader Turner, engaged three 109s, damaging one.

Pilot Officer Johnnie Johnson:

> I became separated from 616 Squadron when over the target so decided to fly with the Beehive during the return flight. When about twenty-five to thirty miles from the French coast and flying at 1,500ft above and behind the Beehive, I saw three aircraft in line astern to the south-west. I then turned inland, above and behind the three aircraft which I then identified as Me 109Fs. I made a quick aileron turn and attacked number three from below and behind, when I was climbing. I gave a second burst with cannon and machine-gun at 150 yards range and saw the tail blown off. The E/A went into an uncontrollable spin. I am claiming this E/A as destroyed. I then broke away as my Number Two had lost me. When over the French coast at 10,000ft I saw an Me 109E over Étaples, diving steeply. I gave chase. It pulled out at 2,000ft and flew straight and level. I drew up and gave a short burst at 150 yards range. I thought I saw something break away from the starboard wing of the E/A, but cannot be certain as my screen was covered in oil from the E/A in the first engagement. I therefore make no claim in this second engagement.

BADER'S SPITFIRE WING

Squadron Leader Burton's log book records that on this day he was 'Chased out by 109s over Gravelines with DB and Cocky'.

Only two Spitfires were lost this day, neither from the Tangmere Wing. Squadron Leader Turner, Pilot Officer Johnson and Sergeant Smith filed the Tangmere Wing's only claims that day; overall, Fighter Command claimed seven 109s destroyed and five damaged. In reality, JG 26 lost one pilot killed, and JG 2 had a missing pilot (although the circumstances are unknown).

By now, the enormously gregarious and enthusiastic Johnnie Johnson was an established member of Wing Commander Bader's 'inner sanctum':

> The Baders' 'Bayhouse' door was always open to us. About once or twice a week we motored there and always found the wing's inner-sanctum gathered about our leader. The conversation rarely strayed far from our limited world of fighters and air fighting. Sipping his lemonade, Bader analysed our recent fights, discoursed on the importance of straight shooting, on the relative merits of machine-guns and cannons, on the ability of our opponents (whom he always held in contempt), on the probably destiny of the pilot who flew with his head in the office and of our own dreadful fate should we

The Bayhouse.

TANGMERE WING WAR DIARY 18 MARCH – 8 AUGUST 1941

ever lose sight of him in combat. He was dogmatic and final in his pronouncements – nobody argued with him. It was a great privilege for us junior officers to be taken into the confidence of a wing commander, and in this fashion the three squadrons were blended into the Tangmere Wing.

Sergeant Jeff West's diary:

> Cloudy morning – raining off and on. Breakfasted promptly and flew on sweep over France. No 2 to Johnny Raikes, tricky. Came home with Roy Marples. Shot up Brighton. Had new Spit VB. Good jobs at 26,000ft. Went like a train. On readiness in afternoon. Had a couple of beers at Royal Oak. On again at 8 pm. Hoppy and I went into town for fish and chips. Brought them back to camp and were put on thirty minutes. Wrote Thelma and Ron's mother.

16 July 1941

Wing Commander Bader 'Tested cannons' in a Spitfire Mk VB on this date, but clearly remained unmoved as he continued flying his usual machine-gun-armed Mk IIA, P7666.

17 July 1941

During the evening, the Tangmere Wing flew a fighter sweep, crossing into France over Hardelot. Just inland, five Me 109Fs approached the Spitfires from their port side, in a slight dive and appearing from the direction of Boulogne. In the ensuing combat, Wing Commander Bader and Squadron Leader Holden each selected a target but were unable to press home their attack as more 109s dived upon them. Quickly withdrawing, the Spitfires regrouped over the Channel and then headed back into France, where two more Me 109s were seen but considered to be a decoy, so were not pursued. At 20,000ft over Le Touquet, 610 Squadron's Pilot Officer Gaze attacked a 109, claiming it as a probable.

19 July 1941

Circus 51 found the Tangmere Wing providing Target Support. Near Dunkirk, Wing Commander claimed a 109 destroyed, sharing another with Flight Lieutenant Dundas, and claimed a probable, as did Dogsbody 2, Sergeant Smith, Flight Lieutenant Casson, and 610 Squadron's Sergeant Raine. Flight Lieutenant Crowley-Milling noted in his log book, 'Fired at three Me 109s. No result. Bad shooting.' 145 Squadron's Sergeant Smith machine-gunned a flak position near Gravelines on the way out of France, concluding the action.

Back at Tangmere there was another 'Thrash', celebrating Flight Lieutenant Dundas receiving the DFC.

Sergeant Jeff West's diary:

> Cloudy morning. Local flying for interception exercise. Yellow Leader. We jumped the other section. Sweep in afternoon but didn't go. YMCA wagon in afternoon. Our Squadron [616] lost our VBs because Wg Cdr flying with us [author's note: who insisted upon flying the less powerful and older IIA]. Getting IIBs in exchange [author's note: hardly a fair exchange!]. Released at about 4.30 pm. Hoppy and I went to Bognor, picture and later Victoria. Obtained quite a lot of fish and chips, then returned to Royal Oak. Again had supper.

<u>20 July 1941</u>
Between 1140 hrs and 1310 hrs, the Tangmere Wing flew a sweep but there was no contact owing to poor visibility over France.

<u>21 July 1941</u>
Between 0740 hrs and 0935 hrs, Wing Commander Bader led the Tangmere Wing on Circus 54, a raid on Lille. Landfall was made at Le Touquet, 0814 hrs, after which the wing's squadrons split up and prowled over France independently. 610 Squadron orbited Béthune before following the Beehive out of France – Sergeant Merriman chased five Me 109s, firing at one, which blew up, while another went down in flames. 610 Squadron reported that one of the four Stirlings involved appeared to have an engine out. 616 Squadron clashed briefly with some 109s, claims for damaged German fighters subsequently being made by Pilot Officer 'Nip' Hepple and Sergeant Beedham. According to 616 Squadron, the sweep was 'disappointing as the enemy refused to fight'. After the sweep, as usual, the wing's Spitfires put down at just about every airfield on the south coast, joining the queues of Spitfires being refuelled at Hawkinge, Friston, Redhill and Shoreham, before returning to Westhampnett and Merston.

Pilot Officer Johnnie Johnson:

> Because the Spitfire was a defensive fighter, range was a problem. Over time, this was extended by auxiliary fuel tanks

but the aircraft was being pressed into an offensive fighter role for which it was not designed. This became an even greater problem from the following year onwards, when the Americans arrived on the scene and began making deeper penetrations – we could only escort them so far, then had to return and refuel. Obviously during that unescorted period, the Germans attacked the bombers. Ultimately the matter was resolved through the arrival of American-built Mustangs, Lightnings and Thunderbolts, purpose-built long-range offensive fighters capable of escorting the bombers to Berlin and back. Our experience of 1941, however, was instrumental in moving all of this forward, although I have always been astonished by the Air Staff's lack of foresight in not having a long-range single-engine fighter from the outset. I suppose before the war it was envisaged that the Blenheim would fulfil this role, but in the event these twin-engine fighters were just not up to taking on the faster and more agile single-engine German fighters.

That evening, between 1950 hrs and 2200 hrs, Wing Commander Bader and the Tangmere Wing participated in a Rodeo, Circus 55, providing a 'Wing patrol over northern France'. Pilot Officer Johnnie Johnson was flying as Red One, leading Red Section, his Red 2 being Sergeant Sidney 'George' Mabbett. Near the target area, 24,000ft over Montreuil, Johnnie positioned his Section to starboard and slightly above and behind Dogsbody Section. Six Me 109s were sighted, flying eastwards. Wing Commander Bader swung his Section around so as to attack the enemy fighters from the rear. Johnnie:

> I then brought my Section slightly below and almost abreast of Dogsbody Section, and at this stage my Number 2 was with me. When about 250 yards from the enemy formation I saw Dogsbody 4 [Pilot Officer Hepple] open fire at the right-hand 109 – which emitted glycol fumes but continued to fly straight, carrying out gentle swings to port and starboard. Unfortunately I did not hear the order to break and pressed home my attack on the right-hand E/A from 150 – 200 yards. After two short bursts (eight machine-guns) the nose of E/A dropped slowly and it eventually went into a vertical dive, the white glycol fumes giving way to thick black smoke. I then broke away and

did not see E/A again. My No 2 was not seen again after this engagement. Very accurate flak experienced when crossing on return journey.

Pilot Officers Johnson and Hepple were credited with a shared probable, and Flight Lieutenant Dundas claimed a 109 damaged over Merville. Squadron Leader Burton's log book recorded that he 'Should have shot down 109, but failed to open fire until too late owing to uncertainty of identity. Sergeant Mabbett missing.'

Sergeant S.W.R. 'Thug' Mabbett had been hit near Montreuil by Unteroffizier Gottfried Dietze of 2/JG 26. It was the German's first kill, and Mabbett's Spitfire, P8690, a Mk VB, was hit in the cockpit area by cannon fire. Fatally wounded, 'Mab', as he was also known, managed to make a successful wheels-up forced-landing near St Omer – expiring almost immediately the aircraft ground to a halt. So impressed were the Germans with this skilful flying when so badly wounded that they buried Sergeant Mabbett at Longuenesse with full military honours.

Above left: Sergeant S.W.R. 'George' Mabbett, from Cheltenham, known as 'Thug' on account of his rugby prowess.

Above right: Sergeant Mabbett was shot down over Montreuil on 21 July 1941, managing to crash-land his Spitfire despite fatal wounds.

TANGMERE WING WAR DIARY 18 MARCH – 8 AUGUST 1941

So impressed were the Germans with Sergeant Mabbett's skill and courage that they buried him with full military honours at St Omer-Longuenesse Souvenir Cemetery.

Seven Spitfires were lost in total that day, six pilots killed, one captured. JG 26 lost one pilot killed, claiming six Spitfires and a Stirling destroyed, while JG 2 claimed five Spitfires but lost one Me 109, the pilot of which was wounded, while another crash-landed at Amiens with combat damage. Fighter Command claimed ten Me 109s destroyed, two probables and ten damaged. The clinical statistics, however, conceal the human tragedy of it all.

Brian Mabbett:

> My elder brother, Sergeant S.W.R. Mabbett, who we all called 'George', was, and still is, my hero. We came from a very poor background in Charlton Kings, Gloucestershire. George, a gentle and kind person, passed for the Grammar School. I remember him as a great brother who excelled at sport and was extremely popular in our village. Between 1936–39 he played rugby for Cheltenham, from the age of 17 onwards, and then, when only 19, he played for both Gloucester City and Gloucester County. The telegram officially notifying my mother of his death arrived on what would have been my brother's 22nd birthday. My father had died just a few months before, and I was just 15. We were proud that the Germans buried him with full military honours at St Omer cemetery. He was a great brother, and no one else could ever compare to him.

22 July 1941

Between 1205 hrs and 1350 hrs, Wing Commander Bader led the Tangmere Wing on a close escort commitment to six Blenheims bombing Le Frait, rendezvousing with the bombers over Tangmere. Crossing the English coast at 10,000ft over Beachy Head, the Beehive headed straight to the target, where 610 Squadron reported seeing bombs 'burst in the target area'. The bombers were escorted home, no flak having been experienced or enemy aircraft seen.

According to the 610 Squadron ORB, that evening the Northolt Polish Wing's 306 and 308 Squadrons arrived at Westhampnett to operate with the Tangmere Wing (although no record of this commitment appears in those units' records). The 610 Squadron diary records that the Tangmere Spitfires, led by Wing Commander Bader, went up at 2100 hrs, the Poles following between 2115 and 2130 hrs. Over base, at 2115 hrs the Tangmere Wing rendezvoused with eleven Coastal Command Bristol Beauforts from Thorney Island. 616 Squadron provided 'low escort with two Polish squadrons, 306 and 308 above with 145 and 610 as high cover'. The Beaufort torpedo bombers arrived in a straggling formation. En route to Le Havre, 616 Squadron, still with the bombers, lost the rest of the wing, sweeping from Le Havre to Cherbourg at 8,000ft. Apart from 'two large stationary ships in the bight between Havre and Cherbourg', no enemy shipping was seen – and those two vessels were not what the RAF pilots sought. The purpose of the operation was succinctly described in Wing Commander Bader's log book: 'Looking for Scharnhorst.' It was a late finish, however, the Spitfires not landing until 2255 hrs.

On this day, the wing concluded re-equipping with the new Spitfire Mk VA and VB.

<u>23 July 1941</u>
First off, at 1155 hrs, Wing Commander Bader led the Tangmere Wing to Manston with orders to rendezvous with six Blenheims over that aerodrome. Unfortunately the bombers were seven minutes early and the Spitfires five late, so all squadrons involved were recalled to Manston for refuelling. At 1351 hrs, the wing was up again, escorting the bombers on a Roadstead, attacking a tanker off Ostend. II/JG 26 intercepted the Beehive, and in the whirling combat, Squadron Leader Turner and Sergeant Grant of 145 Squadron claimed 109s destroyed, and over the target 610 Squadron drove off several Me 109s. Three Blenheims were shot down over France, and a fourth, which was lagging behind on the return journey, crashed into the sea off Deal, sinking immediately – although the Spitfires circled overhead, ready to report the position of survivors, sadly there were none. Again, the Spitfires, short of fuel, landed at various airfields to be refuelled before finally heading home.

TANGMERE WING WAR DIARY 18 MARCH – 8 AUGUST 1941

Wing Commander Bader, however, did not lead the wing on that occasion:

> Took off from Manston with Squadron Leader Burton at approximately 1340 hrs, after 242 Squadron on the expedition to bomb ship off Dunkirk. The weather was very hazy from about 1,000ft upwards but clearer below. We flew from North Foreland and near Gravelines were attacked by a Me 109 out of the sun. We countered and Squadron Leader Burton had a shot at it. It flew low over the water to the French coast. We carried on up to Dunkirk and slightly past where we saw some flak and then a Spitfire (squadron markings XT) flying straight for home in a dive, being attacked by a Me 109. We immediately turned on the Me 109 which saw us and did a left-hand climbing turn back to France, but I got a very close short burst (half a second) at him from underneath and behind him. It definitely hit him and produced a puff of white smoke under his cockpit. I turned away immediately as I had no idea how many were about and did not want to lose Squadron Leader Burton. I claim this Messerschmitt as damaged but would like information from 242 Squadron who told me on landing back at Manston that they had seen two Me 109s go into the sea in that area. We flew back to Manston after this and landed among 242 Squadron, who arrived back at the same time. I claim a damaged aircraft just around Dunkirk out to sea, which may be a destroyed one. I never saw this Messerschmitt after breaking away because visibility was poor.

Squadron Leader Burton's log book records of that sortie, 'Two squirts. Found 109 beating up a Spitfire. Sent 109 quickly back to France.'

That evening, between 1940 hrs and 2115 hrs, 'Dogsbody' led the Tangmere Wing on another Circus, six Blenheims bombing Marzingarbe. After crossing the coast over Le Touquet the wing was constantly engaged by Me 109s – which almost immediately split the Spitfires into sections of four or pairs. Another fifty Me 109s were seen holding back, their leader clearly timing the moment to attack. The 610 Squadron diary recorded that 'all engagements were terrific dogfights'. One of 610's pilots crash-landed at Bexhill with shrapnel in one arm and a cut eye; Wing Commander Bader and Sergeant Raine shared an Me 109 destroyed, Pilot Officer Grey claimed a probable and Sergeant Twitchett damaged another. Sergeant Breeze's Spitfire was damaged but he managed to glide home across the Channel and crash-land at Beachy Head. 616 Squadron met 'plenty of enemy fighters'. Wing Commander Bader also shared a 109 destroyed with Flight Lieutenant Dundas, Flight Lieutenant Casson destroyed another and damaged two more, while Pilot Officer Johnson winged a third.

In his log book, Pilot Officer Johnson noted that there were 'More 109s about than ever before. Wing engaged almost whole time over France.'

The Me 109 claimed destroyed by Flight Lieutenant Buck Casson was 616 Squadron's fiftieth aerial victory – doubtless celebrated by another good 'Thrash'.

24 July 1941
That morning, Wing Commander Bader led the Tangmere Wing escorting bombers attacking shipping off Cherbourg, the sortie being uneventful. Afterwards, Wing Commander Bader flew to Northolt for a conference at Uxbridge, returning later that day.

25 July 1941
Wing Commander Bader again flew to and from Northolt for another conference at 11 Group HQ. There was no commitment for the Tangmere Wing in Dogsbody's absence owing to bad weather.

There were, however, training flights. Pilot Officer Johnnie Johnson practiced 'Surprise attacks', noting in his log book that on this day he had been 'shot down by Buck' (Casson). Other routine flights recorded in his log at this time included escorting a Lysander over the Channel, searching for a ditched Blenheim, and escorting a destroyer 'shelling French coast'.

26 July 1941
At 0545 hrs, Wing Commander Bader led the Tangmere Wing on a 'Channel Sweep', but the patrol was cancelled owing to bad weather, the Spitfires being recalled after just fifteen minutes.

There were no other wing commitments for the remainder of this month, each squadron flying local patrols and protecting convoys, in addition to routine training flights.

27 July 1941
Sergeant Jeff West's diary:

> Weather still broken. Breakfast at 9 am. Not much good. Nothing doing in morning. Had a game of darts. Wrote Mrs Percy and

Mrs Haslam. Quite a poor dinner. Made three separate trips to Royal Oak. On readiness off and on all afternoon, 1, 3, 5, 7, and released.

28 July 1941
On this day, Squadron Leader Stan Turner's 145 Squadron was pulled out of the line and replaced in the Tangmere Wing at Merston by Squadron Leader Lionel Don Finlay DFC's 41 Squadron, which had previously been resting after the Battle of Britain at Catterick.

Thus the Tangmere Wing's identity was significantly changed. The team that had fought together throughout this memorable summer was now no more.

29 July 1941
Still eager to engage the enemy, Flight Lieutenant Lee-Knight and Sergeant Pollock of 610 Squadron took off at 1945 hrs for a Rhubarb, crossing out over Beachy Head at 2,000ft, beneath 10/10ths cloud. Climbing 7,000ft, however, 'big clear patches' could be seen between Dieppe and Le Treport, the weather, therefore, being unsuitable for such an operation, forcing the Spitfires to return to base.

31 July 1941
The 11 Group AOC, Air Vice-Marshal Leigh-Mallory, visited the Tangmere Sector, 'conversing with most of the pilots'.

Sergeant Jeff West's diary:

> Heavily overcast. Squadron was released in morning but I stood-by to test the cannons. Weather poor. Shot up the drome on return from second trip. Wg Cdr was here in his MG. Went down to Royal Oak. Five of the boys called in at tea time for supper – I went back with them – AOC at the Station. Went back to Royal Oak and took Bubbles out. Returned in time for supper. Received letters from Betty, Allan Shaw, Barney Ford and Mrs Tucker – Montreal.

1 August 1941
41 Squadron's CO, Squadron Leader Finlay, was due a rest, and on this day was promoted to wing commander and replaced as 41 Squadron's CO by Squadron Leader L.M. 'Elmer' Gaunce DFC. Gaunce, a Canadian

from Alberta, had first been a soldier before joining the RAF in 1936. He was an experienced fighter pilot, having served as a flight commander in 615 Squadron during the Battle of France, and during the Battle of Britain was awarded the DFC following the destruction of four Me 109s in just over a month. Having already survived being shot down on 18 August 1940, the 'Hardest Day', Gaunce baled out of a blazing Hurricane over Herne Bay on 26 August 1940. Recovered from his burns, he was given command of 46 Squadron at North Weald, leading the squadron into action against the ill-fated Italian attack on England on 11 November 1940. The following month Gaunce was rested, returning to operations when taking command of 41 Squadron, which had flown with distinction from Hornchurch during the Battle of Britain. Neither Squadron Leader Gaunce or 41 Squadron, however, had any experience of offensive wing operations – and were now at the base of a steep learning curve.

41 Squadron relieved 145 at Merston on 28 July 1941. The following pilots are pictured outside the Officers' Mess at Shopwyke House; from left: Pilot Officers Babbage and Draper, Flight Lieutenant Winskill, Squadron Leader Gaunce (CO), Wing Commander Finley (former CO), Flying Officer Williams and Pilot Officer Ranger.

TANGMERE WING WAR DIARY 18 MARCH – 8 AUGUST 1941

Above left: Sergeant Ron Rayner of 41 Squadron on readiness at Merston, his newspaper reporting about 'Bombs on Nazi Aerodrome'.

Above right: Jack Younie, of 41 Squadron's groundcrew.

616 Squadron's Roy Marples was promoted to flight lieutenant and became a flight commander in 41 Squadron.

Surprisingly, there is no record of any practice wing formation flights, enabling 41 Squadron to get to know the 'form'. On this day, two pairs of the squadron's Spitfires flew Rhubarbs, but these were uneventful.

PA 'Jack' Younie, a member of 41 Squadron's groundcrew, remembered that:

> When we arrived at Merston, where we were based before a subsequent move to Westhampnett, we were billeted in huts dispersed around the airfields and at various locations outside. We used to use pushbikes to travel back and forth. The Spitfires were also dispersed around trees along the edge of the airfield. Mainly the job there was sweeping the French coast, and as that year there was two hours' British Summer Time, we were on duty 0330 hrs – 2330 hrs, which gave little time for sleeping! However, the Spitfires were usually away on their sweeps for

about two hours, and that time was used for catching up on a bit of sleep or playing football etc with the pilots on standby for the next sortie. The pilots were also on standby, of course, for any defensive scramble over our own coast.

For us, it was a very busy time as we also had to keep up with our weapons training, aircraft recognition and the other lectures we had to attend. We did have one intense month, during which we were almost constantly on duty non-stop. We also had to put on a night guard, although this was shared with other squadrons. At the end of this non-stop month, we were granted forty-eight hours' leave – most of which I spent in bed!

A couple of incidents spring to mind. We had a new Spitfire delivered and a sergeant-pilot took it up but discovered that the undercarriage would not come down, even despite using the emergency gear. The CO then went up and guided him down, the sergeant made a perfect belly-landing and survived unscathed. We had Spitfires coming back damaged all the time; it was hectic.

I first met Wing Commander Bader when he once flew over from Tangmere to lead our squadron on patrol over France. I did not know who he was, but I directed the aircraft in. He called me over but then turned his back on me when I reached his Spitfire; I wondered what on earth was going on, but then realised who he was as he put his hand on my shoulder and lowered himself down to the ground. I think he picked me because I just happened to be the right height for him to put his hand on my shoulder!

At Cranwell I had qualified to service aircraft radios and radar equipment, in addition to the pilots' microphones and headsets. This was done on a daily basis and also between sorties. We also helped out with rearming and were used by the fitters as ballast to hold the aeroplanes down while their engines were run up. All in all, it was a hard year – but one I will never forget and am proud to have played a small part in the story of 41 Squadron and the Tangmere Wing.

2 August 1941

Five pairs of 41 Squadron Spitfires flew Rhubarbs throughout the day, but without results, among them, between 1055 hrs and 1210 hrs, Flight Lieutenant (later Air Commodore Sir) Archie Winskill, with Sergeant Ron 'Cloudy' Rayner as his No 2; the latter recalled that:

TANGMERE WING WAR DIARY 18 MARCH – 8 AUGUST 1941

Rhubarbs were very dangerous, flying at zero feet to remain off the enemy radar, popping up over the enemy-held coastline and shooting at pretty much anything that moved. I remember once that we shot up a car of some sort and questioning afterwards how on earth we could be sure that the occupant wasn't a civilian, a French doctor, say, an essential vehicle user on an errand of mercy? By flying low and fast, we also hoped to avoid anti-aircraft fire, being gone before gunners could bring their sights to bear, but it was a risky business, very dicey, and I also recall thinking that an expensive aircraft and valuable pilot could be lost just because of a well-aimed single bullet. And, really, what did Rhubarbs achieve? Very little in my view and certainly not commensurate with the number of experienced chaps lost on these nuisance raids.

3 August 1941
At 1430 hrs, three 41 Squadron Spitfires effected a Rhubarb, successfully attacking a railway engine, a signal box and a factory at Le Treport.

4 August 1941
Six Spitfires of 610 Squadron flew a sweep from 1130 hrs – 1245 hrs, but apart from sighting six Spitfires of 616 Squadron over France, it was an uneventful sortie owing to bad visibility. Wing Commander Bader was leading the 616 Squadron formation on 'Sweep. St Omer. La Nieppe. Dull. High escort.'

On this day, Wing Commander Bader swapped his faithful Spitfire Mk IIA, P7666, for a new Mk VA, also a presentation Spitfire, 'Lord Lloyd I', which now sported the wing leader's 'DB' fuselage codes and his wing commander's pennant.

6 August 1941
Sergeant Jeff West's diary:

A beautiful clear morning. Not such a hot breakfast. Called to readiness but put back 15 minutes. Practice flying in morning. Battle tactics. After lunch on convoy patrol and another interception exercise. Hoppy crashed Magister in Cornwall. Seriously injured. Monks hurt. Another convoy at dusk, landing just after 10 pm. Went down to the Royal Oak. Just got in. Stayed for supper with the boys, quite a lively party.

BADER'S SPITFIRE WING

<u>7 August 1941</u>
Between 1710 hrs and 1855 hrs, Wing Commander Bader led the Tangmere Wing, including 41 Squadron, with Wing Commander Finlay at its head, which was flying its first Wing operation, Circus 67, raiding Lille power station. As the wing orbited between Merville and Le Touquet, a large formation of Me 109s dived out of the sun, but dived away when the Spitfires turned into the attack. Individual combats ensued, 41 Squadron's Sergeant Mitchell damaging an Me 109F over Béthune, but Flight Lieutenant Gilbert Draper was shot down over Fruges and captured. Bob Beardsley, one of the Few, was a sergeant-pilot and recalled that sortie:

> On this sortie I was leading a section of four, our rear cover. We were the low squadron of the wing, and as I looked to my rear left I saw an Me 109 closing on my port sub-section, so close that the cannon orifice in the propeller boss was very apparent! The attacking aircraft had not fired, but I called the wing leader to tell him that we had been attacked by 109s. To my amazement, Wing Commander Bader responded 'Only Hurricanes, old boy!' The next second the whole wing was engaged – I saw no more 'Hurricanes'! When the lead squadron was attacked, Bader did actually say 'Sorry, old boy!'

Sergeants West and Brewer of 616 Squadron each claimed a 109 damaged, the Germans persisting in probing attacks over Hazebrouck, Merville and Lille, only breaking off over the French coast.

There was another Circus that evening, to St Omer, but the Tangmere Wing was not involved. Fourteen Spitfires were lost during the day, five pilots being killed and five captured, plus a Canadian Hurricane pilot who was also killed. JG 26 claimed fifteen Spitfires and the Hurricane, JG 2 five Spitfires and a 'Curtiss P-40', so there was an element of overclaiming involved on the German side. The only Luftwaffe casualties were two 109s shot-up and forced-landing, one each from the two groups involved. Fighter Command claimed five Me 109s destroyed, seven probables and eight damaged.

41 Squadron's Flight Lieutenant Archie Winskill recalled this period of operations:

> After taking off, the squadrons of the wing would gradually form up while climbing easterly along the south coast, reaching wing formation at 20,000ft over Beachy Head. We would then head south to the target area. As we crossed the French coast the Me

109s were waiting for us. As sweeps were usually flown at midday, the 109s usually had the advantage of the sun's position. To keep a wing of thirty-six Spitfires together, pilots can only fly at no more than three-quarter throttle, thus the 109s had both height and speed advantage. Harry Broadhurst, Hornchurch wing leader, had a theory for sweeps which was to fly high and at full throttle once you had crossed the French coast – a much sounder principle.

With Bader, once he spotted the enemy there was a semblance of directing his squadrons and deploying them in the air for the attack, but on the whole, when he sighted the first 109s he was after them, the wing just breaking up and it being every man for himself.

Sergeant Jeff West's diary:

> Clear morning. On readiness at 8.30 am. Heard Hoppy died during the night. Weather clouded over. All pilots in Tangmere Wing went to 610 dispersal and had photo taken. Called to readiness at 5 pm – another sweep over France. Lille, 8/10 cloud. Flew Yellow 4, CO's Section. Met by 20 plus over Le Touquet. 41 Squadron's first appearance – pretty bloody rough. RT chatter awful. Lost 10 – 4. 41 Squadron lost 2. I claimed 1 damaged. Also Beedham. Post mortem of do at 610 afterwards. Released at 8 pm. Went down to Royal Oak for a few beers. Stayed to supper.

<u>8 August 1941</u>

Owing to bad weather, there was no operational flying.

Sergeant Jeff West's diary:

> Rained heavily all morning. Eggs for breakfast. Went to Woodfield to see Group Captain re commission. Recommended OK. Went to Chi with Mardon after lunch. Left shoes and film in Chi. Went to Sick Bay at Fontwell to see Smithy. OK. McWatt also there. Beautiful black eyes. 610 and 41 released nearly all day. We stood-by. Letters from Tom Johnson, Doris, Phil, Mollie, Norma, Dobbs, Allan Shaw and cable from Gowers. Finished letter to Mum and Bet. Wrote Doris and Allan Shaw. On duty until 9.30 pm. Went down to Royal Oak. Had supper there with the boys. Cold roast lamb and mint sauce.

Chapter Four

'He never stood-down himself…'

By 8 August 1941, Wing Commander Bader had been flying operationally since joining 19 Squadron at Duxford in February 1940. In that time, he had seen action over Dunkirk, led his controversial 12 Group 'Big Wing' during the Battle of Britain, flown on 'Fighter Nights', and, of course, led the Tangmere Wing since 18 March 1941. During his time as wing leader, Bader had flown at least seventy operational flights, fighter sweeps, patrols, and escorting bombers over enemy occupied France. While thriving on such action and the camaraderie of his wing, the strain was beginning to tell.

Pilot Officer Johnnie Johnson: 'The signs were there. Douglas's reactions were getting slower in the air, and he was becoming increasingly greedy, you know. His awareness and judgement were impaired.'

Indeed, only two days previously Wing Commander Bader had failed to correctly identify the Me 109s Sergeant Bob Beardsley had warned him about, believing them to be Hurricanes, and wasting precious seconds. Fortunately no harm was done – but seconds counted in fast-moving air combat.

Group Captain 'Woody' Woodhall:

> All through that summer, the Tangmere Wing carried out two and frequently three sweeps a day over enemy territory, and Douglas Bader led every one himself. Although he insisted that all his pilots stood-down from operations and were given leave at suitable intervals, to prevent them getting stale, he never stood-down himself.

By this time, Bader, according to his own estimation, had destroyed twenty-eight German aircraft. This was important to him. The measure of a fighter pilot, at least to the public and as a propaganda tool, was how many aircraft he had destroyed. Up there in the 'burning blue', it was RAF aircrews who were able to fight back – and were very much centre stage. The Germans were a formidable foe – and the propagandists sought to give public morale hope and heart by continually emphasising that the RAF was shooting down more aircraft than it was losing. Churchill himself argued that the enemy's prowess should be praised, exaggerated even, to make the British effort appear an even greater achievement. Back then, the newspapers reported the daily score similarly to a cricket test match, although radio was the greatest medium for sharing news. The public saw the RAF fighter pilots and aircrews as glamourous heroes, and the BBC – as always central to British propaganda – lost no time in broadcasting accounts from fighter pilots. During this early war period, those newspaper reports and broadcasts were anonymous, the Air Ministry's policy being to not promote individuals, except when naming decorations or casualties, wishing to avoid a situation whereby morale could unduly suffer if reports concentrated on one or two fighter aces. Indeed, Sir Kingsley Wood, Secretary of State for Air, was clear that fighter pilots were part of the RAF, and that it was important to promote the service as a whole. The fighter ace, then, was a weapon in both combat and in the propaganda war, tales of pilots' derring-do bolstering public confidence and morale. By 1941, however, there were two fighter aces who were so successful, and newsworthy for different reasons, that they were well-known to the public by name: Wing Commanders Douglas Bader, described by the press as the 'Greatest Hero of Them All', and A.G. 'Sailor' Malan.

By the end of July 1941, Wing Commander Malan had destroyed thirty-two enemy aircraft, and had been on operations since the Second World War began on 3 September 1939. Whereas Bader had returned to the RAF as a flying officer in early 1940, Malan was already in a responsible position as a flight commander on 74 Squadron. He too would score over Dunkirk, and during the Battle of Britain when commanding 74 – by which time Bader had caught up in the promotion stakes and was CO of 242 Squadron. Whereas Bader was based in 12 Group throughout the Battle of Britain, and only able to get into action through his 'Big Wing' idea, Malan served in 11 Group, the frontline, for most of that epic struggle. Like Bader, he too had been among the first wing leaders to be appointed, and had led the Biggin Hill Wing on the relentless round of offensive operations during 1941. Malan was obviously newsworthy because of his aerial victories, and, as with Bader (the legless pilot's story being inspirational on so many other levels) for another reason: he was South African – a country divided over support for Britain. The Afrikaner community in particular hated the

British, and in particular the English, which was a legacy of the Boer War and imperialism. Many Afrikaners believed not just that South Africa should remain neutral in this latest global conflict, but that the country should actively take up arms for Germany, fighting against Britain, the old enemy. For that reason the dashing, handsome, Malan was also of great benefit to the propagandists in promoting loyal South Africans' active support of the Allied war effort. As individuals, Bader and Malan, however, could not have been more different; Bader, the loud, forceful, swashbuckling and blood-thirsty pirate, Malan the quiet, almost shy, consummate professional. Whereas being in the public eye was something Bader thrived on, for Malan it was anathema. Neither, though, had any choice in the matter, and being in the spotlight, the press trumpeting fighter pilots' scores, added another dimension of pressure to an already highly charged scenario.

By July 1941, the signs of strain had been recognised in Biggin Hill's exalted wing leader, but the 31-year-old Sailor Malan at first refused to take a break from operations. Then, the demands that he should rest became louder. Malan later said:

> It wasn't an order, they just came up and said how did I feel about it? I thought I was all right, and I refused. The feeling is hard to explain. Since I'd first been approached I had more than doubled my score. I kept thinking 'Just a few more before I go.'

The score was the confirmation of a pilot's ability and prowess, and in Malan's case, like Bader, there was a public expectation for him to continue knocking down German aircraft. Air Chief Marshal Dowding, however, emphasised that the personal score, while important, was not the South African's primary driver:

> I probably knew Sailor better than I knew most officers serving in squadrons during that time of stress known as the Battle of Britain. I looked on him as one of the great assets of the Command – a fighter pilot who was not solely or mainly concerned with his own 'score', but as one whose first thoughts were for the efficiency of his Squadron, and the personal safety of his junior pilots who fought under his command. I know that he was regarded as a heroic figure by the small fry over whom he spread his influence, and I personally shared their opinion.

'HE NEVER STOOD-DOWN HIMSELF...'

At the end of July 1941, Malan was rested from operations. A recent three-week break in the country had made him realise 'how really clapped-out I was'. He also acknowledged that his reflexes had become dull through fatigue, which was potentially dangerous for those he led. By that time, Malan's score stood at thirty-two, making him Fighter Command's top-scoring fighter pilot – a position he would occupy until Wing Commander Johnnie Johnson eventually exceeded that figure in 1944. Instead of continuing the fight, Group Captain Malan went into training, impressing upon new fighter pilots his 'Ten Rules of Air Fighting' and sharing his hard-won and invaluable experience. It was a selfless thing to do, saying much about the man.

When Malan was stood-down, Air Vice-Marshal Leigh-Mallory realised that Wing Commander Bader was equally tired – and more valuable long-term if rested. Bader's somewhat forceful personality resisted even his AOC, however – who backed down.

Johnnie Johnson:

> 'LM' knew that Douglas was tired but he basically *refused* to go. Thelma was worried too and tried to persuade him to come off ops. He wouldn't listen to anyone, not even the AOC, who gave in and agreed to let him continue until the end of the 'season'.

Even the press was concerned, the *Daily Mirror* columnist 'Cassandra' writing that:

> I propose that Douglas Bader be prohibited from ever stepping into an aircraft again. Such men as he – and there are many like him – are too valuable to England. This country cannot afford to lose this splendid strain of manhood. The flower of our people should not be allowed to destroy itself even for the utmost reasons of heroism and bravery. By their valour, by their splendour of spirit, these men kill themselves. Already they have done 10,000 times their share towards winning the war. I say they have done enough. The squadrons may lose great leaders – but the race should be allowed to keep their finest types.

Wing Commander Bader was personally unmoved.

Most, however, had long ago concluded that this human dynamo, who talked of nothing but shooting down Germans, and then more Germans, and who, according to Air Vice-Marshal Tom Pike, 'almost eliminated fear from his pilots', was invincible. Bader was still determined, though, to increase his personal score by September 1941, when he knew he would have to rest. According to Brickhill, he was 'not jealous' of Malan and other aces, 'although he would have loved to have caught them'. To Bader, the Tangmere Wing was all-important, aerial combat the ultimate and most fulfilling thrill. That was undoubtedly so, but remaining on operations was irresponsible and self-serving. Unlike Malan, Bader's primary driver may well have been the ongoing accumulation of his personal score – throughout his whole life, he had to be the best at everything he did, and being the top-scoring RAF fighter pilot was, perhaps, what he was born to be.

According to Brickhill in *Reach for the Sky*, on 8 August 1941, Flight Lieutenant Peter MacDonald MP (who had actually been posted away from Tangmere the previous week) insisted that Wing Commander Bader took a few days off, and booked rooms for the Baders and himself for a golfing break at St Andrew's starting on 11 August. After an argument, Tangmere's wing leader agreed to go. There was time for a few more sweeps, though, weather permitting.

The following day, 9 August 1941, absolutely everything went wrong…

Chapter Five

'Break! For Christ's Sake BREAK!'

According to the Meteorological Office, on Monday, 9 August 1941, a warm front was moving across the United Kingdom, the dawn cloudy at Tangmere, passing over to good visibility but with cloud returning later. The wind was south-westerly, force 2, increasing to 3 or 4. The weather over northern France was similar. Fighter Command operations were 'on'.

The day's main effort was Circus 68, a raid on the power station at Gosnay, by five 226 Squadron Blenheims. As ever, an impressive array of Spitfires supported this effort, the North Weald Wing providing the Escort Wing, Hornchurch the Escort Cover, while Target Support, clearing the way ahead to the target and covering the Beehive's withdrawal, involved two wings: Kenley and Tangmere – some forty-eight fighters in total.

For this now routine offensive operation, Dogsbody Section of 616 Squadron comprised Wing Commander Bader, with Sergeant Jeff West No 2, Flight Lieutenant Hugh Dundas No 3, and leader of the second pair in the 'finger four', and No 4, Pilot Officer Johnnie Johnson. Also leading sections of four within the squadron formation would be

An oft-repeated scene at Westhampnett in summer 1941: 'sanitisation' prior to a sweep, Squadron Leader Burton and Wing Commander Bader removing anything of use to the enemy intelligence-wise: even bus and cinema tickets could provide the enemy useful information.

Above: Dogsbody: Wing Commander Bader with the Spitfire Mk VA he flew on his final operational wartime sortie, W3185. Having only had this aircraft several days, the nose-art adorning his well-known Mk IIA had yet to be applied – and never would be. On 9 August 1941, the Wing Leader's Air Speed Indicator failed almost immediately, but instead of turning back he handed the lead over to Dogsbody 3, Flight Lieutenant Dundas, until reaching the French coast.

Left: Dogsbody 2: Sergeant Jeff West.

'BREAK! FOR CHRIST'S SAKE BREAK!'

Right: Dogsbody 3: Flight Lieutenant Hugh 'Cocky' Dundas DFC.

Below: Dogsbody 4: Pilot Officer Johnnie Johnson.

Squadron Leader Billy Burton (Yellow Section) and Flight Lieutenant Buck Casson (Blue Section).

Westhampnett's Spitfire squadrons, 610 and 616, the latter, as ever, leading, took off at 1040 hrs. High above Chichester, Squadron Leader Holden slid 610 Squadron into its usual position, above and slightly to port of 616. As the two squadrons left Chichester, bound for Beachy Head, there was no sign of Squadron Leader Elmer Gaunce's Merston-based 41 Squadron.

The Beachy Head Forward Relay Station recorded the Tangmere Wing's R/T messages that day. As the wing neared 'Diamond' (Beachy Head), 41 Squadron had still not appeared. Group Captain Woodhall, at Tangmere, was the first to speak, making a test call:

'Dogsbody?'
'OK, OK.'

Bader then made R/T test calls to the commanders of both 610 and 41, using their first names as was his usual practice:

DB: 'Ken?' [Ken Holden]
KH: 'Loud and clear.'
DB: 'Elmer?'

There was no response from Squadron Leader Gaunce, provoking an acerbic remark from the wing leader to 'Woody'. Unable to wait, 616 and 610 Squadrons set course for France and Gosnay, in battle formation. Still climbing, maintaining radio silence, Wing Commander Bader waggled his wings insistently, indicating that 'Dogsbody 3', Flight Lieutenant Dundas, should take the lead. Dundas slid across, tucking his wing tip just two or three feet from Bader's. From this close proximity, Dundas saw the wing leader mouth three words: 'Air Speed Indicator', meaning that this crucial instrument on Spitfire Mk VA W3185 was unserviceable. The wing had to climb at the right speed to ensure pre-planned timings were met, but if the formation leader was unable to measure his air speed, this was impossible. Without doubt, Wing Commander Bader should have handed over to either Dundas or Burton, and gone home, as per standing orders. This, however, was not even a consideration, Bader instead handing the lead over to Dundas until the target area was reached. Fortunately, Dundas had written on the back of his hand the time at which the wing was due over

'BREAK! FOR CHRIST'S SAKE BREAK!'

the French coast, in addition to the speed to be maintained. The 21-year-old flight commander then 'settled down to concentrate on the job', climbing the formation to 28,000ft.

Then, more radio messages:

> DB: 'Ken and Elmer, start gaining height.'
> KH: 'Elmer's not with us.'

> Unidentified, garbled voice on the R/T, believed to be Squadron Leader Gaunce.

> DB: 'Elmer from Dogsbody. I cannot understand what you say, but we are on our way. You had better decide for yourself whether to come or go back.'

Following the last radio transmissions, at least the wing was now aware that more Spitfires were hopefully bringing up the rear, even if some distance away. Dundas led the wing over the French coast right on cue (although there is conflicting evidence regarding whether the coast was crossed south of Le Touquet, or Boulogne, slightly further north). This crucial timing observed, Bader accelerated ahead and informed 'Dogsbody 3' over the RT that he was resuming the lead. The Spitfires' arrival over the coastal flak belt was greeted by dangerous little puff-balls of black smoke which made the formation twist and turn. 'Beetle' (Group Captain Woodhall, Tangmere Control) then informed the wing leader that the Beehive itself was 'on time and engaged'. As the Tangmere Spitfires forged inland, therefore, some distance behind them the bombers and various cover wings were now also bound for France.

Slightly below the condensation trail level, a 610 Squadron pilot reported seeing contrails 'above and to our left'. Squadron Leader Holden consequently led the squadron higher still while 'Beetle' (B) reported:

> B: 'Dogsbody from Beetle. There are twenty plus five miles to the east of you.'
> DB: 'OK, but your transmitter is quite impossible. Please use the other.'
> B: 'Dogsbody is this better?'
> DB: 'Perfect. Ken, start getting more height.'
> KH: 'OK, Dogsbody, but will you throttle back? I cannot keep up.'

DB: 'Sorry Ken, my airspeed indicator is u/s. Throttling back, and I will do one slow left-hand turn so you can catch up.'

KH: 'Dogsbody from Ken, I'm making "smoke" [contrails] at this height.'

DB: 'OK, Ken, I'm going down very slightly.'

'Beetle' then advised 'Dogsbody' of more bandits in the vicinity. 616 Squadron's Flying Officer Roy Marples (RM) saw the enemy first:

RM: 'Three bandits coming down astern of us. I'm keeping an eye on them, now there are six.'

DB: 'OK.'

B: 'Douglas, another twelve plus ahead and slightly higher.'

RM: 'Eleven of them now.'

DB: 'OK, Roy, let me know exactly where they are.'

RM: 'About one mile astern and slightly higher.'

B: 'Douglas, there is another forty plus fifteen miles to the north-east of you.'

DB: 'OK Beetle. Are our friends where they ought to be, I haven't much idea where I am.'

B: 'Yes, you are exactly right. And so are your friends.'

RM: 'Dogsbody from Roy. Keep turning left and you'll see 109s at nine o'clock.'

DB: 'Ken, can you see them?'

KH: 'Douglas, 109s below. Climbing up.'

Things went further awry for the Tangmere Wing when Squadron Leader Lionel 'Elmer' Gaunce's 41 Squadron, which had only recently replaced 145 Squadron at Merston, failed to make the rendezvous with Westhampnett's 610 and 616 Squadrons.

'BREAK! FOR CHRIST'S SAKE BREAK!'

By this time, 616 and 610 Squadron had progressed into a very dangerous French sky indeed, Beetle having already reported some seventy-two bandits, representing odds outnumbering the Spitfires by nearly 3:1. As the Beehive left England, Jafü 2 scrambled Stab/JG 26 and all three Schlageter Gruppen, but kept JG 2 on the ground, in reserve. Clearly this was not to be an uneventful sortie. Tension mounting, the Spitfire pilots switched on their gunsight reflectors and gun buttons to 'Fire'. Anxiously they searched the sky, an ever-watchful eye kept on the 109s positioned 1,000ft above the wing, waiting to pounce. Bader himself dipped each wing in turn, searching the sky below for the 109s Squadron Leader Holden reported.

> DB: 'I can't see them. Will you tell me where to look?'
> KH: 'Underneath Bill's section now. Shall I come down?'
> DB: 'No, I have them. Get into formation. Going down. Ken, are you with us?'
> KH: 'Just above you.'

As Dogsbody Section dived on the enemy, Flight Lieutenant Casson followed with three other aircraft of 'B' Flight. Dogsbody 3, Flight Lieutenant Dundas, had 'smelt a rat' in respect of the Schwärm of I/JG 26 109s that Dogsbody Section was now rapidly diving towards. By this time, the whole of Dogsbody Section was firing, although Dundas, still uneasy and suspecting a trap, had a compelling urge to look behind. Suddenly Pilot Officer 'Nip' Hepple shouted over the R/T:

> 'Blue 2 here. Some buggers coming down behind, astern. Break left!'

It was, as Dundas had suspected, a trap. Wing Commander Bader had been deceived into diving upon the outnumbered 109s below, which were bait – high above lurked more German fighters, hoping that their enemy would fall for the oldest trick in the book. Hoping for an easy victory, Bader had taken the bait. Now, as the Spitfire pilots were in turn ambushed, they hauled their aircraft around in steep turns. The sky behind Dogsbody Section was full of Me 109s, all firing – without Hepple's warning the Spitfires would have been nailed. As the high 109s crashed into 616 Squadron, Squadron Leader Holden decided that it was time for his section to join the fray and reduce the odds. Informing Flight Lieutenant Denis Crowley-Milling of this decision, Holden led his Spitfires down to assist. Flight Lieutenant Casson, following Bader's Section, was well throttled back to keep his flight together.

Squadron Leader Ken Holden, CO of 610 Squadron, who first saw the 109s.

Also attacking from the rear, Casson managed a squirt at a Rotte of 109s. Flying Officer Marples, Number 3 in Casson's Section, then shouted a warning of even more 109s diving upon the wing – while Squadron Leader Billy Burton urged the Spitfires to 'keep turning', thus preventing the 109s (which could not out-turn a Spitfire) getting in a shot. Suddenly the organised chaos became a maelstrom of twisting, turning fighters:

'BREAK! FOR CHRIST'S SAKE *BREAK*!'

The Spitfires immediately 'broke' – hard.

Pilot Officer Johnnie Johnson remembered:

> There was this scream of 'Break!' – and we all broke, we didn't wait to hear it twice! Round. Then a swirling mass of 109s and Spitfires. When I broke I could see Bader, still firing. Dundas was firing at the extreme right 109. There was some cloud nearby and I disappeared into it as quick as possible! I couldn't say how many aircraft were involved, suffice to say a lot. It seemed to me that the greatest danger was a collision, rather

'BREAK! FOR CHRIST'S SAKE BREAK!'

than being shot down, that's how close we all were. We had got the 109s we were bouncing and then Holden came down with his section, so there were a lot of aeroplanes. We were fighting 109Fs, although there may have been some Es among them. There was an absolute mass of aeroplanes just fifty yards apart, it was awful. I thought to myself 'You're going to collide with somebody!' I didn't think about shooting at anything after we were bounced ourselves, all you could think about was surviving, getting out of that mass of aircraft. In such a tight turn, of course, you almost black out, you cannot really see where you are going. It was a mess. I had never been so frightened in my life, *never*!

Officially, Johnnie reported that the combat had occurred at 1130 hrs in the Béthune area, between 18,000 and 20,000ft. 'Frightened' though he was, Dogsbody 4 claimed a 109 destroyed, and shared a second with Sergeant West, Dogsbody 2:

When over the target area at 24,000ft, 610 Leader, Squadron Leader Holden DFC, called the Wing Commander's attention to several 109s flying westwards about 4,000–5,000ft below us, and the Wing Commander sighted these and led his Section into attack. I was flying on the extreme right hand and as there wasn't a 109 for me on that side, I skidded over to the left and attacked a 109F from below and astern – slight deflection. I fired two or three 1 second bursts and observed a large piece fall away from the starboard wing. I then stall-turned to the right, to regain flying speed and Sergeant West came round in a right-hand turn and saw this piece fall off. He attacked this E/A, which he saw go into a vicious flat spin – continuing for several thousand feet before being lost to sight. This aircraft is claimed as destroyed and shared with Sergeant West.

On recovering flying speed I was attacked by three 109s from above and had difficulty in shaking them off – eventually doing so at 9,000ft. I flew along alone, keeping a sharp look-out and eventually saw a 109F about 500ft below, flying straight and level. I attacked this aircraft from astern and below (range 100 yards) and observed black smoke pouring out from the engine. The nose dropped and E/A went into a steep dive, and although my engine cut, I followed him by pushing the stick really hard forward. I managed to get in another burst when almost vertical. E/A continued to dive steeply, and as there was little height for recovery I pulled out at about 4,000ft and turned left. Although I did not see the actual impact, I saw the wreckage and smoke from the crashed E/A in a field near a canal and this is claimed as destroyed. As I was then completely lost I called up 'Swallow' and obtained an excellent homing bearing. I was flying *Progress I*, presented by Blackpool Corporation Transport.

Sergeant West does not appear to have made out a personal combat report; in his diary he wrote:

Fine clear morning. Gradually clouded over. Went on sweep as DB's No 2. Went into attack 15 enemy aircraft 5,000ft below. Got 1 – nearly collided with him on top of stall. He spun down and pieces fell off – seen by Yellow Section. I also spun, then finished off another I shared with Johnnie.

Over the RT, Pilot Officer Johnson could still hear 616 and 610 Squadrons' running battle:

'Get into formation or they'll shoot the bloody lot of you!'

'Spitfire going down in flames, ten o'clock.'

'YQ-C [616 Squadron Spitfire]. Form up on me, I'm at three o'clock to you.'

'Four buggers above us.' This from Hepple.

'All Elfin aircraft [616 Squadron] withdraw. I say again, all Elfin aircraft withdraw.'

'Use the cloud if you're in trouble,' from Billy Burton.

'Are you going home, Ken?' also from Burton.

'Yes, withdrawing,' from Holden.

'Ken from Crow. Are you still about?'

'I'm right behind you, Crow.'

'BREAK! FOR CHRIST'S SAKE BREAK!'

Pilot Officer 'Nip' Hepple, No 3 in Squadron Leader Burton's section.

Pilot Officer 'Nip' Hepple was No 3 in Squadron Leader Burton's Yellow Section, reporting a combat taking place between 300 yards 'to point blank range':

> Shortly after crossing the French coast south of Boulogne, the squadron went into a left-hand orbit. After a few minutes about twenty Me 109Fs were seen to the east of us and several thousand feet below, climbing up over white cloud. Wing Commander Bader led the squadron into attack in a steep dive. When I got to their level the E/A had split up.
>
> I climbed up to the right and saw a 109F come up in front of me. He appeared to be on the top of a stall turn and so I gave him a long burst closing to point blank range. I saw on the side of his aircraft as he turned to the left a large '6' just behind the cross on the fuselage. He then went into a very slow gliding turn to the left and I had a vivid view of his hood flying off and the pilot jumping out of his machine. I watched him falling and turning over and over until he had dropped down to some low white cloud, his parachute had still not opened so I assume he was killed. His aircraft was claimed as destroyed.

> The camouflage was a dirty grey and black. In addition to the usual cross there was a six behind it, the tail was painted orange and the spinner black and white. I was flying an aircraft with 'Watford' and its coat of arms painted on it.

Hepple was credited with a 109 destroyed.

Flying Officer Roy Marples was Blue 3 in Flight Lieutenant Casson's Section, and claimed a 109 probably destroyed:

> When enemy aircraft were sighted beneath us, we were in an excellent tactical advantage as we were up-sun, above them and astern. Blue Section dived to attack, and I attacked the outside aircraft which had broken away, presumably with the intention of coming in behind us. I gave him about a 3 second burst from port quarter, closing in from 200 to 150 yards. He took no evasive action after this burst and I managed to go in behind him with ease, having throttled right back. By this time the E/A was in a power glide turning very gently to starboard. I closed in to astern, 80 yards, and gave him all I had in short bursts and keeping him well in my sights. I am not definitely certain whether I saw anything fly off the E/A but I must have hit him because he took no evasive action, carrying on with his gentle glide.
>
> I am claiming this aircraft as probably destroyed, since I consider that the pilot was dead, and also because he took no evasive action which, under the circumstances, a pilot in his senses would do. I was flying a Spitfire VB with *Cynon Valley* marked on it.

More radio messages:

> 'Are we all here?'
>
> 'Two short.'
>
> 'Dogsbody from Beetle. Do you require any assistance?'
>
> 'Beetle from Elfin Leader. We are OK and withdrawing.'
>
> 'Thank you, Billy. Douglas, do you require any assistance? Steer three-four-zero to the coast.'

'BREAK! FOR CHRIST'S SAKE BREAK!'

Flying Officer Roy Marples, No 3 in Flight Lieutenant Buck Casson's section.

The silence from 'Dogsbody' was ominous. Flight Lieutenant Casson, Blue 1, remembered:

> I watched Wing Commander Bader and 'A' Flight attack and break to port as I was coming in. I was well throttled back in the dive, as the other three had started to fall behind and I wanted to keep the flight together. I attacked from the rear, and after having a squirt at two 109s flying together, left them for a single one which was flying inland alone. I finished nearly all of my cannon ammunition up on this boy, who finally baled out at 6,000ft, having lost most of his tail unit. The other three 'B' flight machines were in my rear and probably one of the lads saw this.
>
> I climbed to 13,000ft and fell in with Billy Burton and three other aircraft, all from 'A' Flight. We chased around in a circle for some time, gaining height all the while, and more

109s were directly above us. Eventually we formed up in line abreast and set off after the wing.

Billy's section flew in pairs abreast, so I flew abreast but at about 200 yards to starboard. We were repeatedly attacked by two Me 109s which had followed us and were flying above and behind. Each time they started diving I called out and we all turned and re-formed, the 109s giving up their attack and climbing each time.

About fifteen miles from the coastline I saw another Spitfire well below us and about half-a-mile to starboard. This machine was alone and travelling very slowly. I called up Billy on the R/T and suggested that we cross over to surround him and help the pilot back as he looked like a sitting duck. I broke off to starboard and made for the solitary Spitfire, but then, on looking back for Billy and the others, was amazed to see them diving away hard to the south-west for a low layer of cloud into which they soon disappeared. I realised then that my message had either been misunderstood or not received. Like a greenhorn, I had been so intent upon watching Billy's extraordinary disappearance to the left, and the lone Spitfire to my right, I lost sight of the Me 109s that had been worrying us. I remember looking for them but upon not discovering their position assumed that they had chased Billy instead. I was soon proved wrong, however, when I received three hits in both fuselage and wing. This occurred just as I broke for some cloud at 5,000ft, which I reached but found too thin for cover, and was pursued by the 109s.

I then picked out two more 109s flying above me and so decided to drop to zero feet, fly north and cross the Channel at a narrow point as I was unsure of the damage sustained and the engine was not running smoothly. I pressed the teat and tried to run for it, but the two Me 109s behind had more speed and were rapidly within range, while the other two flew 1,500ft above and dived from port to starboard and back, delivering quick bursts. Needless to say I was not flying straight and level all this time!

In the event I received a good one from behind, which passed between the stick and my right leg. taking off some of the rudder on its way. It passed into the petrol tank but whether the round continued into the engine I do not know. Petrol began leaking

'BREAK! FOR CHRIST'S SAKE BREAK!'

into the cockpit, oil pressure was dropping low, and with the radiator wide open I could smell the glycol overheating.

As the next attack came, I pulled straight up from the deck in a loop and on my way down, as I was changing direction towards the sea, my engine became extremely rough and seized up as white glycol fumes poured forth. There was no option but to crash-land the aircraft. I tried to send 'Dogsbody' a hurried message, then blew up the wireless and made a belly landing in a field some ten miles south of Calais. The 'Goons', having seen the glycol, were decent enough not to shoot me up as I was landing, but circled about for a time and gave my position away to a German cavalry unit in a wood in a corner of the field. One of the pilots waved to me as he flew overhead, and I waved back just before setting fire to the aircraft. Due to the petrol in the cockpit, and because I was carrying a portfire issued for this purpose, igniting the aircraft was easy. No sooner had I done this than a party of shrieking Goons armed with rifles came chasing over and that was the end of me!

What eventually happened to the lone Spitfire which I went to help out I have no idea. As the 109s followed me, I assume that he got away okay, I certainly hope so.

I will never forget that day, one which I have gone over so often in my daydreams.

Flight Lieutenant Casson had been shot down by Hauptmann Gerhard Schöpfel, Gruppenkommandeur of III/JG 26:

My IIIrd Gruppe attacked a British bomber formation, after which my formation was split up. With the British on their homeward flight, I headed alone for my airfield at Ligescourt, near Crecy. Suddenly I saw a flight of Spitfires flying westwards. I attacked them from above and after a short burst of fire the rear machine nosed over sharply and dived away. While the other aircraft flew on apparently unaware, I pursued the fleeing Spitfire as I could see no sign of damage. The British pilot hugged the ground, dodging trees and houses. I was constantly in his propwash and so could not aim properly. Because of the warm air near the ground my radiator flaps opened and so my speed decreased, it thus took me a long time to get into a good

Left: Flight Lieutenant L.H. 'Buck' Casson DFC, Blue 1.

Below: Hauptmann Gerhard Schöpfel, Gruppenkommandeur of III/JG 26, who shot down Casson.

'BREAK! FOR CHRIST'S SAKE BREAK!'

firing position. Finally I was positioned immediately behind the Spitfire and it filled my gunsight. I pressed the firing button for both cannon and machine-guns, but – click! I had obviously exhausted my ammunition in the earlier air battles. Of course the British pilot had no way of knowing this and I still wanted to strike terror in him for so long as he remained over French soil. I thus remained right behind him, at high speed. Suddenly I was astonished to see a white plume of smoke emit from the Spitfire! The smoke grew denser and the propeller stopped. The pilot made a forced landing in a field east of Marquise. I circled the aircraft and made a note of the markings for my victory report, watched the pilot climb out and waved to him. Just before being captured by German soldiers, he ignited a built-in explosive charge which destroyed the centre-section of his aircraft.

I returned to my field and sent my engineering officer to the site to determine the reason for the forced landing. He found, to my amazement, that the Spitfire had taken a single machine-gun round in an engine cylinder during my first attack. Had I not pressed on after running out of ammunition and therefore forcing the pilot to fly at top speed, he would probably have reached England despite the damage. Just a few weeks before, in fact, I myself had made it back across the Channel after two of my engine's connecting rods had been smashed over Dover. On this occasion over France, however, the British pilot, a flight lieutenant, now had to head for prison camp while I recorded my thirty-third victory.

While Casson was to spend the rest of the war as a prisoner, Schöpfel running out of ammunition had clearly saved his life. With petrol splashing into the cockpit, another hit would have turned the Spitfire into a blowtorch.

Returning to the French coast, Pilot Officer Johnson came 'out of France on the deck, low and fast', his Spitfire roaring over waving civilians, just feet above their fields. At the coast, German soldiers ran to their guns but in a second the fleeting Spitfire was gone. Climbing over the Channel, Dogsbody 4 realised that something might have happened to Wing Commander Bader:

> As I was crossing the Channel, Group Captain Woodhall, who obviously knew that there had been a fight from the radar and

RT, repeated 'Douglas, are you receiving?' This came over the air every five minutes or so. I therefore called up and said 'It's Johnnie here, Sir, we've had a stiff fight and I last saw the Wing Commander on the tail of a 109.' He said, 'Thank you, I'll meet you at dispersal.'

The silence from Dogsbody clearly meant one of two things: either that his radio was unserviceable, or he had somehow been brought down.

Flight Lieutenant Denis Crowley-Milling, 610 Squadron:

The greatest impression I have of that day is the silence on the RT. Douglas *always* maintained a running commentary. Had the worst happened? The colourful language and running commentary had suddenly ceased, leaving us all wondering what had happened. Was he alive or dead? Had his radio failed? I know we were above thick cloud on the way home and asked the Tangmere Controller to provide a homing bearing for us to steer. This was way out in accuracy, however, and unbeknown to us we were flying up the North Sea, just scraping in to Martlesham Heath with hardly any fuel remaining – it was indeed a day to remember!

The crash site of Casson's Spitfire Mk VB, east of Marquise. The centre section was destroyed when the pilot deliberately ignited the port-fire device.

'BREAK! FOR CHRIST'S SAKE BREAK!'

Group Captain Woodhall: anxiously awaited Pilot Officer Johnson's return for news of 'DB'.

So confused had been the fighting, so numerous the aircraft in this incredible maelstrom over St Omer, that only Wing Commander Bader himself had the answers to the questions regarding his present state and whereabouts. The Tangmere wing leader later admitted that he had done

> everything wrong. I signalled 'attacking' and dived down too fast and too steeply. I was tense, and my judgement had gone for some reason which I did not recognise at the time. One never did. I behaved as I had done on my first glimpse of an enemy over the sea off Dunkirk in May 1940. I closed so fast on the 109 that I had no time to fire, and barely time to avoid cutting him in half with my Spitfire. I continued diving and levelled out at 24,000ft. I pulled myself together and had a look around. Nothing in sight, I was alone in the sky. It was always the same. One moment the sky was full of aeroplanes, the next it was empty. I was debating whether to carry on towards the target and hope to find the others or whether to follow my own advice to my pilots when alone, which was to get down to ground level and fly home, when

> I noticed a couple of miles in front and at the same height three pairs of 109s. There was no doubt in my mind what to do. They had come up from St Omer or Merville and were target bound.

Wing Commander Bader had indeed done 'everything wrong'. He should, in fact, have turned about shortly after take-off and immediately his ASI went unserviceable. In his single-minded pursuit of action, Dogsbody had initially wasted precious seconds by not despatching Holden's Section to intercept the enemy that 610 Squadron's CO had sighted – but which he himself could not immediately see. Then, alone over France, Wing Commander Bader committed the cardinal sign of not diving and hedge-hopping home – but once more allowed the possibility of increasing his personal score, and thirst for action, to override his better judgement.

Dogsbody, alone over France, now prepared to attack again:

> I dropped down just below them and closed up. If they saw me and turned I would dive vertically for a few thousand feet and then go home.... They did not see me. I destroyed the back one of the middle pair with a short burst from close range. As he dived away on fire I closed up on his companion in front, and was just opening fire when I saw the two 109s on my left turning towards me – I decided to go home. A few bits were falling off my 109, but I'd nearly been caught that way before when I'd thought I just had time to finish an enemy off and got a cockpit full of bullets instead.
>
> I then made my final mistake. The rule is as old as air fighting: always turn towards your enemy, never turn your back on him. If you do, you lose sight of him and present him with you as a target. The two enemy on my right were still flying straight which was why I turned right towards them, intending to pass over the top of or even behind them, and then dive away for home in the opposite direction. At this stage there was no problem. But the bad judgement that had dogged me all day finally fixed me. I banked over right-handed and collided with the second 109 ... I felt rather than heard a noise behind the cockpit, saw the tail of a 109 out of the corner of my eye passing behind me and then got the impression that someone was grasping the tail of my Spitfire. Down went the nose vertically; I pulled the stick back and there was nothing there

'BREAK! FOR CHRIST'S SAKE BREAK!'

> ... I looked behind and there appeared to be nothing behind the cockpit. In other words, the complete back end, elevator, and fin had disappeared. Time to leave.

At 24,000ft, Douglas was unable to consider escape due to the lack of oxygen outside the cockpit at that height. His dilemma, however, was that the doomed fighter was already travelling in excess of 400 mph, so would soon be subjected to forces so great that baling out would become impossible. Yanking the canopy release mechanism, the hood was sucked away, the cockpit immediately being battered by the airflow. Without legs though, would he be able to thrust his body upwards to get out? As he struggled to get his head above the windscreen, he was nearly plucked out of the cockpit, but halfway he became stuck – the rigid foot of his artificial right leg jamming in the cockpit, the grip vice-like. Ever downwards the fighter plunged, the pilot helpless and continuously battered by the rushing wind, half in and half out of his crashing aeroplane. Desperately gripping his parachute's 'D' ring, Douglas struggled furiously to get out. Eventually, at about 6,000ft, the offending artificial leg's restraining strap broke. Free at last, the pilot was sucked out into mid-air; as the Spitfire continued its dive, he experienced a moment of apparently floating upwards. That terrible buffeting having thankfully ceased, in the silence he was able to think – hand still gripping the 'D' ring, he pulled; there was a slight delay before the parachute deployed and then he was really was floating, gently to earth beneath the life-saving silk umbrella.

At 4,000ft, Wing Commander Bader floated through a layer of cloud, emerging to see the ground still far below. Alarmed by the roar of an aero-engine, he saw a Me 109 fly directly towards him, but the bullets he half expected never came, as the enemy fighter flashed by just fifty yards away. Such a parachute descent, made due to enemy action or some other mishap while flying actively, was often the first a pilot would actually make, there being no formal parachute training. Consequently, Douglas had never before had to consider the practicalities of landing with artificial legs, or indeed on one such leg, as he drifted earthwards. Having had some minutes to ponder this matter, suddenly French soil rushed up to meet him and he hit the ground hard, in an orchard near Blaringhem, to the south-east of St Omer. Many years later, Artur Dubreu, then a 13-year-old French schoolboy, claimed to have been watching the action from his village at Steenbecque:

> I remember the incident vividly. I saw a lot of planes, it was mid-morning on a sunny day. There was a big dogfight and

many contrails in the sky. I saw an aircraft coming down very fast and then a parachute opened. The aircraft crashed in a field and a cloud of black smoke and debris rose over the site. Due to the wind the parachute drifted slightly; it was the first parachute I had ever seen, in fact, so I remember it very well. I wanted to see the pilot, so I ran after the rapidly descending canopy. The parachute seemed to land very fast, but the pilot hit some trees in an orchard which took the shock. The pilot was just sitting there, silk billowing around him. I was horrified to see that he only had one leg, which was twisted at an unnatural angle. There was no blood and, although he seemed to be stunned from the landing, he did not appear otherwise concerned about his legs. I could not understand it at all. I was the first on the scene but before I could help a German officer ran into the field, took charge and told me to clear off, which I did as I was very frightened of the soldiers. The Germans then carried the pilot to their waiting car.

For Wing Commander Douglas Bader, the air war was over: his personal period of operational service had lasted just eighteen months. As Douglas Bader himself said, 9 August 1941 was 'A lousy day indeed' – although upon repatriation in 1945, he wrote in his log book, 'Good fight near Béthune. Shot down 1 Me 109 and collided with another. PoW. 2 Me 109s destroyed. Total E/A destroyed, 30.'

Pilot Officer Johnson recalled the scene back at Westhampnett: 'Group Captain Woodhall was waiting for me on the airfield, and when Dundas, West, Hepple and the others came back the consensus of opinion was that the wing commander had either been shot down or involved in a collision.'

In his flying log book, Pilot Officer Johnson wrote that on this

Flight Lieutenant Denis Crowley-Milling: 'The greatest impression I have of that day is the silence on the RT. Douglas *always* maintained a running commentary… Was he alive or dead?'

'BREAK! FOR CHRIST'S SAKE BREAK!'

In 1996, Artur Dubreu describes to the author how and where, as a thirteen-year-old schoolboy, he had watched Wing Commander Bader's parachute descent.

penetration over France there had been 'more opposition than ever before'. Squadron Leader Burton's log book recorded 'Had a bad time with 109s on way out and had to get into cloud.' As the clock ticked on, it became clear from fuel considerations that the two Spitfires reported missing during the radio chatter over France were unlikely to return to Westhampnett. Reasoning that if flying damaged machines the pilots might land at one of the coastal airfields, Tangmere telephoned each in turn, receiving negative responses from all.

Douglas Roberts was a Radio Telephone (Direction Finding) Operator at the Tangmere 'Fixer' station located on West Malling airfield in Kent:

> We were told that Wing Commander Bader was missing and so listened out for several hours. Our system was basic when compared to modern equipment today, but nevertheless very efficient. The aerial system was a double dipole which, when rotated, would indicate either a true bearing or a reciprocal. Despite our diligence, nothing was ever heard from 'Dogsbody'.

Soon, Dundas, Johnson, Hepple and West were flying back over the Channel, searching for any sign of Wing Commander Bader or Flight Lieutenant Casson in the water. At Le Touquet, Dundas led the Section north, parallel to the coast and towards Cap Griz-Nez. Avoiding flak from various enemy vessels, especially near Calais, a steep turn at zero feet returned the Spitfires to Le Touquet. At one point, Hepple broke away to machine-gun a surfacing submarine, but otherwise the only item to report was an empty dinghy sighted by Sergeant West. To Johnnie Johnson, that empty, life-saving, rubber boat was somehow symbolic of their fruitless search. With petrol almost exhausted, the section landed at Hawkinge. No news had yet been received of either missing pilot. Immediately the aircraft were refuelled, the 616 Squadron pilots took off again, intending to head back across the Channel to France. Shortly after take-off, however, Group Captain Woodhall cancelled the sortie, fearing that a second trip was too risky as the enemy might now be waiting. Swinging round to the west, Dundas led the Spitfires back to Westhampnett. For Dundas, the thought of Bader dead was 'utterly shattering'. Buck Casson's loss was also a serious blow to Dundas's morale; they had joined the squadron together at Doncaster. When the fact dawned on him that he was now the only member of the old guard left, Dundas found this a 'terrifying thought'. Regarding Bader, as a loyal lieutenant, Dundas felt some degree of responsibility. He drove back to Shopwyke House 'alone and utterly dejected'.

With no news other than the fact that her husband had apparently vanished, Group Captain Woodhall had the unenviable duty of driving over to the Bay House and informing Thelma that Douglas was missing. John Hunt, a young Intelligence Officer, was already there, having arrived to give some support only to discover that Thelma had yet to receive the bad news, which upon arrival Woody softened by adding that Douglas Bader was indestructible and therefore probably a prisoner. Later, Dundas arrived and with Jill, Thelma's sister, persuaded Mrs Bader to take some sherry – which

Douglas Roberts waited in vain for a radio transmission from 'Dogsbody' on 9 August 1941.

'BREAK! FOR CHRIST'S SAKE BREAK!'

she only brought up again. As Dundas drove back to Shopwyke House he cried. Back at the Mess, he and Johnnie Johnson shared a whole bottle of brandy. Despair had overtaken the inner sanctum.

At Fighter Command HQ, that rambling old house Bentley Priory, Air Marshal Douglas was given the bad news: 'Douglas Bader's missing'. 'Agitated', the Air Marshal immediately liaised with his SASO, Air Vice-Marshal Evill and ascertained what was known: Wing Commander Bader had led two squadrons of his wing on a Circus, and dived to attack some 109s over Béthune. After that encounter, the other Spitfire pilots had emerged without their leader, who had simply disappeared. 'But,' as Air Marshal Douglas wrote, 'no one had seen him go.'

So what, then, had actually happened to Wing Commander Bader?

Chapter Six

'Nothing is certain, nor ever will be'… or is it?

Just as the Circus 68 Target Support mission had been routine for the Tangmere Wing, so too was the subsequent interception by JG 26. Having urgently responded to the Alarmstart, it was 109s from the Schlageter Geschwader that the Tangmere Wing had fought that day high above Béthune.

After the action, which developed into a running battle between Béthune and the French coast, the German pilots claimed a total of fourteen Spitfires destroyed. Fighter Command actually lost eleven aircraft, so the enemy claims were, as usual, fairly accurate; six Spitfire pilots were killed, three were captured, one evaded and another crash-landed back in England. This narrative, however, has consistently evidenced how Fighter Command's claims were almost always substantially exaggerated – and this day's fighting was no different: twenty-one Me 109s, including one shared, were claimed destroyed, along with ten probables and eight damaged. The reality is harsh; JG 26 only lost one aircraft in action that day: Unteroffizier Albert Schlager of 3/JG 26, whose Me 109F-4 (8350) was shot down over the Aire – Hazebrouck area (which is to say Béthune/St Omer) and killed when his parachute failed to open. Unquestionably, it was Pilot Officer 'Nip' Hepple of 616 Squadron who had shot Schlager down, having recorded a detailed personal combat report upon return to Westhampnett, in which the German's parachute failure is clearly described. While other accounts claim that 8/JG 26's Leutnant Luckhardt was wounded when hit south-east of Guines, this is not so; Luckhardt was wounded two days previously. So, Schlager's was the only 109 destroyed that day, and we know by whom.

Among the successful German pilots was JG 26's Kommodore, Oberstleutnant Adolf Galland, who had recorded victory number seventy-six, a Spitfire north-west of St Pol, at 1132 hrs. Shortly afterwards,

'NOTHING IS CERTAIN, NOR EVER WILL BE'… OR IS IT?

Oberleutnant 'Pips' Priller, Staffelkapitän of 1/JG 26, arrived at Galland's Audembert HQ to tell his Kommodore about the captured legless Wing Commander Bader, urging Galland 'you must come and meet him'. After capture, Bader had been removed to hospital, the Clinique Sterin in St Omer, where the 'Herr Ving Commander' was actually visited several times by two JG 26 pilots; he shared a bottle of champagne with them in the doctor's room and concluded that they were 'types' whom he would have liked in the Tangmere Wing. Brickhill stated that the Germans recovered Bader's missing leg from his Spitfire's crash site, but in fact French eyewitnesses confirm that the artificial limb fluttered down on its own and landed close to Wing Commander Bader's parachute. The villagers handed the article in to the German authorities, after which Galland's engineers made running repairs on the leg to afford the Wing Commander some mobility. A few days later, Galland sent his Horsch staff car to fetch Bader for a visit to the Geschwaderstab Schwärm at their Audembert airfield.

While visiting JG 26, Wing Commander Bader was interested to know what had happened when he was brought down. His impression was of a collision with an Me 109, although he had not actually seen the aeroplane with which he had supposedly collided. Galland was puzzled, however, as none of his aircraft had been involved in such a collision. As previously explained, only one 109 pilot had been killed: Unteroffizier Alfred Schlager, who crashed near Aire, some ten miles south-east of St Omer. The Germans therefore conceded it possible that Bader may have collided with Schlager who had not survived to make any report. More likely, though, so far as Galland was concerned, was that Wing Commander Bader had been shot down by one of two pilots, either Oberfeldwebel Walter Meyer (6/JG 26) or Leutnant Kosse (5/JG 26) who had recorded their eleventh and seventh victories respectively over St Omer that morning. According to Adolf Galland, for Bader it was an 'intolerable idea' that his master in the air was an NCO pilot. Tactfully, therefore, a 'fair-haired, good looking flying officer' was selected from the victorious German pilots and introduced to Bader as his champion. Kosse was the only officer of that rank to make a claim that morning, and so it is likely that it was he who Bader met at Audembert. However, neither German pilots' victory report was conclusive. As Galland later wrote 'it was never confirmed who shot him down'.

Indeed, the thought that the enemy had beaten him in aerial combat was unthinkable to Bader, and he continued insisting that he was the victim of a collision. Upon repatriation, he recorded his impression of events after having fired a three-second burst at a 109 and breaking right:

> I collided with an Me 109 which took my tail off, it appeared as far as the radio mast but was actually probably only the empennage. This was at about 24,000ft and I do not think it did the Me 109 much good. The collision was my fault.

Among the officers present at the reception thrown for Bader by JG 26 was Hauptmann Gerhard Schöpfel:

> My meeting with Wing Commander Bader was memorable and one which I well recall. Our Oberst Joachim-Friedrich Huth had lost a leg in the First World War, and when the report about Bader being shot down reached him he was sure that spare artificial legs existed in England. There followed a number of telephone calls, during which Bader's capture was reported to the Red Cross, and it was decided that an RAF aircraft should be offered free passage to deliver the spare legs to our airfield at an appointed time and date. So far as I know, this was initially confirmed by England.

On 13 August 1941, several RAF RT stations heard a general broadcast in German on 500KCs from Ushant, announcing that Wing Commander Bader was a prisoner and that he had lost his right artificial leg while baling out. It was requested that a new leg was delivered by parachute – safe conduct was granted to the delivery aircraft. Flight Lieutenant Crowley-Milling remembered that:

> the loss of Douglas Bader had left us all stunned. A few of us, including Dundas and Johnson, were with Thelma Bader in their married quarters at Tangmere when the telephone rang. After speaking, Thelma came back to join us and very calmly said 'Douglas is safe and a prisoner'. Even from a purely humanitarian perspective, this was good news, surely, but George Reid, of 616 Squadron's groundcrew, felt differently: 'So far as I am concerned, after Wing Commander Bader was shot down, a happy feeling settled on 616, Westhampnett, Tangmere and, I daresay, Chichester. Good days arrived, the sun came out and life was grand.'

'NOTHING IS CERTAIN, NOR EVER WILL BE'... OR IS IT?

The British press reported 'Legless Air Ace is Safe – Say Germans': 'Wing Commander Bader jumped from his burning machine after being shot down by a German fighter over the Channel last Saturday, the news agency states.' Already, the facts were becoming distorted.

When the signal was received from Germany offering free passage for an RAF aircraft to deliver Wing Commander Bader's spare legs, Group Captain Woodhall responded so enthusiastically that he even offered to fly a Lysander to Audembert himself. However, the Air Ministry rejected the proposal out of hand.

Gerhard Schöpfel recalled events across the Channel:

Thelma Bader: 'Douglas is safe and a prisoner'.

> I was at the Geschwader-gefechtsstand in Audembert, having flown in from my base at Ligescourt, home of my III/JG 26. Soon after our meeting, Bader wanted to inspect one of our Me 109s. Galland invited him to climb into a Geschwader-maschine and Bader commented that he would like to fly it, but of course this could not be allowed.

Many photographs were taken by the Germans of this visit, which numerous non-flying JG 26 personnel would later recall as the most memorable incident of their entire war. Among the snapshots taken is a photograph of Wing Commander Bader sitting in the cockpit of a 109, a German officer stood on the wing (in *Reach for the Sky*, and consequently many other books, the object in this officer's left hand is described as a 'pistol' – other photographs from the same series show that in fact Oberst Joachim Huth is holding his leather gloves).

Schöpfel continues:

> When told of our arrangement via the Red Cross regarding his spare legs, he was not surprised when no plane arrived as he felt

Left: Oberst Joachim-Friedrich Huth, an experte in both world wars and who himself had lost a leg during the First World War.

Below: Oberst Huth, holding his leather gloves and not a pistol, as is widely believed, showing Wing Commander Bader the cockpit of a 109.

'NOTHING IS CERTAIN, NOR EVER WILL BE'... OR IS IT?

Wing Commander Bader being received at Audembert by Oberstleutnant Galland and his officers, including Hauptmann Schöpfel (in forage cap).

Wing Commander Bader being shown around the airfield at Audembert by Oberstleutnant Galland and his officers.

that high authority in England would take time to sanction such things. He hoped, however, that his own wing would find a way. One or two days later, our radar announced a beehive approaching. The Blenheims flew over St Omer where they dropped a few bombs on our I Gruppe. Also dropped, however, was a crate containing Bader's legs which was attached to a parachute.

On 19 August 1941, a new leg, toilet requirements and a letter from Air Vice-Marshal Leigh-Mallory was dropped under a parachute by an 18 Squadron Blenheim on a Circus to the enemy aerodrome at St Omer-Longuenesse. Naturally, the Tangmere Wing provided Close Escort. The Germans fired at the descending object but fortunately missed. The RAF then broadcast on 500 KCs, confirming to the enemy that the leg had been dropped, and the location. At 1549 hrs, an acknowledgement was received from Ushant, confirming that the leg had been collected.

Josef Niesmark was a member of JG 26's groundcrew:

> The crate in which Wing Commander Bader's spare legs were dropped was taken as a souvenir by a soldier of No 1 Army Group. Wherever he was posted throughout the war, the crate went with him, eventually arriving in Kloster Handrupp, Germany. In 1945, the soldier was posted elsewhere and was unable to take the crate, so I took possession of it. It was not possible, however, to keep it with me during the remainder of the war, so I hid it, together with some other souvenirs, in a Handrupp church. Of course, we were retreating, moving from place to place, eventually surrendering at Flensburg. At the end of June 1945, I was released from a British PoW camp but did not at first return to Germany. When I did, much later, I went to Handrupp to collect the crate and contents. However, the church in which I had left it had been taken over by Polish soldiers, so I was too frightened to enter and collect my belongings. So there ended the story of the crate and my unusual association with Douglas Bader.

Wing Commander Bader, mobile once more, would prove an unappeasable prisoner, making innumerable escape attempts and constantly antagonising the Germans, ending up in the notorious Colditz Castle. Gerhard Schöpfel: 'Some time after Wing Commander Bader's capture, I visited the

'NOTHING IS CERTAIN, NOR EVER WILL BE'... OR IS IT?

Above and below: The crate in which Wing Commander Bader's replacement artificial legs were dropped by parachute during a Circus on 19 August 1941.

Interrogation Centre at Dulag Luft, Oberusal. Out of interest I had a look at his interview notes – it did not surprise me to discover that he gave nothing away!'

Exactly how Wing Commander Bader had been brought down over France, however, remained unexplained.

Upon repatriation in 1945, Bader made out a combat report, concluding, as quoted previously, that his impression was a collision. As we have seen, Flight Lieutenant Buck Casson, also of 616 Squadron, was also shot down and captured on 9 August 1941. The two men were friends, so not unnaturally, very soon after the war Group Captain Bader, as he had become, wrote to Buck inquiring what events had befallen him that fateful day. Buck replied, the content of his letter being his recollections quoted in the previous chapter. Clearly the former Tangmere wing leader accepted Buck's account without question, and thought no more of it.

Indeed, as late as 1981, the year before his death, Group Captain Sir Douglas Bader was still interested in confirming what had happened. In March 1981, Sir Douglas Bader apparently opened the Schofield Air Show, Sydney, where, by chance, he was introduced to former Luftwaffe fighter pilot, 'Max Mayer'. The pair exchanged pleasantries, but no more. The following day Bader was astonished to read in the press an article based upon an interview which Mayer had given a journalist after his meeting with Sir Douglas and in which he claimed to have shot down the Tangmere wing leader. So who was 'Max Mayer'? Having contacted Sydney's *The Daily Telegraph Mirror* in 1995, I received a copy of the article in question, written by a C.J. McKenzie. Mayer claimed to have shot Bader down with 'one cannon burst, which ripped away the tail of Bader's Spitfire'. Mayer continued 'I saw him spiralling down, I saw his face. I followed him down because I had to confirm the kill. When I saw his parachute coming up I turned away. I reported where he had crashed.' McKenzie was advised, by one of Bader's entourage not to 'bring that up or you'll get an argument'. Mayer claimed that it was the second time he and Bader had shaken hands, the first having been in the Clinique Sterin in St Omer: 'He was surprised when he found out it was me. He was a Wing Commander. I was a mere Leutnant. He was very warm towards me and we shook hands strongly.'

Already it was possible to identify major inaccuracies in Max Mayer's story. Firstly it would be impossible, of course, to identify a pilot's face in the circumstances discussed. Secondly, Mayer gives the impression that at the time, so far as the Germans were concerned, his claim was accepted. Refer again to Adolf Galland: 'It was never confirmed who shot down Douglas

'NOTHING IS CERTAIN, NOR EVER WILL BE'... OR IS IT?

Oberfeldwebel Walter Meyer, who claimed a Spitfire destroyed over St Omer on 9 August 1941, and who did not survive the war.

Bader'. Furthermore, whereas Mayer claims to have been a Leutnant, the Walter *Meyer* who claimed a Spitfire destroyed that day was an NCO – and was killed in 1943. Max Mayer also claimed to have destroyed thirty-four enemy aircraft, a tally including victories not only on the Kanalfront, but also over Russia and North Africa. Such a score had, he stated, won him the coveted Knight's Cross. Anyone checking the list of fighter pilots who were Ritterkreuztrager would discover no reference to a Martin Maxwell 'Max' Mayer. After the Second World War, Max Mayer claimed to have flown with the French Air Force in Algiers, but there is no record of such a pilot, a non-French national, having flown with the French Air Force.

Following the newspaper article, Group Captain Bader wrote to Mayer:

> Dear Max Mayer,
> You will recall that we met on Saturday, March 28th, at the Schofield Air Show near Sydney. We were both pleased to meet each other because we were ex-fighter pilots (on opposite sides) and we had an agreeable conversation for some minutes.
>
> The next morning, March 29th, I read an article in one of the newspapers quoting an interview with you, during the course of which you said that you had shot me down over France on August 9th, 1941 and had followed me down until you saw me bale out. Having read that, I was hoping to see you that day, so that we could discuss it. None of us could find you on Sunday. We tried on the Monday to contact you, but were unsuccessful. Then I left to go elsewhere in Australia. Dolfo Galland, who commanded JG 26, has become a great friend of mine since the war. He cannot tell me about the incident on August 9th 1941.

My impression was that I turned across a Me 109 and that it collided with the back of my Spitfire, removing the tail. On the other hand, if the pilot of the Me 109 had fired his guns at that moment, he could have blown my tail off. The result would have been the same.

Please write and tell me your account of this incident, if you can remember it. You told the Australian press that you followed my Spitfire down until you saw me bale out. I imagine you knew it was me because you saw, when I baled out, that one leg was missing. I know that you had lived in Australia for 25 years but cannot think why you did not tell me all this when we talked to each other on March 28th. We could have had a tremendous laugh about it and really enjoyed it.

I shall greatly look forward to hearing from you,

Best wishes,
Yours sincerely,
Douglas Bader

The reporter involved, C.J. McKenzie, observed that:

Bader actually met Mayer at Mascot Airport (Sydney Kingsford Smith International), not at the Schofields Air Show. It had taken me some time to tee-up the meeting and Bader knew precisely who he was meeting and why. I introduced Mayer in those terms. He knew also why I was there, why the photographer was there, yet he seems to express surprise at the story of 29 March 1981. He says, after reading the story, 'I was hoping to see you that day so we could discuss it.' What day does he mean? And discuss what? He says further that he tried to find Mayer on the Sunday and Monday. He had only to phone *The Sunday Telegraph* to have been put in contact with Mayer. The meeting between the two was brief, not as Bader says 'an agreeable conversation for some minutes'. Indeed, I was embarrassed by Bader's attitude. It is not always easy in words to give the right tone to something said. Bader's use of the word 'Kraut', instead of 'German', surprised me. The way he said it was, in my view, intended to be insulting or at least denigrating. Max Mayer died some years ago.

'NOTHING IS CERTAIN, NOR EVER WILL BE'... OR IS IT?

There is no doubt, though, that 'Martin Maxwell Mayer' was not the man he claimed to be, nor indeed the man who shot down Douglas Bader.

During exhaustive research into this engagement, I corresponded with another Bader biographer, his brother-in-law, Wing Commander 'Laddie' Lucas, himself a wartime fighter ace:

> When having dinner at Douglas Bader's house in the country, Adolf Galland told me categorically that DB had been shot down over the Pas-de-Calais in 1941. Galland stated that there had not been a collision. I can say in fact that, in my own humble experience, receiving a volley or two of cannon shells from an Me 109 could certainly sound like a collision with a London bus! I put this view to Douglas, who responded: 'In that case, old cock, because it was me, why didn't they have the bugger responsible goose-stepping down the Under-den-Linden?'

That may have been an exaggeration, but Sir Douglas certainly had a point.

On 5 March 1982, Group Captain Sir Douglas Bader was the subject of an episode of the popular weekly biographical show, *This is Your Life*, presented by Eamonn Andrews. The programme included various key personalities from Bader's war, including, naturally, his great friend Air Vice-Marshal Sir Denis Crowley-Milling, who had flown under Sir Douglas's command in both 242 Squadron during the Battle of Britain and later the Tangmere Wing, and featured a reunion of 616 Squadron's famous 'Dogsbody Section', which flew with Bader on that fateful day, 9 August 1941. Joining Sir Douglas on stage were Squadron Leader Jeff West, all the way from Hamilton, New Zealand (No 2), Group Captain Sir Hugh Dundas (No 3) and Air Vice-Marshal Johnnie Johnson (No 4). Squadron Leader Sir Alan Smith, who although not flying on Circus 68 had flown as 'Dogsbody 2' many times, was also on stage for this Tangmere Wing segment of the show. Squadron Leader West described the events as he saw them on Bader's last wartime flight:

> We were over the other side, and Douglas said 'Come on, chaps, there's a gaggle of 109s down here, there's plenty for all, chaps!' One was just coming up and I was about to press the tit when I saw he was going to do it on the same one, so I had to pull across and take another one, and I'm afraid I lost him. I shot this other thing down and span on top of it, and when I recovered from the spin the sky was empty and I lost sight of you.

Jokingly, Group Captain Bader replied 'I think he'd shot me down!', to raucous laughter and enthusiastic applause.

It was an innocent remark, without any sinister or opaque connotations, but therein, as they say, lies a tale.

In addition to highlighting the exaggerated Fighter Command Combat claims during summer 1941, this narrative has also included examples of 'friendly fire' – which were not uncommon. Indeed, wartime fighter ace and distinguished test pilot Squadron Leader Neville Duke commented that:

> Friendly fire was indeed a frequent occurrence. It sometimes came about by accidental intrusion into your line of fire in the scramble to get at the enemy, as well as mistaken aircraft recognition – e.g. the spirited dogfight between American P.40 Warhawks and Spitfires of 601 Squadron over Tunisia. Americans were at fault, but 601 was flying some clipped wing Spits, adding to the confusion!

Group Captain Sir Douglas Bader appearing on 'This is Your Life' with presenter Eamon Andrews and former members of 'Dogsbody Section': from left, Air Vice-Marshal Johnnie Johnson (obscured), Squadron Leaders Jeff West and Sir Alan Smith, and Group Captain Sir Hugh Dundas.

'NOTHING IS CERTAIN, NOR EVER WILL BE'... OR IS IT?

On the programme, Sir Douglas joked that West may have shot him down!

General Galland also appeared on the popular biographical programme, admitting that the Germans did not know who had shot Sir Douglas down.

Above and below: A Me 109F under fire.

'NOTHING IS CERTAIN, NOR EVER WILL BE'... OR IS IT?

Similarly, on 9 August 1941, the Tangmere Wing fought Me 109Fs – still comparatively new, and, again as previously documented, very different looking to the earlier, angular, 109E with its square wingtips. The Franz also lacked the Emil's tail-struts, had a smaller tail, a rounded nose profile and, most importantly, wingtips; arguably, it looked not dissimilar to a Spitfire.

A significant point is that Fighter Command's pilots, given their claims, truly believed that German aircraft were being shot down in droves. When, therefore, Buck Casson wrote to his old wing leader in 1945, describing his own recollections, neither man appreciated the crucial significance of this statement:

> After having a squirt at two 109s flying together, I left them for a single one flying inland alone. I finished nearly all of my cannon ammunition up on this boy, who finally baled out at 6,000ft, having lost most of his tail unit.

Had Group Captain Bader been aware that his was actually the only Spitfire lost in that combat, and Schlager's the only 109, he would surely have interpreted Buck's account differently.

It has already been conclusively proven that Pilot Officer Hepple shot down JG 26's only casualty on the day in question, Unteroffizier Albert Schlager, and that 109, therefore, was not involved in a collision. In 1995,

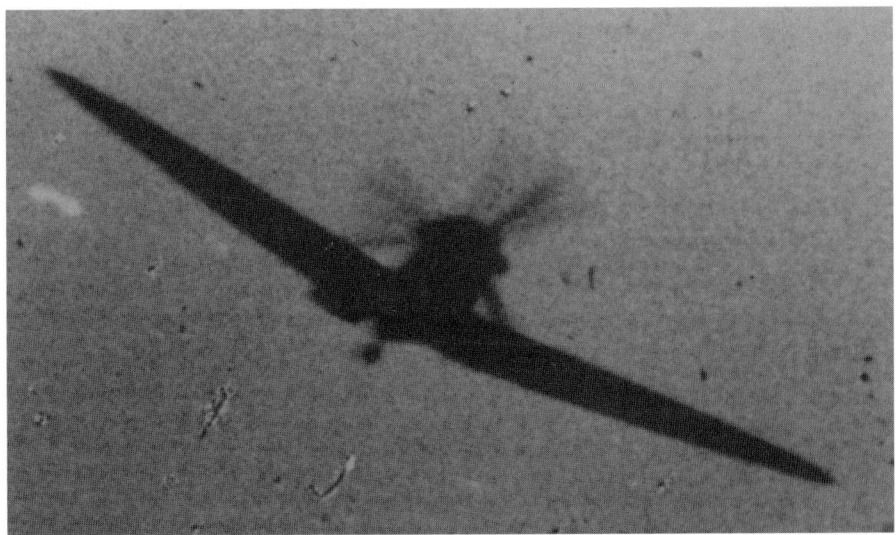

A Spitfire under fire on 27 June 1941 – the similarities with the Me 109F are clear.

BADER'S SPITFIRE WING

I was shown the alleged crash-site of a German fighter near Aire by a French local historian, but I was unprepared to agree the landowner's extortionate demand for excessive payment in return for permission to excavate the site. In June 2004, enthusiasts did excavate this site, discovering identity plates confirming this to be Schlager's aircraft – and among items recovered was the tailwheel assembly, proving that the tail unit was present when the 109 crashed. Buck Casson could not, therefore, have shot Schlager down.

Wing Commander Bader's Spitfire, W3185, was the only other aircraft brought down in this engagement; given his description of losing his tail and being trapped in the cockpit before baling out some thousands of feet below, the implication of Buck Casson's statement is obvious: the Tangmere wing leader was the victim of 'friendly fire'.

Having been captured himself on 9 August 1941, Buck Casson never made out a combat report at the time, and nor did he do so upon repatriation. Had he done so, this would have been in the public domain by the 1970s, and had that been the case, perhaps a researcher may have made the connection back then. As explained, the only written record was Buck's private correspondence with Group Captain Bader shared with me in 1987, and which I first published in 1992 (*The Invisible Thread:*

In 1996, a local French historian showed the author Unteroffizier Schlager's crash-site, and is pictured here with Professor Bernard-Marie Dupont at that time.

'NOTHING IS CERTAIN, NOR EVER WILL BE'... OR IS IT?

A Spitfire's Tale, Ramrod Publications). It was only immediately afterwards, while deconstructing the events of 9 August 1941, for my original book on the Tangmere Wing, *Bader's Tangmere Spitfires* (Haynes PSL), that I made the likely connection with 'friendly fire'. Unfortunately, it was not possible to put the evidence before Sir Douglas himself, who had died suddenly, on 5 September 1982, just six months after the *This is Your Life* programme. In 1995, while writing my book, I was, however, able to put the evidence to two surviving members of Dogsbody Section, receiving these responses:

Air Vice-Marshal Johnnie Johnson:

> I would be very surprised if an experienced and careful fighter pilot such as Buck Casson would make such a mistake, but do agree from his description of events that he has almost certainly seen DB come down. You must put this to Buck.

Group Captain Sir Hugh Dundas:

> I urge you very strongly to keep the theory to yourself and, most particularly, not to put it before Buck Casson, as you say you have it in mind to do.... Nothing is certain, nor ever will be ... I hate to think of the distress this would cause Buck and his family, quite unnecessarily and to no one's benefit. I do hope that you will consider my advice on this matter very seriously indeed.

A letter to Squadron Leader West in New Zealand went unanswered; he died on 4 April 1998.

Squadron Leader Casson, however, had long been well-known to me as a friend, and so it was eventually agreed with Johnnie that the somewhat sensitive matter should, in fact, be put before him.

In a letter dated 6 September 1995, Buck commented: 'I didn't see DB bale out ... I had no idea he had been shot down or had collided with a Me 109.' And on 10 April 1996:

> When I met up with DB at Dulag Luft there was no question whatsoever of us colliding with each other over France, nor was there the slightest mention of it when we saw each other at Warburg. You will appreciate that I well-knew the difference between a Me 109 and a Spitfire in the heat of a dogfight.

Squadron Leader L.H. 'Buck' Casson DFC AFC: 'I shot down a 109 that day'; he died in 2003, coincidentally the same year as his victor, Gerhard Schöpfel, that 'fateful day', 9 August 1941.

'NOTHING IS CERTAIN, NOR EVER WILL BE'... OR IS IT?

> I was nowhere near DB when he was shot down or apparently collided with a 109. As a matter of interest, I saw the pilot of the Me 109 I shot down bale out, but did not see his parachute open.

In a subsequent telephone conversation, Buck was adamant: 'I was an experienced fighter pilot and well knew what a 109 looked like. I shot down a 109 that day.'

The fact is, however, that no enemy aircraft were involved in a collision, and the tail unit of the only 109 to fall was not shot away. These are inescapable facts.

In the event, back in 1995, I agreed with Sir Hugh that if made public the matter would cause Buck and his family 'distress' – which I could never have been party to at any price. Consequently, I did not publish the story in *Bader's Tangmere Spitfires*, but did float the idea therein that unspecified 'friendly fire' could have been responsible for Wing Commander Bader's unresolved demise. Frustrating though that was, it was the right thing to do and something I do not regret.

If Buck did thumb the trigger at the wrong moment all those years ago, and the available evidence, on balance, supports that probably being the case, given the chaotic combat's circumstances it was perfectly understandable and a not uncommon occurrence in aerial combat. Squadron Leader Lionel Harwood 'Buck' Casson DFC AFC, whose detailed story I told in *A Few of the Many* (Ramrod Publications, 1995), a friend with a fine service record in war and peace, died on 8 October 2003 – his reputation (rightly) and my integrity, intact.

The last word, however, goes to Group Captain Sir Hugh Dundas, who commented on *This is Your Life* that:

> We hadn't heard from him [Douglas]. We thought he might be in the 'drink', so we refuelled and I got Johnnie and Jeff and another chap and we flew up and down the French coast for a bit when it sunk in that he really was missing. And I must say that was a very, very devastating moment for all of us. The thought of him lost forever was devastating. I should have known better: he's been organising our lives ever since!

Chapter Seven

Bader's Bus Company: Still Running

Whatever happened that day over France, now so long ago, the fact remained that Tangmere's apparently invincible leader had fallen and was a prisoner of war. Exactly one month later, the award of a Bar to Douglas's DFC was gazetted. The citation read: 'This fearless pilot has recently added a further four enemy aircraft to his previous successes; in addition he has probably destroyed another four and damaged five hostile aircraft. By his fine leadership and high courage Wing Commander Bader has inspired the wing on every occasion.' Now, nearly four years of privation and adversity awaited 'Dogsbody' behind the barbed wire.

Pilot Officer Johnnie Johnson: 'Bader's Bus Company Still Running'. The war went on, and Johnson survived as the RAF's official top-scoring fighter pilot of the Second World War.

BADER'S BUS COMPANY: STILL RUNNING

For Fighter Command, and not least the Tangmere Wing, however, the war went on: beneath the 'Bader's Bus Company' sign on 616 Squadron's pilots' hut, a wag added 'Still Running'.

Wing Commander Bader was succeeded as wing leader by Wing Commander Paddy Woodhouse, previously commander of an American 'Eagle' squadron and beforehand CO of 610 Squadron at Tangmere. On 14 August 1941, Woodhouse led the Tangmere Wing for the first time, Circus 72, a raid on Boulogne's E-Boat base. Flying high cover, the squadrons of 'Greenline Bus' were out of formation and split up. Attacked from below over Calais by 4/JG 26's Me 109Es, two Spitfires were shot down, Sergeant McKee of 616, and 41 Squadron's Flight Lieutenant Archie Winskill.

Air Commodore Sir Archie Winskill: 'I baled out and was fortunate to receive help from the French, which ultimately enabled me to escape over the Pyrenees and return home via Spain and Gibraltar.'

Coincidentally, Sergeant McKee also successfully evaded capture.

Sir Archie added: 'While I was hiding on a farm in the Pas-de-Calais, I was visited by a British agent, Sidney Bowen, who was from an escape organisation based in Marseilles. He asked why more Spitfires were crashing in France than 109s – I had no answer for him.'

It was a fair question.

Group Captain Woodhall, however, wrote that:

> The Circus operations made the enemy react quite seriously, and although we had some losses, the balance was considerably in our favour. They also had the undoubted effect of pinning down a German fighter force on the Western Front, which would otherwise have been sent to the Russian Front when Hitler launched his attack to the east in June 1941.

That was certainly true: JG 2 and JG 26 served on the Kanalfront throughout the war. Bader's first biographer, Paul Brickhill, that myth-making Australian journalist and ex-Spitfire pilot, however, was patently wrong when he claimed that 'Leigh-Mallory's tactics began to pay: Göring was pulling fighter squadrons out of Russia.' That was not true. The two Kanalgeschwadern, to their great credit, were never reinforced by other fighter units. The CAS, Air Chief Marshal Portal, had made clear to Air Marshal Douglas, when doubts were raised regarding the Non-stop Offensive's effectiveness, that the objective was to relieve the pressure on Russia. That being so, the offensive can only be considered a failure. Indeed, the daylight air fighting over the

Kanalfront in 1941 failed to even grab a sentence in either the *Luftwaffe War Diaries* or the official Air Ministry publication *The Rise and Fall of the German Air Force 1933–1945*. Nonetheless, a perusal of this book's appendices, covering combat losses and claims, clearly indicate that in 1941, considerable effort was expended over the Kanalfront – by both sides.

Basil Collier, the official historian, considered that the RAF's daylight 'operations failed ... to achieve their primary object, though the part they played in developing qualities which stood our pilots in good stead on other occasions deserves to be remembered' – if, of course, they survived. Writing in 1966, Air Marshal Douglas, however, commented that:

> Our losses in these operations over the next two and a half months were admittedly heavy, although mere statistics do not give the complete picture. I have always felt that totting up the number of aircraft shot down by either side and so trying to strike a balance is a very short-sighted way of delivering judgement on the results of an air operation ... there were major fighter operations, involving at times large numbers of squadrons, and if the results were not spectacular by 'a quantitative standard' they were nevertheless very effective.

These statements, however, are difficult to reconcile considering that in the Air Marshal's 1948 despatch, he clearly emphasised that the 'primary objective' was 'the destruction of enemy aircraft'. That being so, the statistics arising concerning the combat losses and claims can only be considered a primary measure of the Non-stop Offensive's outcome.

The outcome of the Non-stop Offensive was far from as optimistic as Brickhill claimed in his global best-seller *Reach for the Sky*...

BADER'S BUS COMPANY: STILL RUNNING

The Circus operations had really got going on 14 June 1941, between which date and 31 December 1941, Fighter Command lost 411 fighters either over the Channel or enemy occupied France. During the same period, Air Marshal Douglas's pilots claimed the destruction of 731 German fighters, favourable figures if not interrogated further. The reality, however, was that JG 2 and JG 26 had only lost 103 fighters, casting a somewhat different complexion on the matter. The RAF had lost 298 more aircraft, and were losing by 4:1. Among those RAF pilots either killed, missing or captured were some highly experienced and skilled fighters and leaders – not least Wing Commander Bader. Fighter Command was also overclaiming by a ratio of 7:1. The problem was that the Luftwaffe was already receiving a new fighter, the FW 190, which was far superior to anything else in service at that time – things would, unfortunately, get a whole lot worse in 1942. That said, on 7 December 1941, the United States Pacific Fleet was attacked at Pearl Harbor in an undeclared act of aggression by the Japanese, and four days later Hitler declared war on America, finally ending years of isolation and neutrality, bringing 'Uncle Sam' into the war against the Axis. Thereafter, Britain became a crucial base, into which American men and materiel poured, and from where, on 17 April 1942, the American General Ira Eaker led a formation of B-17 'Flying Fortress' bombers to attack the Rouen-Sotteville marshalling yards. Arguably from that day onwards, an Allied victory was inevitable. To what extent the Non-stop Offensive contributed to that outcome, however, can only be considered questionable.

From June 1941 onwards, the Government Code and Cypher School at Bletchley Park was providing the Allied high command 'Ultra Secret' intelligence from intercepting and decoding encrypted German communications. Thus, Luftwaffe orders of battle and requests for replacement aircraft etc were well-known to the CAS and, no doubt, Air Marshal Douglas, who would, therefore, have had some appreciation of how the Non-stop Offensive was actually going. This information, however, could not possibly be made known to aircrew or, indeed, the public, for fear of revealing this clandestine advantage to the enemy and, of course, damaging morale. And in spite of losses, Fighter Command's morale in 1941 was high.

Flight Lieutenant Frank Twitchett, who had flown in the Tangmere Wing's 145 Squadron as a sergeant-pilot in 1941, summed things up well:

> The feeling that we were going over to the offensive ourselves gave everyone a great fillip in the sense that we had finished having our backs to the wall and were finally going to deal out

some of the punishment which we felt Jerry richly deserved. Perhaps if we had looked forward to the enormous effort of the couple of years following 1941, we might have seen things differently. A very good friend of mine once summed up the Non-stop Offensive by saying that at that point in time we were sure that we would win the war, but were unsure how; sooner or later we would prevail and emerge victorious. Fortunately, his prophecy came true.

Air Vice-Marshal Johnnie Johnson: 'The thing was, we had to do *something*, and that was it, this "reaching out", "leaning into France".'

During the Battle of Britain, the Germans had found that inflexibly tying their fighters to the bomber escort role meant that Jagdfliegern were less effective at destroying RAF fighters, and were themselves more vulnerable. The Kanaljäger were lethal, however, when allowed to roam on Freie Hunten, fighter sweeps, and the inclusion of Me 109 fighter-bombers in

Frank Twitchett, of the Tangmere Wing's 145 Squadron, survived the war, and later questioned the Non-stop Offensive's value; pictured here with living history enthusiast and aviation poet Larry McHale at a symposium organised by the author in 1996, Flight Lieutenant Twitchett died in 1998, soon after this photograph was taken at Worcester Guildhall.

their formations meant that Fighter Command could not ignore these high-altitude incursions. Indeed, Squadron Leader Geoffrey Wellum, a Spitfire pilot with 92 Squadron at Biggin Hill during October 1940, recalled that period as 'the most exhausting' – it was also when, for a short period, the Germans wrested aerial superiority from Fighter Command over south-east England. Clearly, then, there were lessons to be learned from the German experience during the summer and autumn of 1940, which, when reversing the scenario in 1941, Fighter Command ignored. Moreover, the fixation of Air Marshal Douglas and Air Vice-Marshal Leigh-Mallory with 'Big Wings' was even less effective in 1941, in offence, than it had been for defence in 1940. Unfortunately, all too many young RAF fighter pilots paid the price – and their courage and spirit were never in doubt.

Among the Tangmere Wing's shining lights who would not survive what Johnnie Johnson once described as 'The Great Adventure', was Squadron Leader Billy Burton, 616 Squadron's CO. Without doubt, this Cranwellian would have been destined for great things in the service, and today is a rather forgotten hero.

41 Squadron's Ron Rayner also survived the war, decorated with the DFC, and was highly critical of 1941's Rhubarb operations in particular. 'Cloudy' left us in 1999.

After the war, Group Captain Bader and General Galland became great friends, attending lectures, signings and air shows worldwide together as celebrity guests.

Gerhard Schöpfel also survived, ultimately serving as JG 26's Kommodore with 40 aerial victories, and is pictured here in 1989 (centre) with two Kanaljäger experten, Adolf Glunz (65 victories, left), and Otto Stammberger (7). Herr Schöpfel died in Bergisch-Gladbach, aged 90, in 2003, coincidentally the same year as Buck Casson, who he shot down on 9 August 1941.

Above left: After Tangmere Wing days, Sir Alan Smith fought with distinction over Malta, receiving the DFC; he died in 2013 (via Mark Hiller).

Above right: The widow of Wing Commander Billy Burton, now the late Mrs Jean Allom, proudly displaying her first husband's iconic Irvin flying jacket and photographed by the author in 1995.

Jean Allom:

On 5 September 1941, Billy's DFC was gazetted, and on 1 October he was at last taken off operations and posted to 11 Group HQ as 'Squadron Leader Tactics'. He hated leaving 616 but it was obvious to all that he was desperately tired; after that long summer of operational flying, he badly needed a rest.

I piled our few worldly goods into his little Morris Minor and set off for Uxbridge to try and find us somewhere to live. Tangmere was now in the past, but that summer remains among my most vivid memories, perhaps because it was the first and last that Billy and I were ever to spend together.

Early in 1942, Billy Burton was promoted to wing commander and posted to the Middle East, leading the Kittyhawk-equipped 239 Wing on tank-busting sorties. A bar to the DFC followed on 23 February 1943, and Wing Commander Burton was appointed to the DSO for 'brilliant leadership'. On 6 April 1943, this tour of operational duty was concluded, during which Billy had also been awarded the French Croix de Guerre for a daring low-level attack on a desert fort where General Leclerc was besieged by German forces, enabling the French commander to escape. In May 1943, Air Commodore Harry Broadhurst, leader of the Desert Air Force (DAF) returned to England on leave, along with several of his more senior commanders, including Wing Commander Burton.

Jean Allom:

> Billy was to return to North Africa in a Hudson flown by Group Captain Gordon Yaxley, a much-decorated officer and senior to my husband. In actual fact, there were two group captains aboard, as while Billy was in England, Broadhurst had told him of his promotion and to put up his fourth stripe.
>
> In retrospect, there seems to have been doom hanging over this flight as the Hudson should never have been flying that day – it was due to return several days earlier. The delay was caused by those servicing the aircraft discovering some desert insects therein, and so it had to be fumigated. Of course, the date on which the flight was to return to Gibraltar was then scheduled to take place, 3 June 1943, was one on which there was maximum Luftwaffe activity over the Bay of Biscay as Churchill was expected to be flying back to the UK. Only two days before, in fact, a Dakota had been shot down over the Bay – all aboard were lost, including the actor Leslie Howard. Also, regarding Billy's flight, Broadhurst had been summoned to a top-level conference in London, so was not returning with them. He told me later that he would never in a million years have agreed to the flight going by day, although I understand that Billy tried to do everything possible to dissuade Yaxley, but the latter and more senior man insisted upon doing so – with disastrous consequences. It is impossible to understand why such an experienced officer as Yaxley took such a foolhardy course of action.

At 1050 hrs, the 117 Squadron Hudson concerned was intercepted and shot down over the Bay of Biscay by a Ju 88C flown by Leutnant Heinz Olbrecht of 15/KG 40. Three of the RAF crew, a group captain and four wing commanders (including Billy Burton, whose promotion was not yet official), and two squadron leaders all perished. Between them, these officers had three DSOs, three DFCs, and an MC. All remain missing to this day, and such a grievous blow was the loss to the DAF that the news was suppressed. Many others who flew in the Tangmere Wing that 'stirring' summer of 1941 would not survive to see Total Victory in 1945.

Finally, two of 'Dogsbody Section' and the inner sanctum who did survive, but are sadly no longer with us, have left us their impressions of Douglas Bader's leadership during those Tangmere Wing days.

Former wartime members of 616 Squadron commemorating the Battle of Britain during the 1990s, including Squadron Leader Buck Casson (third from right), Group Captain Denis Gillam (fifth from right), and Group Captain Sir Hugh Dundas (second left). The friendships and bonds forged in war always remained.

BADER'S SPITFIRE WING

Air Vice-Marshal Johnnie Johnson, who finished the Second World War as the RAF's top-scoring fighter pilot:

> It was the most exciting period of our lives, when we were privileged to fly with Douglas Bader down at Tangmere in 1941, and from him learned something about the elusive qualities of leadership and how to conduct ourselves in battle. It was there, of course, that the 'Finger Four' was worked out, which was adopted throughout Fighter Command, and which was really Cocky Dundas's idea.

Group Captain Sir Hugh Dundas:

> I had plenty of opportunity to observe leadership in war – and recognise the genuine article when I saw it… The personal experience of war, all those years ago, has never gone away, and I am sure never will … never quite and never will be

After repatriation in 1945, Bob Morton became a teacher, and continued flying with the RAFVR until 1953; he always hoped that Spitfire Mk V still awaited his test flight at Westhampnett…

forgotten.… Leadership in war is not something that can be taught or learned in the normal way. A great wartime leader does not tell people what to do, he *shows* them. I became personally aware of this phenomenon through my association with Douglas Bader.

I first met him in September 1940, and later lived and flew with him through the somewhat hectic spring and summer of 1941 … Douglas Bader came into my life at a critical moment. I had just got back to my squadron after being very comprehensively and frighteningly shot down, and the squadron to which I had returned was the one I had joined eighteen months before as a starry-eyed 18-year-old pilot, was more or less unrecognisable, with over half the pilots having either fallen victim, one way or another, to the Battle of Britain. Now, re-formed, we were about to go into action again with the Duxford Wing, commanded by Squadron Leader Douglas Bader. The atmosphere that morning in the Nissen hut allocated to us at the dispersal point at Fowlmere … could probably be best described as 'frightened'. Indeed, I was terrified to the bone at the prospect of an encounter with the Luftwaffe such as my last one had been.… Far from itching to be up and at them, I was praying with an intensity that would have been a credit to Medieval mystics, that there would be no action for Dundas that day. Well, that extreme form of sickness was alleviated, if not altogether cured, by the appearance and presence of Douglas Bader. He stomped into the hut and wrought his magic. He lifted our spirits. He made us *want* to follow him into the hostile sky. He told us how he felt about it all and wanted us to feel the same. He didn't *tell* us, he *showed* us. Although we only flew in the Duxford Wing a few times in the dying phase of the Battle of Britain, it was enough to open my eyes to *leadership*.

The process was continued, at much greater length and at closer quarters, when Bader was leading the Tangmere Wing and elected to keep his Spitfire with our squadron, elected also to have me fly beside him on every sortie. We crossed over to France together at the sharp end of the wing more than sixty times between May and mid-August 1941, when he went down over St Omer. It was hard slogging, and there was a steady drain of pilots shot down or damaged and unable to make it back across the Channel. In one period of twenty-one days our squadron lost twelve pilots, more than half our establishment, and it was no different in the other two squadrons of the wing – and yet, morale and spirit were sky-high, buoyed up and sustained by the example of the man who led us.

I wish I could tell you how he did it … I cannot, of course. He was brave, no doubt about that, and visibly demonstrably so, and yet he was far from being reckless. He demanded commitment to the fight from individuals and units, and yet he was understanding of others less robust in sprit and nature than himself. He put a metaphorical armour around us and hoped that we would go forward with him. He drove himself tirelessly, but kept a careful eye on others to make sure they were not driven beyond the limits of their own endurance. He could and did admit you to his personal friendship, and yet he always maintained that invisible barrier which sets aside a commander from those he commands. From my worm-like position I was able to observe him closely, and he showed me how a man should behave at war, and what the word *leadership* truly meant.… I had his example always before me.

After repatriation, Group Captain Bader left the RAF to resume a career in civil aviation – and made his greatest contribution as an ambassador for and inspiration to the disabled community, for which he was knighted in 1976. Sadly, the great man died suddenly in 1982 – but his legacy lives on through the Douglas Bader Foundation, a charity founded as a living memorial continuing to inspire and assist the amputee community in Sir Douglas's name.

BADER'S BUS COMPANY: STILL RUNNING

On 9 August 2001, the sadly also now late Lady Bader OBE unveiled this statue of Sir Douglas at Goodwood airfield, formerly known as Westhampnett and from where his final operational flight was made. The piece is the work of the sculptor Kenneth Potts, and was created using certain of the author's photographs for reference. Commissioned by Lord March, the work symbolises the pugnacious optimism, courage and spirit of the 'Tangmere Wing of all the talents' – which remains inspirational whatever the actual outcome of Air Marshal Douglas and Air Vice-Marshal Leigh-Mallory's Non-stop Offensive.

There we will leave the legless, swashbuckling Wing Commander Douglas Bader and 'Dogsbody Section', the Tangmere Wing, the 109s – always higher, faster, diving to attack before zooming away – the Beehives of a handful of bombers and hundreds of Spitfires; the conundrum of whether 'Dogsbody' was the victim of 'friendly fire', as does seem likely; the oil-stained and wreckage-strewn sea, the shocking visions of burning aircraft crashing violently to earth, the parachute-filled sky, the devastating telegrams home, regretting to inform that….

We will leave all of that, those vapour-trail filled, shot- and shell-riven, blue skies of summer 1941 – for that was then, now eighty years ago.

Today, none of it, the survivors having now passed, is a living memory. But it is history, Churchill's 'flickering lamp' having now shone upon those heady days, bringing them back to life in the time it took the reader to complete this book. There will never be another opportunity to harvest such first-hand accounts as appear within it. That being so, this is a permanent record – through which the 'Tangmere Wing of all the talents' lives on…

Appendix 1

Below are details of the Tangmere Wing's operations during the time Wing Commander D.R.S. Bader DSO DFC was wing leader between 18 March and 9 August 1941. This appendix largely comprises details concerning the wing's combat losses and claims, and was largely contributed by John Foreman to my original *Bader's Tangmere Spitfires* (1996).

145 Squadron

Operational Record, 18 March – 9 August 1941

20.03.41.
Flying accident: Spitfire P7603 forced-landed at Shoreham, Sgt Weber safe.

05.05.41.
Fg Off J.H.M. Offenberg: one He 60 destroyed, one Me 109 probable, Pointe de Barfleur.

13.05.41.
Flying accident: Spitfire P8071 forced-landed at Manston, Fg Off J.H.M. Offenberg safe.

21.05.41.
Spitfires P7493 and P7737 both Cat. E, collided over Westhampnett during return from evening Circus. Flt Lt Stevens and Fg Off Owen killed.

04.06.41.
Fg Off Clarke: Ju 87 destroyed, Le Havre.
Flying accident: Spitfire P8323 Cat. E, abandoned near Worthing, Pt Off Sabourin safe.

APPENDIX 1

<u>11.06.41.</u>
Flying accident: Spitfire P8230 damaged while landing at Manston, Sgt Robillard safe.

<u>18.06.41.</u>
12 Spitfires. 17:35–19:45 hrs. Circus No. 15 to Bois de Licques.
Spitfire P8254 Cat. E: shot down by Me 109, Sgt Palmer missing.
Spitfire P8328 Cat. E: shot down by Me 109, Sgt Turnbull missing.

<u>21.06.41.</u>
12 Spitfires. 11:33–13:10 hrs. Circus No. 16 to Longuenesse aerodrome.
Fg Off J. Macachek and Sqn Ldr H.F. Burton (latter CO 616) shared Me 109 destroyed, Bridge, Kent.
Spitfire P8341: Cat. B, damaged by Me 109 off Ramsgate, Sgt F.J. Twitchett slightly wounded.
10 Spitfires. 15:50–17:35 hrs. Circus No. 17 to Desvres aerodrome.
Sgt Grant: Me 109 destroyed, Le Touquet.
Spitfire P8339: Cat. B, damaged by Me 109, Flt Lt M.A. Newling unhurt.

<u>22.06.41.</u>
10 Spitfires. 15:07–16:50 hrs. Circus No. 18 to Hazebrouck.
Sgt J. Robillard: Me 109 destroyed, Port Phillipe.

<u>25.06.41.</u>
12 Spitfires. 15:47–17:40 hrs. Circus No. 23 to Longuenesse.
Flt Lt Arthur: Me 109 destroyed, Le Touquet.
Sgt Grant: Me 109 destroyed, Le Touquet.

<u>26.06.41.</u>
12 Spitfires. 10:45–12:25 hrs. Sweep (Circus No. 24 aborted).
Sgt W.J. Johnson: Me 109 destroyed, Gravelines.
Spitfire P8314 Cat. E: shot down by Me 109, Gravelines, Sgt Macbeth missing.

<u>27.06.41.</u>
12 Spitfires. 20:50-22:30 hrs. Circus No. 25 to Lille.
Flt Lt M.A. Newling: Me 109 probable, Lille.

<u>28.06.41.</u>
12 Spitfires. 07:44–10:00 hrs. Circus No. 26 to Commines.
Fg Off J. Macachek: Me 109 probable, near Cassel.

02.07.41.
12 Spitfires. 11:49–13:30 hrs, Circus Lille.
Spitfire P8536 Cat. E: Sgt J.G.L. Robillard reported missing, but evaded and later returned home safely.

05.07.41.
12 Spitfires. 12:19–15:00 hrs. Circus.
Fg Off J. Macachek: Me 109 destroyed, one damaged, Lille.

06.07.41.
12 Spitfires. 13:52–15:20 hrs. Circus.
Spitfire W3366: Flt Lt M.A. Newling lost in action.

07.07.41.
8 Spitfires. 14:36–16:35 hrs. Circus.
Spitfire X4667: Cat. E, shot down by Me 109. Sgt Silvester forced-landed wounded.

08.07.41.
10 Spitfires. 14:40–16:35 hrs. Circus.
Spitfire R7263: Pt Off Pine lost.
Spitfire R7218: Fg Off J. Macachek lost.

09.07.41.
8 Spitfires. 13:05–14:45 hrs. Circus Mazingarbe.
Spitfire P8070: Sgt McFarlane killed during solo head-on attack against four Me 109s.

14.07.41.
8 Spitfires. 09:35–11:25 hrs. Circus.
Sqn Ldr P.S. Turner: Me 109F destroyed, NE France.
Spitfire W3185: Cat. A, Sqn Ldr P.S. Turner unhurt.

23.07.41.
10 Spitfires. 13:31-21:24 hrs. Roadstead, Hague.
Sqn Ldr P.S. Turner: Me 109E destroyed, Ostend.
Sgt R.J.C. Grant: Me 190E destroyed, Ostend.
10 Spitfires. 19:38-21:24 hrs. Circus Mazingarbe.
Sgt F.J. Twitchett: Me 109 destroyed, Mazingarbe.

APPENDIX 1

Spitfire P8712: Fg Off D.N. Forde missing in action.
Spitfire: Cat. B, forced-landed Beachy Head. Pt Off Breeze unhurt.

610 Squadron

Operational Record, 18 March 18 – 9 August 1941

19.03.41.
12 Spitfires. 16:20 hrs. Defensive patrol.
Sgt Payne: Me 109 destroyed, S of Dungeness.
One Spitfire, serial number unknown, Cat. B to Me 109, forced-landed Hailsham, Sgt Hale wounded.

23.03.41.
Spitfire P7685: Cat. E, hit hill near West Dean. Pilot, Plt Off ISO Gaze, killed, brother of PO FAO Gaze of the same Squadron.

03.04.41.
Flt Lt Morris and Sgt Ballard: Ju 88 destroyed (shared) S of Beachy Head.

15.04.41
4 Spitfires. 18:10–19:30 hrs. Defensive patrol.
Pt Off Ross and Sgt Richardson: Ju 88 destroyed (shared) off St Catherine's Point.
Spitfire P7684: Pt Off Ross missing in action.
Spitfire DW-R: Damaged by Ju 88, Sgt Richardson safe.
Spitfire P7613: Flying accident, forced-landed at Westhampnett, Sqn Ldr Woodhouse safe.

22.04.41.
1 Spitfire. 08:40 hrs.
Sgt Payne: Ju 88 destroyed, E of Bognor Regis.

25.04.41.
2 Spitfires. 07:25 hrs.
Sqn Ldr Woodhouse and Pt Off Stoop: Ju 88 destroyed, S of Brighton.

08.05.41.
Two Spitfires. 12:00 hrs. Patrol.

Sgt Mains: Me 109 destroyed, one Me 109 probable, Dover Straits.
Spitfire, serial number unknown, damaged by Me 109 in above action, Sgt Mains unhurt.

10.05.41.
Spitfire P7777: Flying accident, crash-landed at Westhampnett, Sgt Davis safe.

11.05.41.
2 Spitfires. 00:21-01:43 hrs. Night interception.
Sgt Warden: Ju 88 destroyed, Guildford.
WO Pegge: He 111 destroyed, Guildford.

12.05.41.
1 Spitfire. 22:30-22:51 hrs. Night interception.
Sgt Payne: Ju 88 destroyed, S of Brighton.

06.06.41.
Spitfire P8660: Flying accident, crash-landed at Westhampnett, Sgt Davis safe.

17.06.41.
12 Spitfires. 18:5-20:45 hrs. Circus No. 14 to Choques.
Flt Lt R.A. Lee-Knight: Me 109 destroyed, near Gris Nez.
Spitfire P8526: Cat. A, crash-landed at Merston, Sgt Mains unhurt.

18.06.41.
12 Spitfires. 17:38-20:20 hrs. Circus No. 15 to Bois de Licques.
Sgt Merriman: Me 109 destroyed, 20 miles S of Dungeness.

21.06.41.
12 Spitfires. 11:30–13:10 hrs. Circus No. 16 to Longuenesse aerodrome.
Flt Lt R.A. Lee-Knight: Me 109 destroyed, another damaged, both off Gravelines.
12 Spitfires. 15:00–17:33 hrs. Circus No. 17 to Desvres aerodrome.
Pt Off Scott: Me 109 destroyed, Le Touquet.

22.06.41.
12 Spitfires. 15:05–16:55 hrs. Circus No. 18 to Hazebrouck.
Sqn Ldr K. Holden: Me 109 destroyed, Hazebrouck.

APPENDIX 1

Pt Off Horner: Me 109 destroyed, Hazebrouck.
Sgt Raine: Me 109 destroyed, Hazebrouck.

25.06.41.
12 Spitfires. 11:57–14:14 hrs. Circus No. 22 to Hazebrouck.
Pt Off Scott: Me 109 destroyed, Gravelines.
Flt Lt Crowley-Milling: Me 109 probable, Gravelines.
Spitfire, serial unknown: Cat. A, damaged by Me 109, Sgt Davies wounded.
11 Spitfires. 15:47–17:32 hrs. Circus No. 23 to Longuenesse.
Wg Cdr Aitken: Me 109 destroyed, near St Omer. (This was The Hon. J.W.M. Aitken, CO of 68 Squadron, the son of Lord Beaverbrook, the Minister for Aircraft Production.)
Pt Off Horner: Me 109 destroyed, near St Omer.
Sqn Ldr Holden: Me 109 damaged, near St Omer.
Sgt Raine: Me 109 probable, near St Omer, and one damaged on airfield.
Spitfire P8399: Cat. E, failed to return, Pt Off Scott missing.
Spitfire, serial unknown: Cat. A, damaged by Me 109, Sgt Raine unhurt.

26.06.41.
10 Spitfires. 10:45–12:30 hrs. Sweep (Circus No. 24 aborted).
Pt Off F.A.O. Gaze: Me 109 destroyed, Gravelines.
Sqn Ldr Holden: Me 109 damaged, Gravelines.
Flt Lt Lee-Knight: Me 109 damaged, Gravelines.
Spitfire, serial unknown: Cat. A, crash-landed, Pt Off Gaze unhurt.

02.07.41.
12 Spitfires. 11:46–13:50 hrs. Circus to Lille.
Sgt Mains: Me 109 destroyed, N France.
Pt Off F.A.O. Gaze: Me 109 damaged, N France.

03.07.41.
12 Spitfires. 10:40–12:18 hrs. Circus to St Omer.
Flt Lt Lee-Knight and Pt Off J.R. Stoop: Me 109 destroyed, shared, Hazebrouck.
Flt Lt Lee-Knight: Me 109 damaged, Hazebrouck.
Sgt Merriman and Sgt R.D. Bowen (latter of 616): Hs 126 probable, Hazebrouck.

05.07.41.
12 Spitfires. 12:15–13:36 hrs. Circus.
Sgt Mains: Me 109 destroyed, Lille.

Spitfire, serial unknown: Cat. B, crash-landed near Telscombe Station, Pt Off Wilcox unhurt.
Spitfire P8521: Cat. A, Overshot at Hawkinge, Sgt Mains safe.

06.07.41.
12 Spitfires. 13:31–15:20 hrs. Circus.
Sqn Ldr Holden: Me 109 destroyed, NE France.
Sqn Ldr Holden and Pt Of F.A.O. Gaze: Me 109 destroyed, shared, NE France.

08.07.41.
2 Spitfires. 11:55–12:35 hrs. Interception.
Sgt Merriman: Me 109 destroyed and one probable, S of Portsmouth.
12 Spitfires. 14:40–17:10 hrs. Circus.
Flt Lt Lee-Knight. Me 109 destroyed, NE France.
Spitfire P8504: Pt Off F.G. Horner missing (captured).
Spitfire DW-H: Pt Off J.R. Stoop missing (rescued, wounded).

10.07.41.
12 Spitfires. 11:36–13.55 hrs. Circus.
Sqn Ldr Holden: Me 109 destroyed, NE France.
Spitfire P8520: Pt Off P. Ward-Smith missing (captured).
Spitfire P8523: Sgt Blackman lost, killed at Maizieres, St Pol.
Spitfire P8374: Sgt L.H. Anderson lost.

11.07.41.
8 Spitfires. 11:08–12:18 hrs. Sweep.
Sgt Merriman: Me 109 probable, NE France.
Sgt Grey: Me 109 damaged, NE France.

14.07.41.
Spitfire P8656: Cat. E, crash-landed and overturned, three miles E of Heathfield. Sgt R.W. Richardson injured.

17.07.41.
8 Spitfires. 19:00-20:25 hrs. Sweep.
Pt Off F.A.O. Gaze: Me 109 destroyed, Hardelot.

19.07.41.
8 Spitfires. 13:10–15:28 hrs. Circus.
Sgt W. Raine: Me 109 probable, Dunkirk.

APPENDIX 1

21.07.41.
12 Spitfires. 07:40–09:40 hrs. Circus to Lille.
Sgt Merriman: Two Me 109Fs destroyed, N France.

23.07.41.
8 Spitfires. 19:38–21:45 hrs. Circus to Mazingarbe.
Wg Cdr D.R.S. Bader and Sgt W. Raine: Me 109 destroyed, shared, Mazingarbe.
Pt Off J.E.I. Grey: Me 109 probable, Mazingarbe.
Spitfire DW-S: Cat. B, Sgt Philpotts wounded.

07.08.41.
12 Spitfires. 17:11–18:50 hrs. Circus to Lille.
Spitfire DW-A: Cat. B, crash-landed at Friston. Sgt McWatt wounded.

616 Squadron

Operational Record, 18 March – 9 August 1941

27.03.41.
2 Spitfires. 14:00 hrs. Scramble.
Flt Lt C.H. Macfie: Me 110 damaged, Littlehampton.
Spitfire P7732: Flying accident, forced-landed at Durrington, Sgt Sellars safe.

21.04.41.
12 Spitfires. 09:00-09:15 hrs. Channel Patrol.
Spitfire P7812: Missing after action St Catherine's Point, Sgt Sellars lost.

24.04.41.
2 Spitfires. 14:35–15:41 hrs. Rhubarb.
Flt Lt C.H. Macfie: Me 109 destroyed on ground, Maupertus airfield.
Spitfire P7736: Shot down by flak, Maupertus airfield, Sgt McDevette killed.
Spitfire P7771: Flying accident, bellylanded at Tangmere, Sgt Mabbett safe.

05.05.41.
2 Spitfires. 07:24-08:00 hrs. Interception.
Fg Off L.H. Casson and Fg Off R. Marples: Ju 88 damaged, shared, S of Tangmere.

Spitfire P7753: Cat. E to return fire from Ju 88, Fg Off Casson baled out near Littlehampton.

08.05.41.
2 Spitfires. 12:00 hrs. Patrol.
Wg Cdr D.R.S. Bader: Me 109 probable, Dover Straits.
Spitfire P7827, QJ-A: Cat. B to Me 109 during above action, Fg Off H.S.L. Dundas crash-landed at Hawkinge.

09.05.41.
Spitfire P7829: Flying accident, bellylanded at Westhampnett, pilot believed safe.

17.05.41.
2 Spitfires. 16:35 hrs. Interception.
Fg Off H.S.L. Dundas: Me 109 destroyed off Shoreham.

18.06.41.
12 Spitfires. 17:35–19:45 hrs. Circus No. 15 to Bois de Licques.
Spitfire, serial number unknown: Cat. B, overshot, Tangmere, Pt Off Leckie injured.

19.06.41.
12 Spitfires. 16:57–18:25 hrs. Operation *Derby* to Le Havre.
Flt Lt C.H. Macfie: Me 109 damaged near Le Havre.

21.06.41.
12 Spitfires. 11:39–13:24 hrs. Circus No. 16 to Longuenesse aerodrome.
Sqn Ldr H.F. Burton and Fg Off Macachek (latter of 145 Sqn): Me 109 destroyed, shared, Bridge, Kent.
12 Spitfires. 15:52–17:33. Circus No. 17 to Desvres aerodrome.
Wg Cdr D.R.S. Bader: Me 109 destroyed North of Boulogne.
Spitfire P7730: Cat. E, shot down near Boulogne by Me 109, Pt Off Brown missing.

22.06.41.
12 Spitfires. 15:09–16:56 hrs. Circus No. 18 to Hazebrouck.
Fg Off R. Marples: Me 109 destroyed off Gravelines.
Fg Off L.H. Casson and Sgt Beedham: Me 109 destroyed, shared, off Gravelines.

APPENDIX 1

<u>23.06.41.</u>
12 Spitfires. 19:53–21:40 hrs. Circus No. 20 to Desvres aerodrome.
Spitfire P7435: Cat. E, damaged by Me 109 and abandoned over Channel, Sgt Beedham rescued.

<u>25.06.41.</u>
10 Spitfires. 11:58–13:55 hrs. Circus No. 22 to Hazebrouck.
Wg Cdr D.R.S. Bader: Me 109 destroyed, Gravelines.
Wg Cdr D.R.S. Bader and Sgt J. West: Me 109 destroyed, shared, Gravelines.
Fg Off H.S.L. Dundas: Me 109 damaged, Gravelines.
Fg Off R. Marples: Me 109 damaged, Gravelines.
Spitfire, serial number unknown: Cat. B, damaged by Me 109, Sgt McCairns unhurt.
Spitfire, serial number unknown: Cat. B, damaged by Me 109, crash-landed at Hawkinge, Sgt R.A. Morton unhurt.
12 Spitfires. Circus No. 23 to Longuenesse.
Wg Cdr D.R.S. Bader: Me 109 destroyed, St Omer.
Spitfire P8272: Cat. E, shot down by Me 109 near St Omer, Sgt Jenks missing.
Spitfire P7327: Cat. E, shot down by Me 109 near St Omer, Sgt Brewer missing.

<u>26.06.41.</u>
12 Spitfires. 10:45–12:10 hrs. Sweep (Circus No. 24 aborted).
Pt Off J.E. Johnson: Me 109 destroyed over Gravelines.
Fg Off L.H. Casson: Me 109 damaged over Gravelines.
Spitfire P7815, YQ-N: Cat. E, crashed during forced landing at Bacton, Norfolk, Sgt R.A. Morton unhurt.

<u>02.07.41.</u>
12 Spitfires. 11:50–13:43 hrs. Circus to Lille.
Pt Off P.W.E. Hepple: Me 109 destroyed, N France.
Sgt A. Smith: Me 109 destroyed and one damaged, both N France.

<u>03.07.41.</u>
12 Spitfires. 10:40–12:18 hrs. Circus to St Omer.
Sgt R.D. Bowen and Sgt E.W Merriman (latter of 610 Sqn): Hs 126 probable, shared.
Spitfire P7980: Missing in action, Sgt Crabtree captured, later escaped and returned home.

10 Spitfires. 15:00–16:25 hrs. Circus to Hazebrouck.
Sgt D.W. Beedham: Me 109 probable, Hazebrouck.

04.07.41.
9 Spitfires. 14:16–16:50 hrs. Circus to Choques.
Pt Off J.E. Johnson: Me 109 damaged, five miles south of Gravelines.
Sgt R.A. Morton: Me 109 damaged.

05.07.41.
12 Spitfires. 12:17–15:00 hrs. Circus.
Spitfire P8651: Missing over Lille, Flt Lt C.H. Macfie lost, captured.

06.07.41.
12 Spitfires. 13:33–15:20 hrs. Circus.
Wg Cdr D.R.S. Bader: Me 109 destroyed, N France.
Pt Off J.E. Johnson: Me 109 destroyed, S of Dunkirk.
Sgt A. Smith: Me 109 probable, NE France.
Sgt D.W. Beedham: Me 109 damaged, NE France.
Spitfire P8500: Missing in action, Sgt J.A. McCairns evaded and returned home.

07.07.41.
10 Spitfires. 14:43–16:23 hrs. Circus.
Spitfire, serial number unknown: Cat. E to Me 109, Sgt Bowen crash-landed at Hawkinge, unhurt.
Spitfire, serial not known: Flying accident, Cat. A, damaged during landing at Friston, Sgt J.G. West safe.

08.07.41.
12 Spitfires. 05:35–07:30 hrs. Circus.
Spitfire P7837: Cat. A, damaged while landing at Westhampnett, Pt Off Johnson safe.
Spitfire P7856: Cat. A, hit sea during sweep, landed at Hawkinge, Fg Off Marples safe.

09.07.41.
8 Spitfires. 13:03–15:15 hrs. Circus to Mazingarbe.
Sqn Ldr E.P. Gibbs: Me 109 destroyed and one probable, NE France.
Sgt A. Smith: Me 109 damaged, NE France.
Spitfire P8070: Missing in action, Sqn Ldr E.P. Gibbs lost but evaded and safely returned.

APPENDIX 1

Spitfire P8386: Shot down by Me 109 near St Omer, Sgt R.A. Morton captured.

10.07.41.
8 Spitfires. 11:38–13:50 hrs. Circus.
Flt Lt H.S.L. Dundas: Me 109F destroyed, NE France.
Sgt J.G. West: Me 109F destroyed, NE France.
Pt Off P.W.E. Hepple: Me 109F damaged, NE France.

11.07.41.
8 Spitfires. 14:56–16:59 hrs. Rhubarb.
Sgt A. Smith: Two Ju 87s destroyed on ground, Norrent-Fontes.

12.07.41.
7 Spitfires. 09:29–11:19 hrs. Circus.
Sgt A. Smith: Me 109F probable, NE France.
Pt Off P.W.E. Hepple: Me 109F damaged, NE France.

14.07.41.
12 Spitfires. 09:35–11:25 hrs. Circus.
Pt Off J.E. Johnson: Me 109F destroyed over Fanquembergues.
Sgt A. Smith: Me 109E damaged, NE France.

19.07.41.
9 Spitfires. 13:11–15:26 hrs. Circus.
Wg Cdr D.R.S. Bader and Fg Off H.S.L. Dundas: Me 109F destroyed, shared, Dunkirk.
Wg Cdr D.R.S. Bader: A further Me 109F destroyed, and a probable, Dunkirk.
Flt Lt L.H. Casson: Me 109 probable, Dunkirk.

21.07.41.
11 Spitfires. 07:43–09:44 hrs. Circus to Lille.
Wg Cdr D.R.S. Bader: Me 109 destroyed, N France.
Pt Off P.W.E. Hepple: Me 109 probable, N France.
Sgt D.W. Beedham: Me 109 damaged, N France.
11 Spitfires. 19:52–22:00 hrs. Circus to Mazingarbe.
Wg Cdr D.R.S. Bader: Me 109F damaged, N France.
Pt Off P.W.E. Hepple and Pt Off J.E. Johnson: Me 109 probable, shared, N France.

Flt Lt H.S.L. Dundas: Me 109 damaged, N France.
Spitfire W3376: Shot down by Me 109 near St Omer, Sgt S.W.R. Mabbett killed.

23.07.41.
10 Spitfires. 19:41–21:46 hrs. Circus to Mazingarbe.
Flt Lt L.H. Casson: Me 109 destroyed, and one damaged, Mazingarbe.
Pt Off J.E. Johnson: Me 109 damaged, Mazingarbe.
Sqn Ldr H.F. Burton: Me 109 damaged, Mazingarbe.

07.08.41.
12 Spitfires. 17:14–18:45 hrs. Circus to Lille. Sgt D.W. Beedham: Me 109F damaged. Sgt J.G. West: Me 109F damaged.

09.08.41.
14 Spitfires. 10:42–12:53. Circus to Gosnay.
Pt Off J.E. Johnson: Two Me 109Fs destroyed, NE France.
Pt Off P.W.E. Hepple: Me 109F destroyed, NE France.
Sgt J.G. West: Me 109F destroyed, NE France.
Wg Cdr D.R.S. Bader and Sgt J.G. West: Me 109 destroyed, shared, NE France.
Wg Cdr D.R.S. Bader: Me 109F destroyed, NE France.
Fg Off R. Marples: Me 109F probable, NE France.
Spitfire W3185, D-B: Missing, Wg Cdr D.R.S. Bader DSO* DFC captured near St Omer.
Spitfire W3458: Missing, Flt Lt L.H. Casson shot down and captured near Marquise.

41 Squadron

Operational Record, 28 July – 9 August 1941

28.07.41.
Arrived at Merston and relieved 145 Squadron.

07.08.41.
12 Spitfires. 17:10–18:50. Circus to Lille.
Sgt Mitchell: Me 109F probable, Béthune.
Spitfire, serial unknown: Flt Lt Draper missing, later reported as having been captured.

Appendix 2

Below the combat losses of JG 26 Schlageter, between 18 March and 9 August 1941, are listed. This German fighter group often fought the Tangmere Wing over northern France. Source: *The JG 26 War Diary: Volume One, 1939–1945* – see Bibliography.

8 April 1941
Lt Horst Reech, 5/JG 26, KIA, Me 109E-7 (WN2754), Morlaix, shot down by Blenheim.
Fw. Karl Schieffer, 5/JG 26, safe, forced-landed, Me 109E-7 (WN6500), Brest, shot down by Blenheim.

14 June 1941
Lt Robert Menge, 3/JG 26, KIA, Me 109E-7 (WN6490), Marquise, shot down by Spitfire.
Lt Karl Schrader, 3/JG 26, wounded, Me 109E-7 (WN3758), Marquise – Audembert, shot down by Spitfire.
Oblt Kahse, 1/JG 26, rescued, Me 109E-7 (WN4105), Channel, shot down by Spitfire.

16 June 1941
Gefr Karl Dietz, 1/JG 26, KIA, Me 109E-7 (WN3817), Marquis/Samer, shot down by Spitfire.
Lt Gustav Hüttner, 8/JG 26, KIA, Me 109E-7 (WN8125), East Montreuil/Calais, shot down by Spitfire.

17 June 1941
Fw Bernhard Adam, KIA, 2/JG 26, Me 109E-7 (WN N/K), Channel/Boulogne, shot down by Hurricane.

BADER'S SPITFIRE WING

21 June 1941

Lt Heinz Gries, KIA, 8/JG 26, Me 109F-2 (WN6732), Etaples, shot down by Spitfire.

Uffz Heinz Catmienke, KIA, 8/JG 26, Me 109F-2 (WN6733), West of Le Touquet, shot down by Spitfire.

Gefr Christian Knees, KIA, 9/JG 26, Me 109F-2 (WN N\K), Le Touquet, shot down by Spitfire.

Uffz Oto Ewald, POW, 6/JG 26, Me 109E-7 (WN6462), SE Ramsgate, shot down by Spitfire.

Obfw Franz Lüders, POW, 6/JG 26, Me 109E-7 (WN6497), As above.

Lt Hans-Joachim Geburtig, wounded, 8/JG 26, Me 109F-2 (WN5521), Samer, shot down by Spitfire.

Obstlt Adolf Galland, safe, forced-landed, Kommodore, Me 109F-2 (WN5776), Calais (1236 hrs), shot down by Spitfire.

Obstlt Adolf Galland, wounded, Kommodore, Me 109F-2 (WN6713), NE Boulogne (1637 hrs), shot down by Spitfire.

Fw Bruno Hegenaur, Stab/JG 26, Me 109F-2 (WN N/K), St Omer, shot down by Spitfire.

22 June 1941

Lt Hans Glasmacher, KIA, 2/JG 26, Me 109E-7 (WN6219), Clairmarais, shot down by Spitfire.

24 June 1941

Lt Erdmann Neumann, KIA, 9/JG 26, Me 109F-2 (WN N/K), South of Gravelines, shot down by Spitfire.

25 June 1941

Fw Bartholomaeus Eierstock, KIA, 9/JG 26, Me 109F-2 (WN12664), Dunkirk, shot down by Spitfire.

Oblt Heinrich Gottlob, wounded, 1/JG 26, Me 109E-7 (WN7690), Hardinghem, shot down by Spitfire.

27 June 1941

Uffz Otto Freidrich, KIA, 4/JG 26, Me 109E-7 (WN4183), St Omer, shot down by Spitfire.

28 June 1941

Oblt Gustav Sprick, KIA, SK 8/JG 26, Me 109F-2 (WN5743), Gravelines-St Omer, wing collapsed in combat, crashed.

APPENDIX 2

Uffz Hans Friedrich, safe, 3/JG 26, Me 109E-7 (WN7970), Calais, shot down by Spitfire.

Ofhr F Graf von Uiberacker, wounded, 1/JG 26, Me 109E-7 (WN3776), St Omer, shot down by Spitfire.

Lt Johannes Schmidt, wounded, 3/JG 26, Me 109E-7 (WN7689), Le Touquet, shot down by Spitfire.

Oblt Harald Grawatsch, wounded, Stab II/JG 26, Me 109E-7 (WN6487), SE St Omer, shot down by Spitfire.

2 July 1941

Oblt Martin Rysavy, KIA, SK 2/JG 26, Me 109E-7 (WN3213), East of Calais, flak – friendly fire.

Obstlt Adolf Galland, wounded, Kommodore, Me 109F-2 (WN N/K), St Omer area, shot-up by Spitfire.

Hptmn Rudolf Bieber, KIA, Stab I/JG 26, Me 109F-2 (WN7686), St Omer, shot down by Spitfire.

Lt Joachim Kehrhahn, KIA, 3/JG 26, Me 109F-2 (WN6476), NE St Pol, shot down by Spitfire.

8 July 1941

Uffz Albrecht Held, KIA, 1/JG 26, Me 109F-2 (WN9157), North St Omer, wing collapsed in combat.

Uffz Karl Finke, KIA, 6/JG 26, Me 109E-7 (WN3711), South of Ypres, shot down by Spitfire.

10 July 1941

Uffz Erich Hammon, KIA, 2/JG 26, Me 109E-7 (WN3855), Dover Strait, shot down by Spitfire.

Hptmn Rolf Pingel, POW, GK I/JG 26, Me 109F-2 (WN12764), Dover, shot down by Sterling and Spitfire.

Lt Heinz Reiche, wounded, 5/JG 26, Me 109E-7 (WN6459), Guines, shot down by Spitfire.

12 July 1941

Lt Horst Ullenberg, SK 2/JG 26, Me 109E-7 (WN3739), Coquelles, shot down by Spitfire.

14 July 1941

Gefr Robert Kleinecke, KIA, 9/JG 26, Me 109F-2 (WN6735), Marquise, shot down by Spitfire.

BADER'S SPITFIRE WING

<u>19 July 1941</u>
Lt Heinz Rahardt, wounded, 2/JG 26, Me 109F-2 (WN8346), Courtrai/Beselere, shot down by Spitfire.

<u>21 July 1941</u>
Ogfr Heinrich Gleixner, KIA, 4/JG 26, Me 109E-7 (WM6512), Lille, shot down by Spitfire.
Ogr Ernt Krämer, KIA, 9/JG 26, Me 109F-2 (WN8847), Radinghem, shot down by Spitfire.
Uffz Alfred Barthel, wounded, 5/JG 26, Me 109E-7 (WN4954), Manighem, shot down by Spitfire.

<u>9 August 1941</u>
Uffz Albert Schlager, KIA, 3/JG 26, Me 109F-4 (WN8350), near Aire, shot down by Spitfire.

Appendix 3

Below are listed the known combat losses of JG 2 Richthofen, between 18 March and 9 August 1941. Other machines were lost, but the cause unclear from surviving German records.

19 May 1941
I/JG 2, Me 109E-7 (WN6506), pilot n/k, baled out unhurt after combat with enemy fighters near Cherbourg.
I/JG 2, Me 109E-7 (WN6439), pilot n/k, baled out and rescued from Channel after combat off Portland.
1/JG 2, Me 109E-7 (WN6439), Uffz Kaspar Amashausend, shot down and killed by enemy fighters 5 km South of Portland.

9 June 1941
7/JG 2, Me 109E-7 (WN5983), White 15 +, Oblt Werner Machold (SK), shot down by AA fire, Swanage area, pilot missing.

17 June 1941
III/JG 2, Me 109F-2 (WN5504), Uffz Heinz Seuffert, shot down and killed in combat with enemy fighters West of Cherbourg.

18 June 1941
II/JG 2, Me 109F-2 (WN5504), pilot n/k, shot-up by enemy fighters and forced-landed at St Ingelvert airfield.
I/JG 2, Me 109E-7 (WN4220), pilot n/k, as above, near Sangatte.

19 June 1941
II/JG 2, Me 109E-4 (WN1431), pilot n/k, Le Havre, damaged in combat.

20 June 1941
1/JG 2, Me 109F-2 (WN n/k), Lt Martin Laube, wounded in combat with enemy fighters over the Channel.

21 June 1941

5/JG 2, Me 109F-2 (WN6724), Uffz Lorenz Dessoy, shot down and wounded by enemy fighters, baled out over Channel, rescued 12 km north-west of Le Treport.

22 June 1941

Stab/JG 2, Me 109F-2 (WM5749), pilot n/k, damaged in combat with enemy fighters and forced-landed at St Omer/Arques airfield.

9/JG 2, Me 109F-2 (WN8220), Le Martin Adolph, killed in combat with enemy fighters, 3 kms north-north-west of Les Hemmes, 1635 hrs.

9/JG 2, Me 109F-2 (WN5479), Uffz Wilhelm Schaaf, shot down in flames over Dunkirk and killed.

23 June 1941

II/JG 2, Me 109F-2 (WN6763), pilot n/k, damaged in combat with enemy fighters and forced-landed at Abbeville/Drucat airfield.

4/JG 2, Me 109F-2 (WN6756), Fw Georg Bock, pilot shot down by enemy fighters and killed at St Condette, 2 km South of Boulogne.

II/JG 2, Me 109F-2 (WN12643), pilot n/k, damaged in combat with enemy fighters, forced-landed on beach at Berck-sur-Mer.

9/JG 2, Me 109F-2 (WN5763), Uffz Hans-Johann Staub, shot down and killed north-west of St Omer.

7/JG 2, Me 109F-2 (WN6755), Lt Wolfgang Diekmann, shot down and killed at St Bourthes, 1400 hrs.

24 June 1941

9/JG 2, Me 109F-2 (WN n/k), Fw Helmut Krause, shot down in combat over Calais, pilot missing.

Stab II/JG 2, Me 109F-2 (WN n/k), Lt Heinz Bolze, shot down and killed 1 km South of Audruicq.

25 June 1941

7/JG 2, Me 109F-2 (WN n/k), Fw Wolfgang Falkinger, shot down over Channel 10 km North of Calais and reported missing.

II/JG 2, Me 109F-2 (WN6762), pilot n/k, damaged in combat with enemy fighters and forced-landed at Calais – Marck airfield.

7/JG 2, Me 109F-2 (WN12709), Lt Christian von Schlieffen, posted missing after combat with enemy fighters over Desvres.

APPENDIX 3

26 June 1941

4/JG 2, Me 109F-2 (WN6759), Uffz Maximillian Meindl, posted missing after combat with enemy fighters over Boulogne. Found dead at Coudekerque (Bruges) following day.

5/JG 2, Me 109F-2 (WN12668), Uffz Walter Reich, killed in combat over Boulogne.

9/JG 2, Me 109F-2 (WN n/k), Fw Paul Paetau, seriously wounded in combat with enemy fighters over De Panne.

2 July 1941

4/JG 2, Me 109F-2 (WN6758), Oblt Hans-Jurgen Hepe (SK), baled out wounded after combat with enemy fighters, 1 km south-west of Cassell.

III/JG 2, Me 109F-2 (WN7518), pilot n/k, damaged in combat with enemy fighters and forced-landed near Fruges.

III/JG 2, Me 109F (WN5330), Fw Heinz Jahner, baled out wounded after combat with enemy fighters over Norrent-Fontes.

3 July 1941

Stab/JG 2, Me 109F-4 (WN7066), Major Wilhelm Balthasar (Kommodore), killed near Aire when a wing on his aircraft failed in combat.

7/JG 2, Me 109F-2 (WN5497), Lt Jakob Augustin wounded in combat with enemy fighters over Lùmbres.

4 July 1941

II/JG 2, Me 109F-4 (WN7049), pilot n/k, damaged by enemy fighters and forced-landed near St Quentin.

4/JG 2, Me 109F-2 (WN12819), Lt Hans Gerlach, shot down and killed by enemy fighters near Béthune.

4/JG 2, Me 109F-2 (WN6749), Fw Edgar Brandt, shot down by enemy fighters near Ligescourt and baled out wounded.

8 July 1941

8/JG 2, Me 109F-1 (WN5726), Uffz Karl Kilian, shot down at killed by enemy fighters at Hesmond, 5 km East of Montreuil.

9 July 1941

3/JG 2, Me 109F-2 (WN12812), Lt Helmut Specht, shot down and killed over St Pol.

BADER'S SPITFIRE WING

<u>10 July 1941</u>
II/JG 2, Me 109F-2 (WN6761), pilot n/k, damaged by enemy fighters and forced-landed at Desvres.

<u>11 July 1941</u>
4/JG 2, Me 109F-2 (WN12822), Uffz Valentin Nawrot, shot down and killed by enemy fighters near Boulogne.

<u>12 July 1941</u>
7/JG 2, Me 109F-2 (WN n/k), Uffz Erich Fröhner, severely wounded in combat with enemy fighters near Hazebrouck.

<u>20 July 1941</u>
6/JG 2, Me 109F-2 (WN12689), Lt Hans-Joachim Dette, shot down and killed by enemy fighters over Abbeville.

<u>21 July 1941</u>
6/JG 2, Me 109F-2 (WN12665), Fw Hans Pirkel, wounded in combat with enemy fighters and forced-landed at St Frévent.
II/JG 2, Me 109F-2 (WN5463), pilot n/k, damaged in combat with enemy fighters and forced-landed near Amiens.

<u>23 July 1941</u>
Stab II/JG 2, Me 109F-2 (WN9662), Lt Günther Behrendt (Adjutant), shot down by enemy fighters over Grigny, 1 km North of Hesdin, and baled out wounded.
3/JG 2, Me 109E-7 (WN n/k), Fw Helmut Schöneman, shot down by enemy fighters and killed at Delettes, 15 km South of St Omer.

<u>24 July 1941</u>
3/JG 2, Me 109E-7 (WN7665), Uffz Walter Vock, shot down by enemy fighters and killed 2 km West of Brest.
1/JG 2, Me 109E-7 (WN6963), Ofw Rudolf Täschner, wounded in combat with enemy fighters near La Rochelle, 1420 hrs.
3/JG 2, Me 109E-7 (WN7671), Lt Julius Meimberg (SK), shot down by enemy fighters and wounded, forced-landed at Brélès, 12 km north-west of St Renan).
2/JG 2, Me 109E-7 (WN6461), Lt Rudolf Schleicher, shot down and killed by enemy fighters at Le Rest, north-east of Plouvien, 1530 hrs.

APPENDIX 3

3/JG 2, Me 109E-7 (WN6457), Fw Erwin Richey, shot down and killed by enemy fighters 1½ km West of Bourg-Blanc (Brest), 1530 hrs.

2/JG 2, Me 109E-7 (WN7693), Uffz Friedrich Schumann, shot down by enemy fighters and killed off Brest, 1530 hrs.

I/JG 2, Me 109E-7 (WN6507), Obgfr Willi Reinz, shot down and killed by enemy fighters 3 km West of Lanilis (Brest), 1515 hrs.

<u>6 August 1941</u>

Erg/JG 2, Me 109E-7 (WN3802), Uffz Helmut Rainer, shot-down and killed on take-off by four RAF Whirlwind fighters, crashed near Théville.

Erg/JG 2, Me 109E-4 (WN1460), pilot n/k, shot down by enemy fighters and baled out over Théville.

<u>7 August 1941</u>

II/JG 2, Me 109F-2 (WN12667), pilot n/k, shot down by enemy fighters and forced-landed at Audembert.

Appendix 4

Oberkommando der Luftwaffe (OKL)
Combat claims, Kanaljäger, Kanalfront (continental time).
18 March 1941 – 9 August 1941

18 March 1941
Oblt Hermann-Friedrich Joppien, Stab I/JG 51, Hurricane, 5 km. South of Lewes, 8,500 m, 1228 hrs.
Oblt Rudolf Busch, Stab I./JG 51, Hurricane, South of Lewes, 8,500 m, 1229 hrs.

19 March 1941
Hptmn Herbert Ihlefeld, Stab I(J)/LG 2, Spitfire, 10 km East of Hastings, 1908 hrs.
Hptmn Herbert Ihlefeld, Stab I(J)/LG 2, Spitfire, 10 km. East of Hastings, 1910 hrs.
Hptmn Heinz Bretnütz, Stab II/JG 53, Spitfire, North of Dungeness, 1720 hrs.

24 March 1941
Lt Friedrich Geißhardt, 1(J)/LG 2, Spitfire, mid-Channel, 1945 hrs.

25 March 1941
Hptmn Herbert Ihlefeld, Stab I(J)/LG 2, Spitfire, Dungeness, 1230 hrs.

27 March 1941
Lt Friedrich Geißhardt, 1(J)/LG 2, Spitfire south-west of Folkestone, 1815 hrs.
Fw Otto Niemeyer, 4/JG 77, Beaufort, 35 km north-west of Morlaix, 2032 hrs.
Uffz Willi Hagel, 4/JG 77, Beaufort, 40 km north of Morlaix, 2032 hrs.

APPENDIX 4

31 March 1941

Lt Enzio von Saalfeld, 7/JG 51, Hurricane, Dungeness-Cap Gris Nez, 5,500 m, 1055 hrs.

Maj Günther von Maltzahn, Stab/JG 53, Spitfire, north-west of Calais, 1135 hrs.

1 April 1941

Fw Georg Bock, 4/JG 2, Hampden, Lannilis, 25 km north-east of Brest, 1527 hrs.

4 April 1941

Maj Adolf Galland, Stab/JG 26, Spitfire, Dover-Canterbury, 1,200 m, 1750 hrs.

Ofw Robert Menge, 3/JG 26, Spitfire, Dover-Deal, 1750 hrs.

Fw Josef Wurmheller, 5/JG 53, Spitfire, 10 km North of Wissant

6 April 1941

Fw Eberhard Bauer, 5/JG 2, Blenheim, 40 km North of Morlaix, 1245 hrs.

Oblt Hans-Jürgen Hepe, 4./JG 2, Blenheim, 6 km North of Plouescat, 1340 hrs.

Hptmn Karl-Heinz Greisert, Stab II/JG 2, Blenheim, Brest, 1600 hrs.

Ofw Walter März, 5/JG 26, Avro Anson, Brignogan, 1340 hrs.

8 April 1941

Oblt Harry Koch, 5/JG 26, Blenheim, Ile de Batz, 1325 hrs.

Lt Hans Kolbow, 5/JG 51, Spitfire, Sheerness, 100 m, 1316 hrs.

9 April 1941

Hptmn Josef Fözö, Stab II/JG 51, Spitfire, 3 km North of Mardyck, 300 m, 1200 hrs.

Fw Josef Wurmheller, 5/JG 53, Spitfire, South of Dover, 1721hrs.

Fw Josef Scheuchenpflug, 5/JG 53, Spitfire, South of Dover, 1721 hrs.

Hptmn Heinz Bretnütz, Stab II/JG 53, Blenheim, West of Southend 1910 hrs.

10 April 1941

Lt Horst Ulenberg, 2/JG 26, 1 PRU Spitfire, North of Ile d' Ouessant, 0922 hrs.

Lt Horst Ulenberg, 2/JG 26, 1 PRU Spitfire, Plouescat, 1925 hrs.

BADER'S SPITFIRE WING

<u>11 April 1941</u>
Oblt Hermann Staiger, 7/JG 51, Spitfire, Dungeness, 1340 hrs.

<u>12 April 1941</u>
Fw Bernhard Lausch, 8/JG 51, Hurricane, Cap Gris Nez, 1355 hrs.

<u>15 April 1941</u>
Obstlt Adolf Galland, Stab/JG 26, Spitfire, 30 km West of Dover: 3,800 m, 1750 hrs.
Obstlt Adolf Galland, Stab/JG 26, Spitfire, between Dover and Margate, 4,500 m, 1800 hrs.
Obstlt Adolf Galland, Stab/JG 26, Spitfire, between Dover and Margate, 4,500 m, also 1800 hrs.
Maj Werner Mölders, Stab/JG 51, Spitfire, south-west of Boulogne, 1800 hrs.
Hptm. Hermann-Friedrich Joppien, Stab I/JG 51, Spitfire, 5 km south-east of Dungeness, 9,500 m, 1233 hrs.
Ofw Franz Barten, 11/JG 51, Spitfire, between St Omer and Boulogne, 7,800-5,000 m, 0845 hrs.

<u>16 April 1941</u>
Oblt Horst Geyer, Stab/JG 51, Spitfire, south-west of Le Touquet, 1825 hrs.
Maj Werner Mölders, Stab/JG 51, Spitfire, 5 km West of Berck-sur-Mer, 1832 hrs.
Oblt Wilfried Balfanz, Stab/JG 51, Spitfire, Dungeness, 1840 hrs.
Maj Werner Mölders, Stab/JG 51, Hurricane, south-west Dungeness, 1842 hrs.
Oblt Hartmann Grasser, Stab/JG 51, Spitfire, Berck-sur-Mer, 1842 hrs.
Lt Heinz Bär, 1/JG 51, Hurricane, Le Touquet, 3-4,000 m, 1825 hrs.
Oblt Hermann-Friedrich Joppien, Stab I./JG 51, Hurricane, 4 km. south-west of Dungeness, 1830 hrs.
Lt Georg Seelmann, 11/JG 51, Hurricane, south-east of Dungeness, 1835 hrs.
Maj Günther von Maltzahn, Stab/JG 53, Spitfire, Dungeness, 1840 hrs.
Lt Herbert Schramm, 7/JG 53, Spitfire, Military Canal, Romney, 1200 hrs.

<u>17 April 1941</u>
Uffz. Emil Babenz, 3/JG 26, Beaufort, North of Brest, 1800 hrs.
Fw Friedrich Heimann, 5/JG 51, Spitfire, 25 km West of Cap Gris Nez, 0850 hrs.

APPENDIX 4

<u>18 April 1941</u>
Fw Helmut Schönemann, ErgSt/JG 2 Spitfire, 25 km WSW of Brighton, 2040 hrs.
Oblt Martin Rysavy, 2/JG 26, Blenheim, 70 km West of Ras de Sein, 0948 hrs.

<u>19 April 1941</u>
Maj Günther von Maltzahn, Stab/JG 53, Spitfire, between Dover and Calais, 1909 hrs.

<u>20 April 1941</u>
Oblt Wilfried Balfanz, Stab/JG 51, Spitfire, West of Sheerness, 1826 hrs.
Oblt Hermann-Friedrich Joppien, 1/JG 51, Spitfire, 20 km North of Cap Gris Nez, 1212 hrs.
Oblt Otto Böhner, 6/JG 53, Spitfire, South of Dover, 1228 hrs.

<u>21 April 1941</u>
Lt Kurt Votel, 1/JG 2, Spitfire, 50 km South of Isle of Wight, 1012 hrs.
Lt Erich Rudorffer, 2/JG 2, Blenheim, 30 km North of Jersey, 1503 hrs.
Oblt Wilfried Balfanz, Stab/JG 51, Spitfire, East of Canterbury, 1943 hrs.
Lt Heinz Bär, 1/JG 51, Hurricane, Ashford, 6,500m, 20.07hrs.
Oblt Hermann-Friedrich Joppien, Stab I/JG 51, Hurricane, north-west of Ashford, 2010 hrs.

<u>24 April 1941</u>
Uffz. Kaspar Amhausend, 1/JG 2, Spitfire, North of Théville, 1607 hrs.

<u>25 April 1941</u>
Oblt Gerhard Michalski, Stab II/JG 53, Spitfire, 5 km West of Walcheren, 1547 hrs.

<u>26 April 1941</u>
Oblt Karl Führing, Stab IV/JG 51, Hurricane, between Le Portel-Boulogne, 1310 hrs.
Oblt August-Wilhelm Schumann, 5/JG 52, Spitfire, north-west of Littlestone, 1417 hrs.
Lt Wolfgang Tonne, 3/JG 53, Spitfire, South of Boulogne 1310 hrs.

<u>28 April 1941</u>
Maj Werner Mölders, Stab/JG 51, Hurricane, Dungeness,1310 hrs.

BADER'S SPITFIRE WING

29 April 1941
Uffz Wilhelm Mink, 5/JG 51, Blenheim, Military Canal, Romney, 1020 hrs.
Gefr Hermann Aubrecht: 5/JG 51, Blenheim, Military Canal, Romney, 1020 hrs.
Oblt Hermann Staiger, 7/JG 51, Hurricane, 5 km North of Dünkirchen, 1012 hrs.
Fw Werner Bielefeldt, 7/JG 51, Hurricane, 10 km. South of Dünkirchen, 1030 hrs.
Obfhr Hans-Herbert Märtens, 7/JG 51, Hurricane, 20 km North of Dünkirchen, 1035 hrs.
Oblt Friedrich-Karl Müller, Stab III/JG 53, Spitfire, Dungeness

1 May 1941
Lt Gustav Denk, 6/JG 52, Blenheim, Location n/k, 1428 hrs.

3 May 1941
Hptmn Heinz Bretnütz, Stab II/JG 53, Spitfire, Dungeness, 1703 hrs.

4 May 1941
Maj Werner Mölders, Stab/JG 51, Hurricane, West of Deal, 1217 hrs.
Hptmn Heinz Bretnütz, Stab II/JG 53, Lysander, North of Deal, 1253 hrs.

6 May 1941
Maj Werner Mölders, Stab/JG 51, Hurricane, Dover, 1200 hrs.
Lt Heinz Bär, 1/JG 51, Spitfire, 15-20 km north-west of Calais, 200 m, 1410 hrs.
Lt Fritz Nächster, 2/JG 51, Spitfire, Calais, 200 m, 1412 hrs.
Lt Walter Krieger, 6/JG 51, Spitfire, north-east of Calais, 300 m, 1425 hrs.
Ma. Friedrich Beckh, Stab IV/JG 51, Spitfire, 20 km North of Cap Blanc Nez, 1355 hrs.
Oblt Karl-Gottfried Nordmann,12/JG 51, Spitfire, 25 km north-west of Calais, 1355 hrs.
Lt Bernd Gallowitsch, 10/JG 51, Spitfire, 5 km West of Dover, 1415 hrs.

7 May 1941
Oblt Gordon Gollob, 4/JG 3, Spitfire, Gravelines, 1125 hrs.
Fw Georg Mayr, 4/JG 52, Spitfire, 3-5 km. East Deal, 5-600 m, 0753-56 hrs.
Gefr Adolf Glunz, 4/JG 52, Spitfire, 3-5 km, East of Deal, 5-600 m.

APPENDIX 4

Fw Rolf Helber, 5/JG 51, Spitfire, 5 km South of Gravelines, 600 m, 1126 hrs.
Oblt Otto Böhner, 6/JG 53, Spitfire, West of Deal, 0630 hrs.
Lt Hans Möller, 6/JG 53, Spitfire, West of Deal, 0631 hrs.
Fw Josef Wurmheller, 5/JG 53, Spitfire, Deal, 0747 hrs.
Oblt Franz Götz, 9/JG 53, Spitfire, West of Dover, 1653 hrs.

8 May 1941
Uffz Heinz Küpper, 2/JG 3, Spitfire, Dungeness, 1230 hrs.
Maj Werner Mölders, Stab/JG 51, Spitfire, Dover 1220 hrs.
Oblt Horst Geyer, Stab/JG 51, Spitfire, Dover, 1220 hrs.
Oblt Horst Geyer, Stab/JG 51, Spitfire, Dover, 1220 hrs.
Oblt Horst Geyer, Stab/JG 51, Spitfire, Dover, 50 m, 1225 hrs.
Hptmn Hermann-Friedrich Joppien, Stab I/JG 51, Hurricane, Folkestone, 8,000 m, 1802 hrs.
Lt Erwin Fleig, 1/JG 51, Hurricane, Dungeness, 800–1.000 m, 1802 hrs.
Hptmn Hermann-Friedrich Joppien, Stab I./JG 51, Hurricane north-east Dungeness, 7,500 m, 1803 hrs.

9 May 1941
Oblt Willy Stange, 8/JG 3, Spitfire, 15 km, Cap Gris Nez, 7,000 m, 1607 hrs.
Maj Günther von Maltzahn, Stab/JG 53, Spitfire, North of Calais.

11 May 1941
Fw Karl Pfeiffer, 3/JG 2, Spitfire, 5 km south-west of Portland, 800-500 m, 2050 hrs.
Uffz Theodor Zingerle, 8/JG 2, Spitfire, Portland, 2041hrs.
Lt Jakob Augustin, 8/JG 2, Spitfire, Portland, 2041 hrs.
Lt Heinz Bär, 1/JG 51, Spitfire, East of Deal, 50 m, 2140 hrs.

12 May 1941
Lt Wolf von Bülow, 5/JG 2, Blenheim, 30 km, West of Boulogne, 1125 hrs.

14 May 1941
Oblt Ernst-Günther Heinze, 8/JG 53, Spitfire, 20 km, Dünkirchen-Ostende, 1840 hrs.
Fw Hans Oechler, 8/JG 53, Spitfire, 20 km, Dünkirchen-Ostende, 1840 hrs.

15 May 1941
Ofw Hans Stechmann, 9/JG 3, Hurricane, Cap Gris Nez, 2055 hrs.

BADER'S SPITFIRE WING

Fw Georg Schentke, 9/JG 3, Hurricane, Cap Gris Nez, 2055 hrs.
Oblt Heinz Schumann, Stab I/JG 51Hurricane, Folkestone, 2004 hrs.

16 May 1941
Hptmn Walter Oesau, Stab III/JG 3, Spitfire, South of Folkestone, 1545 hrs.
Oblt Heinz Altendorf, 7/JG 53Hurricane, 5 km West of Ramsgate, 1605 hrs.

17 May 1941
Maj Wilhelm Balthasar, Stab/JG 2, Hurricane, Dover Straits, 1855 hrs.
Hptmn Heinz Bretnütz, Stab II/JG 53, Hurricane, 30 km South of Harwich, 1918 hrs.
Uffz Alfred Seidl, 8/JG 53, Spitfire, Deal, 1030 hrs.

19 May 1941
Maj Wilhelm Balthasar, Stab/JG 2, Blenheim, South of Isle of Wight, 2020 hrs.
Oblt Johannes Steinhoff, 4/JG 52, Spitfire, North of Dover, 1240 hrs.
Gefr Adolf Glunz, 4/JG 52, Spitfire, Canterbury, 3,000 m, 12.40 hrs.
Fw Georg Mayr, 4/JG 52, Spitfire, North of Dover, 1244 hrs.
Oblt Johannes Steinhoff, 4/JG 52, Spitfire, North of Dover, 1245 hrs.

21 May 1941
Oblt Willy Stange, 8/JG 3, Spitfire, 10 km. West of Calais, 1745 hrs.
Uffz Günther Keil, 8/JG 3, Hurricane, South of Calais, 1750 hrs.
Fw Otto Weßling, 9/JG 3, Blenheim, North of St. Pol.
Oblt. Wilfried Balfanz, Stab/JG 51, Hurricane, north-west of Dünkirchen, 1820 hrs.
Oblt Erich Hohagen, 4/JG 51, Hurricanee, 30 km north-west of Dünkirchen, 1,000–1,500 m, 1755 hrs.
Uffz Wilhelm Mink, 5/JG 51, Hurricane, East of Ramsgate, 1805 hrs.
Maj Friedrich Beckh, Stab IV/JG 51, Hurricane, 10 km North of Calais, 1800 hrs.
Lt Bernd Gallowitsch, 10/JG 51, Hurricane, 10–15 km, East of Deal, 1805 hrs.

25 May 1941
Uffz Kurt Niedereichholz, 1/JG 3, Hurricane, South of Ramsgate, 1610 hrs.
Fw Eberhard von Boremski, 9/JG 3, Hurricane, West of Calais, 0755 hrs.
Uffz Karl-Heinz Wallrath, 8/JG 3, Hurricane, 1455 hrs.
Lt Horst Ulenberg, 2/JG 26, PRU Spitfire, Over sea, 60 km North of Brest, 0901 hrs.

APPENDIX 4

28 May 1941
Hptmn Walter Oesau, Stab III/JG 3, Hurricane, North of Calais, 1925 hrs.
Oblt Johann Knauth, 10/JG 51, Spitfire, 15 km North of Calais, 7,500 m, 1925 hrs.
Uffz. Kurt Braasch, 5/JG 53, Spitfire, Boulogne, 1923 hrs.

31 May 1941
Uffz Hans Schleef, 7/JG 3, Blenheim, location n/k, 1743 hrs.

9 June 1941
Ofw Robert Menge, 3/JG 26, Spitfire, East of Dover, 1410 hrs.
Lt Wolfgang Kosse, 5/JG 26, Blenheim, Kanalenge, 1710 hrs.
Oblt Walter Schneider, 6/JG 26, Wellington, Knokke, 1745 hrs.
Oblt Hans-Jürgen Westphal, 8/JG 26, Spitfire, Dover, 1412 hrs.

11 June 1941
Fw Wolfgang Falkinger, 7/JG 2, Lysander, 5 km. West of Dawlish, 1905 hrs.
Lt Johannes Schmidt, 3/JG 26, Hurricane, mid-Channel, 1325 hrs.
Hptmn Johannes Seifert, 3/JG 26, Hurricane, mid-Channel, 1330 hrs.
Oblt Kurt Ebersberger, 4/JG 26, Spitfire, Nieuport, 1655 hrs.

13 June 1941
Obstlt Adolf Galland, Stab/JG 26, Hurricane, 5 km West of Dover, 3.500 m, 1315 hrs.
Obstlt Adolf Galland, Stab/JG 26, Hurricane, 10 km. north-east of Ashford, 2,000 m.

14 June 1941
Uffz Gerhard Oemler, 9/JG 26Blenheim, north-west of Calais, 0725 hrs.

16 June 1941
Obstlt Adolf Galland, Stab/JG 26, Hurricane, West of Boulogne, 3,000 m, 1635 hrs.
Fw Erwin Leibold, 3/JG 26, Spitfire, West of Boulogne, 1,800 m, 1622 hrs.
Hptm. Rolf Pingel, Stab I./JG 26, Blenheim, south-east of Boulogne, 1635 hrs.
Oblt Josef Priller, 1/JG 26, Spitfire, Boulogne, 1635 hrs.
Lt Robert Unzeitig, 1/JG 26, Spitfire, north-west of Boulogne, 1637 hrs.
Uffz. Albrecht Held, 1/JG 26, Brewster, south-west of Boulogne, 1641 hrs.

BADER'S SPITFIRE WING

Oblt Josef Priller, 1/JG 26, Blenheim, south-west of Boulogne, 1645 hrs.
Oblt Heinrich Gottlob, 1/JG 26, Spitfire, south-east of Dungeness, 1650 hrs.
Hptmn Rolf Pingel, Stab I/JG 26, Spitfire, South of Dungeness, 1652 hrs.
Lt Horst Ulenberg, 2/JG 26, Spitfire, South of Folkestone, 1732 hrs.
Oblt Martin Rysavy, 2/JG 26, Spitfire, South of Hythe, 1820 hrs.
Fw Ernst Jäckel, 2/JG 26, Spitfire, south-east of Dungeness, 1830 hrs.
Oblt Hans-Jürgen Westphal, 8/JG 26, Spitfire, Boulogne-Etaples, 1625 hrs.
Oblt Gustav Sprick, 8/JG 26, Spitfire, Dungeness, 1635 hrs.
Oblt Hans-Jürgen Westphal, 8/JG 26, Spitfire, 40 km West of Boulogne, 1700 hrs.

17 June 1941
Obstlt. Adolf Galland, Stab/JG 26, Hurricane, 15 km West of St. Omer, 3,500 m, 1938 hrs.
Obstlt Adolf Galland, Stab/JG 26, Hurricane, 5 km south-east of Boulogne, 3,500 m, 1940 hrs.
Oblt Christian Eickhoff, 2/JG 26, Spitfire, north-west of Cap Gris Nez, 1940 hrs.
Oblt Josef Priller, 1/JG 26, Hurricane, West of Cap Gris Nez, 1942 hrs.
Lt Johann Aistleitner, 1/JG 26, Hurricane north-west of Boulogne, 1947 hrs.
Oblt Martin Rysavy, 2/JG 26, Hurricane, north-west of Cap Gris Nez, 1952 hrs.
Hptmn Walter Adolph, Stab II/JG 26, Hurricane, Boulogne, 1950 hrs.
Lt Ernst Janda, 4/JG 26, Hurricane, Cap Gris Nez, 1950 hrs.
Uffz. Bartolomäus Eierstock, 9/JG 26, Spitfire, north-west of Cap Gris Nez, 1935 hrs.
Oblt Hans-Jürgen Westphal, 8/JG 26, Spitfire, Etaples, 6,000 m, 1940 hrs.
Hptmn Gerhard Schöpfel, Stab III/JG 26, Hurricane, location not known, 1940 hrs.
Oblt Gustav Sprick, 8/JG 26, Hurricane, North of Etaples, 1942 hrs.
Ofw Max Martin, 8/JG 26, Hurricane, North of Etaples, 1945 hrs.
Oblt Hans-Jürgen Westphal, 8/JG 26, Spitfire, Dover Straits, 1945 hrs.
Lt Erdmann Neumann, 9/JG 26, Spitfire, Dover Straits, 1952 hrs.
Oblt Gustav Sprick, 8/JG 26, Hurricane, Dover Straits, 1958 hrs.
Hptmn Josef Haiböck, Stab III/JG 26, Spitfire, St Omer, 2000 hrs.
Lt Egon Mayer, 7/JG 2, Spitfire, Noth of Cherbourg, 1750 hrs.

18 June 1941
Obstlt Adolf Galland, Stab/JG 26, Spitfire, 1½ km East of Ardres, 6,500 m, 1818 hrs.

APPENDIX 4

Oblt. Gustav Sprick, 8/JG 26, Spitfire, 1820 hrs.
Gruppenabschuss, II & III/JG 26, Spitfire, north-west Cap Gris Nez, 2,000 m, 1835 hrs.

19 June 1941
Uffz Bartolomäus Eierstock, 9/JG 26, Spitfire, north-west of Cap Gris Nez, 3,500 m, 1935 hrs.

21 June 1941
Ofw Kurt Bühligen, 4/JG 2, Spitfire, Boulogne-Hardelot, 1636 hrs.
Oblt. Helmut-Felix Bolz, 5/JG 2, Hurricane, Boulogne-Hardelot, 1640 hrs.
Oblt Jürgen Hepe, 4/JG 2, Spitfire, Boulogne-Hardelot, 1645 hrs.
Oblt Jürgen Hepe, 4/JG 2, Spitfire, West of Le Touquet, 1647 hrs.
Uffz Willi Morzinek, 4/JG 2, Spitfire
Lt Siegfried Schnell, 4/JG 2, Spitfire, West of Le Touquet, 1648 hrs.
Lt Siegfried Schnell, 4/JG 2, Spitfire, West of Le Touquet, 1649 hrs.
Lt Martin Brachmann, 5/JG 2, Spitfire, West of Le Touquet, 1650 hrs.
Ofw Kurt Bühligen, 4/JG 2, Spitfire, Boulogne-Le Touquet, 1650 hrs.
Ofw Kurt Bühligen, 4/JG 2, Spitfire, Boulogne-Le Touquet, 1651 hrs.
Hptmn Karl-Heinz Greisert, Stab II/JG 2, Spitfire, Boulogne-Hardelot, time n/k.
Obstlt Adolf Galland, Stab/JG 26, Spitfire, South of St. Omer, 3,500 m, 1232 hrs.
Obstlt Adolf Galland, Stab/JG 26, Spitfire, north-west of St. Omer, 3,500 m, 1236 hrs.
Obstlt Adolf Galland, Stab/JG 26, Spitfire, North of Etaples, 5,000 m, 1637 hrs.
Oblt Josef Priller, 1/JG 26, Spitfire, south-west of Ramsgate, 1240 hrs.
Fw Ernst Jäckel, 2/JG 26, Spitfire, West of Boulogne, 1630 hrs.
Oblt Martin Rysavy, 2/JG 26, Spitfire, Cap Gris Nez – Boulogne, 200 m, 1631hrs.
Oblt Eberhard Mätzke, 4/JG 26, Spitfire, North of Lederzeele, 3,500 m, 1320 hrs.
Uffz Bartholomäus Eierstock, 9/JG 26, Spitfire, location n/k, 1250 hrs.
Lt Johannes Naumann, 9/JG 26, Hurricane, West of Boulogne, 1635 hrs.
Ofw Max Martin, 8/JG 26, Spitfire, West of Boulogne, 1640 hrs.
Oblt. Gustav Sprick, 8/JG 26, Hurricane, West of Boulogne, 1642 hrs.
Oblt Gustav Sprick, 8/JG 26, Spitfire, 20 km south-west of Boulogne, 1655 hrs.

BADER'S SPITFIRE WING

22 June 1941
Hptmn Wilhelm Balthasar, Stab/JG 2, Blenheim, location n/k, 1600 hrs.
Hptmn Wilhelm Balthasar, Stab/JG 2, Blenheim, location n/k, 1602 hrs.
Oblt Rudolf Pflanz, Stab/JG 2, Spitfire, location n/k, 1609 hrs.
Oblt Erich Leie, Stab/JG 2, Spitfire, St. Omer – Arques,1610 hrs.
Lt Theo Eicher, 4/JG 2, Spitfire, location n/k, 1610hrs.
Hptmn Karl-Heinz Griesert, Stab II/JG 2, Spitfire, location n/k, 1615 hrs.
Lt Siegfried Schnell, 4/JG 2, Spitfire, location n/k, 1620 hrs.
Hptmn Rolf Pingel, Stab I/JG 26,Spitfire, West of Dünkirchen, 1610 hrs.
Hptmn Walter Adolph, Stab II/JG 26, Spitfire, location n/k, 1600 hrs.
Oblt Hans-Jürgen Westphal, 8/JG 26, Spitfire, off Gravelines, 1610 hrs.
Oblt. Gustav Sprick, 8/JG 26, Spitfire, off Gravelines, 1620 hrs.

23 June 1941
Hptmn Wilhelm Balthasar, Stab/JG 2, Blenheim, 10 km North of Dünkirchen, 2030 hrs.
Hptmn Wilhelm Balthasar, Stab/JG 2, Blenheim, 10 km North of Dünkirchen, 2033 hrs.
Uffz Karl-Heinz Rotte, 6/JG 2, Blenheim, location n/k, 1246 hrs.
Uffz Willi Morzinek, 4/JG 2, Spitfire, East of Dungeness, 1400 hrs.
Fw Edgar Brandt, 4/JG 2, Spitfire, location n/k, 2018 hrs.
Oblt Jürgen Hepe, 4/JG 2, Blenheim, location n/k, 2019 hrs.
Lt Siegfried Schnell, 4/JG 2, Spitfire, location n/k, 2019 hrs.
Lt Hans Gerlach, 4/JG 2, Spitfire, location n/k, 2020 hrs.
Lt Siegfried Schnell, 4/JG 2, Blenheim, location n/k, 2020 hrs.
Lt Siegfried Schnell, 4/JG 2, Blenheim, location n/k, 2022 hrs.
Lt Walter Höhler, 7/JG 2, Spitfire, location n/k, 2030 hrs.
Lt Egon Mayer, 7/JG 2, Spitfire, no other details.
Lt Egon Mayer, 7/JG 2, Spitfire, second claim, no other details.
Hptmn Johannes Seifert, Stab I/JG 26, Spitfire, Samer, 1350 hrs.
Oblt Josef Priller, 1/JG 26, Spitfire, South of Somme Mouth, 1335 hrs.
Oblt Heinrich Gottlob, 1/JG 26, Spitfire, north-west of Calais, 2050 hrs.
Oblt Kurt Ebersberger, 4/JG 26, Spitfire, St Omer, 2040 hrs.
Hptmn Gerhard Schöpfel,Stab III/JG 26,Blenheim, Over Channel, 10 km North of Dünkirchen, 2030 hrs.

24 June 1941
Hptmn Wilhelm Balthasar, Stab/JG 2, Spitfire, location n/k, 2050 hrs.
Oblt Erich Leie, Stab/JG 2, Spitfire, East of Calais, 2055 hrs.

APPENDIX 4

Oblt Erich Leie, Stab/JG 2, Spitfire, North of Calais, 2057 hrs.
Lt Heinz Bolze, Stab II/JG 2, Spitfire, location n/k, 2038 hrs.
Lt Siegfried Schnell, 4/JG 2, Spitfire, location n/k, 2044 hrs.
Lt Egon Mayer, 7/JG 2, Spitfire, location n/k, 2042hrs.
Fw Wolfgang Falkinger, 7/JG 2, Spitfire, 20 km north-north-west of Calais, 4,000 m, 2055 hrs.
Hptmn Hans Hahn, Stab III/JG 2, Spitfire, north-west of Calais, 2100 hrs.
Uffz Willi Stratmann, 7/JG 2, Spitfire, north-north-west of Calais, 2100 hrs.
Fw Josef Brenner, 7/JG 2, Spitfire, north-north-west of Calais, 2105 hrs.
Ofw Walter Meyer, 6/JG 26, Spitfire, Calais, 2040 hrs.
Ofw Willy Roth, 4/JG 26, Spitfire, Gravelines, 7,000 m, 2055 hrs.
Oblt Gustav Sprick, 8/JG 26, Spitfire, off Gravelines, 2058 hrs.

25 June 1941
Oblt Rudolf Pflanz, Stab/JG 2, Spitfire, location n/k, 1255 hrs.
Fw Günther Seeger, Stab/JG 2, Spitfire, South of Calais, 1257 hrs.
Hptmn Wilhelm Balthasar, Stab/JG 2, Spitfire, location n/k, 1300 hrs.
Oblt Erich Leie, Stab/JG 2, Spitfire, North of Boulogne, 1630 hrs.
Hptmn Wilhelm Balthasar, Stab/JG 2, Spitfire, location n/k, 1645 hrs.
Uffz Willi Morzinek, 4/JG 2, Spitfire, south-east of Dünkirchen, 1255 hrs.
Lt Siegfried Schnell, 4/JG 2, Spitfire, location n/k, 1632 hrs.
Lt Günther Behrendt, 4/JG 2, Spitfire, location n/k, 1635 hrs.
Lt Siegfried Schnell, 4/JG 2, Spitfire, location n/k, 1640 hrs.
Lt Christian von Schlieffen, Stab III/JG 2, Spitfire, location n/k, 1258 hrs.
Hptmn Hans Hahn, Stab III/JG 2 Spitfire, Marquise, 1631 hrs.
Lt Egon Mayer, 7/JG 2, Spitfire, location n/k, 1635hrs.
Lt Walter Höhler, 7/JG 2, Spitfire, location n/k, 1635 hrs.
Ofw Rudolf Krull, 7/JG 2, Spitfire, location n/k, 1640 hrs.
Oblt Martin Rysavy, 2/JG 26, Spitfire, South of Dünkirchen, 1240 hrs.
Oblt Martin Rysavy, 2/JG 26, Spitfire, south-west of Dünkirchen, 1256 hrs.
Oblt Josef Priller, 1/JG 26, Spitfire, West of Gravelines, 1300 hrs.
Lt Johannes Schmidt, 3/JG 26, Spitfire, 10 km North of Dünkirchen, 1645 hrs.
Oblt Walter Schneider, 6/JG 26, Spitfire, South of Dünkirchen, 1640 hrs.

26 June 1941
Stabs-Fw Erwin Kley, 1/JG 2, Blenheim, location n/k, 0915 hrs.
Lt Siegfried Schnell, 4/JG 2, Spitfire, location n/k, 1142 hrs.
Fw Edgar Brandt, 4/JG 2, Spitfire, location n/k, 1143 hrs.

BADER'S SPITFIRE WING

Oblt Helmut-Felix Bolz, 5/JG 2Spitfire, location n/k, 1155 hrs.
Hptmn Hans Hahn, Stab III/JG 2, Spitfire, Dünkirchen, 1135 hrs.
Lt Horst Sternberg, 5/JG 26, Spitfire, Dünkirchen, 1150 hrs.
Hptmn Walter Adolph, Stab II/JG 26, Spitfire, Mardyck, 1155 hrs.

27 June 1941
Hptmn Balthasar, Stab/JG 2, Spitfire, location n/k, 2203 hrs.
Hptmn Wilhelm Balthasar, Stab/JG 2, Blenheim, location n/k, 2207 hrs.
Lt Siegfried Schnell, 4/JG 2, Spitfire, location n/k, 2130 hrs.
Lt Siegfried Schnell, 4/JG 2, Spitfire, location n/k, 2132 hrs.
Oblt Josef Priller, 1/JG 26, Spitfire, south-west Gravelines, 1000 hrs.
Uffz Albrecht Held, 1/JG 26, Spitfire, North of Dünkirchen, 1007 hrs.
Fw. Ernst Jäckel, 2/JG 26, Spitfire, East of Sangatte, 1010 hrs.
Hptmn Rolf Pingel, Stab I/JG 26,Spitfire, near Roubaix, 2143 hrs.
Oblt Kurt Ebersberger, 4/JG 26, Spitfire, near Marquise, 1659 hrs.
Hptmn Gerhard Schöpfel, Stab III/JG 26, Hurricane, location n/k, 1705 hrs.

28 June 1941
Uffz Emil Babenz, 3/JG 26, Spitfire, West of Lille, 0825 hrs.
Hptmn Gerhard Schöpfel,Stab III/JG 26, Spitfire, Audruicq, 0850 hrs.
Ofw Reische, 1[F]/123, Spitfire, location n/k, 4,000 m, 1550 hrs.
Lt Bethke, 1/JG 52, location n/k, Stirling1610 hrs.
Lt Mikosek, 1/JG 52, Stirlimng, location n/k, 200-300 m, 1620 hrs.

30 June 1941
Fw Erwin Richey, 3/JG 2, Spitfire, location n/k, 1828 hrs.
Fw Karl Pfeiffer, 3/JG 2, Spitfire, location n/k, 1845 hrs.
Oblt Josef Priller, 1/JG 26, Spitfire, 10 km north-west of St Inglevert, 1856 hrs.

30 June 1941
Hptmn Rudolf Bieber, Stab I/JG 26, location n/k, Spitfire, time n/k.

2 July 1941
Fw Günther Seeger, Stab/JG 2, Blenheim, South of Paradière/south-east Merville, 2,500 m, 1245 hrs.
Ofw Rudolf Täschner, 1/JG 2, Spitfire, location n/k, 1245 hrs.
Oblt Jürgen Hepe, 4/JG 2, Spitfire, location n/k, 1255 hrs.
Lt Bruno Stolle, 8/JG 2, Spitfire, West of Armentières, 5,000 m, 1235 hrs.

APPENDIX 4

Fw Heinz Jahner, 9/JG 2, Spitfire, location n/k, 1237 hrs.
Lt Egon Mayer, 7/JG 2, Blenheim, location n/k, 1238 hrs.
Lt Friedrich Kellner, 7/JG 2, Spitfire, location n/k, 1245 hrs.
Hptmn Hans Hahn, Stab III/JG 2, Spitfire, Hazebrouck, time n/k.
Lt Egon Mayer, 7/JG 2, Spitfire, location n/k, 1355hrs.
Obstlt Adolf Galland, Stab/JG 26, Blenheim, Merville, 4.000 m, 1230 hrs.
Hptmn Rudolf Bieber, Stab I/JG 26, Blenheim, South of Merville airfield, 1235 hrs.
Oblt Josef Priller, 1/JG 26, Spitfire, 10 km West of Lille, 1245 hrs.
Lt Horst Ulenberg, 2/JG 26, Spitfire, East of Bouckerque, 1250 hrs.
Hptmn Rolf Pingel, Stab I/JG 26, Hurricane, South of Dünkirchen, 1250 hrs.
Oblt Walter Schneider, 6/JG 26, Spitfire, Mardyck, 1255 hrs.
Hptmn Gerhard Schöpfel, Stab III/JG 26, Spitfire, South of Lillers, 2,500-3,000 m, 1250 hrs.
Ofw Max Martin, 8/JG 26, Spitfire, St Omer, 1410 hrs.

3 July 1941
Oblt Rudolf Pflanz, Stab/JG 2, Spitfire, location n/k, 1150 hrs.
Lt Julius Meimberg, 3/JG 2, Spitfire, location n/k, 1539 hrs.

Fw. Karl Pfeiffer, 3/JG 2, Spitfire, North of Hazebrouck, 1547 hrs.
Lt Egon Mayer, 7/JG 2, Spitfire, location n/k, 1146 hrs.
Lt Egon Mayer, 7/JG 2, Spitfire, location n/k, 1536hrs.
Lt Siegfried Schnell, 9/JG 2, Spitfire, Dünkirchen-Gravelines, 1540 hrs.
Lt Karl-Joachim Harder, 2/JG 26, Spitfire, South of Bouckerque, 1545 hrs.
Lt Johannes Naumann, 9/JG 26, Spitfire, location n/k, 1145 hrs.

4 July 1941
Fw Erwin Richey, 3/JG 2, Spitfire, location n/k, 1505 hrs.
Lt Günther Behrendt, 4/JG 2, Spitfire, location n/k, 1505 hrs.
Hptmn Karl-Heinz Greisert, Stab II/JG 2, Spitfire, location n/k, 1510 hrs.
Uffz Karl Nowak, 9./JG 2, Blenheim (shared with Flak battery), location n/k, 1504 hrs.
Lt Siegfried Schnell, 9/JG 2, Spitfire, location n/k, 1505 hrs.
Lt Siegfried Schnell, 9/JG 2, Spitfire, location n/k, 1507 hrs.
Lt Siegfried Schnell, 9/JG 2, Spitfire, location n/k, 1515 hrs.
Lt Siegfried Schnell, 9/JG 2, Spitfire, location n/k, 1643 hrs.
Oblt Josef Priller, 1/JG 26, Spitfire, 10 km south-west of St Omer, 1455 hrs.
Gefr Ernst Christof, 1/JG 26, Spitfire, West of St Omer, 1458 hrs.

BADER'S SPITFIRE WING

Hptmn Johannes Seifert, 3/JG 26, Spitfire, 6 km North of Béthune, 1520 hrs.
Ofw Erwin Busch, 9/JG 26, Spitfire, location n/k, 1505 hrs.

5 July 1941
Oblt Helmut-Felix Bolz, 5/JG 2, Spitfire, location n/k, 1315 hrs.
Lt Egon Mayer, 7/JG 2, Spitfire, location n/k, 1236 hrs.
Lt Bruno Stolle, 8/JG 2, Blenheim, location n/k 1330 hrs.
Lt Horst Ulenberg, 2/JG 26, Spitfire, St Herberthout, 6,000 m, 1325 hrs.
Oblt Josef Priller, 1/JG 26, Spitfire, north-west of Dünkirchen, 1340 hrs.
Lt Robert Unzeitig, 1/JG 26, Spitfire, West of Dünkirchen, 1340 hrs.

6 July 1941
Oblt Erich Leie, Stab/JG 2, Spitfire, 30 km North of Grand Fort Phillipe, 1435 hrs.
Fw Günther Seeger, Stab/JG 2, Spitfire, 10 km Est of Dover, 1445 hrs.
Ofw Hans Tilly, 3/JG 2, Spitfire, location n/k, 1440 hrs.
Ofw Rudolf Täschner, 1/JG 2, Spitfire, location n/k, 1440 hrs.
Ofw Rudolf Täschner, 1/JG 2, Spitfire, location n/k, 1445 hrs.
Lt Siegfried Schnell, 9/JG 2, Spitfire, location n/k, 1440 hrs.
Lt Horst Ulenberg, 2/JG 26, Spitfire, 5 km north-west of Dünkirchen, 2,500 m, 1448 hrs.
Oblt Walter Otte, 3/JG 26, Spitfire, Houten, 1436 hrs.
Lt Horst Ulenberg, 2/JG 26, Spitfire, north-west of Dünkirchen, 1425 hrs.
Lt Friedrich Uiberacker, 1/JG 26, Spitfire, north-west of Dünkirchen, 1455 hrs.
Hptmn Walter Adolph, Stab II./JG 26, Spitfire, between Wormhoudt and Calais, 5,000 m, 1445 hrs.

7 July 1941
Ofw Kurt Bühligen, 4/JG 2, Spitfire, location n/k, 1532 hrs.
Lt Erich Rudorffer, Stab II/JG 2, Spitfire, East of Boulogne, 1535 hrs.
Lt Erich Rudorffer, Stab II/JG 2, Spitfire, East of Boulogne, 1540 hrs.
Hptmn Hans Hahn, Stab III/JG 2, Hurricane, 7 km West of Le Touquet, 3,000 m, 1536 hrs.
Hptmn Hans Hahn, Stab III/JG 2, Hurricane, 7–10 km West of Le Touquet, 3,000 m, 1537 hrs.
Oblt Josef Priller, 1/JG 26, Spitfire, North of Gravelines, 1000 hrs.
Oblt Walter Otte, 3/JG 26, Spitfire, mid-Channel, 1045 hrs.
Oblt Josef Priller, 1/JG 26, Spitfire, West of the Somme's Mouth, 1047 hrs.

APPENDIX 4

Lt Robert Unzeitig, 1/JG 26, Spitfire, south-west of Boulogne, 1056 hrs.
Uffz Albrecht Held, 1/JG 26, Spitfire, south-west of Boulogne, 1058 hrs.
Lt Hans-Georg Dippel, 2/JG 26, Spitfire, Samer, 1520 hrs.

8 July 1941
Lt Helmut Specht, 3/JG 2, Hurricane, Béthune, 600 m, 0635 hrs.
Lt Siegfried Schnell, 9/JG 2, Spitfire, south-west of Bergues, 4,000 m, 0645 hrs.
Lt Siegfried Schnell, 9/JG 2, Spitfire, south-west Bergues, 1545 hrs.
Ofw Magnus Brunkhorst, 9/JG 2, Spitfire, location n/k, 1548 hrs.
Hptmn Hans Hahn, Stab III/JG 2 Spitfire, Calais-Marck, 1552 hrs.
Uffz Albrecht Held, 1/JG 26, Spitfire, Merckeghem, 0635 hrs.
Lt Johann Aistleitner, 1/JG 26, Spitfire, 10 km north-west of Cap Gris Nez, 1,200 m, 0640 hrs.
Oblt Josef Priller, 1/JG 26, Spitfire, North of St Omer, 1530 hrs.
Uffz Ulrich Grebe, 1/JG 26, Spitfire, soth-east of Dünkirchen, 1540 hrs.
Uffz. Ulrich Grebe, 1/JG 26, Spitfire, North of Dünkirchen, 1545 hrs.
Oblt Werner Kahse, 1/JG 26, Spitfire, 20 km, north-north-west of Coxyde, 1545 hrs.
Uffz Hans-Jürgen Fröhlich, 2/JG 26, Spitfire, north-east of Calais, 1550 hrs.
Lt Paul Schauder, 3/JG 26, Spitfire, 8 km north-east Gravelines, 1550 hrs.
Hptmn Walter Adolph, Stab II/JG 26, Spitfire, Gravelines, 1530 hrs.
Ofw Walter Meyer, 6/JG 26, Spitfire, Hazebrouck, 1540 hrs.
Uffz Karl Finke, 6/JG 26, Spitfire, South of Ypern, time n/k.

9 July 1941
Lt Erich Rudorffer, Stab II/JG 2, Spitfire, south-west of St Omer, 1340 hrs.
Lt Erich Rudorffer, Stab II/JG 2, Hurricane, north-west of St Omer, 1345 hrs.
Uffz Valentin Nawrot, 4/JG 2, Spitfire, North of St Omer, 1345 hrs.
Lt Martin Brachmann, 5/JG 2, Spitfire, Calais, 1404 hrs.
Oblt Werner Stöckelmann, Stab III/JG 2, Spitfire, location n/k, 1357 hrs.
Lt Siegfried Schnell, 9/JG 2, Spitfire, location n/k, 1357 hrs.
Lt Siegfried Schnell, 9/JG 2, Spitfire, location n/k, 1359 hrs.
Uffz. Karl Nowak, 9/JG 2, Spitfire, location n/k, 1400 hrs.
Lt Siegfried Schnell, 9/JG 2, Spitfire, location n/k, 1405 hrs.
Lt Egon Mayer, 7/JG 2, Spitfire, location n/k, 1405 hrs.
Lt Siegfried Schnell, 9/JG 2, Spitfire, location n/k, 1610 hrs.
Lt Siegfried Schnell, 9/JG 2, Spitfire, location n/k, 1620 hrs.
Lt Siegfried Schnell, 9/JG 2, Spitfire, location n/k, 1622 hrs.

BADER'S SPITFIRE WING

Oblt Josef Priller, 1/JG 26, Spitfire, South of Aire, 1400 hrs.
Oblt Christian Eickhoff, 2/JG 26, Spitfire, 10 km south-west of St Omer, 1405 hrs.
Oblt Josef Priller, 1/JG 26, Spitfire, 2 km South of Calais, 1410 hrs.
Lt Horst Ulenberg, 2/JG 26, Spitfire, 10 km North of Etaples, 1415 hrs.
Ofw Max Martin, 8/JG 26, Spitfire, St Omer, 1410 hrs.

10 July 1941
Fw Günther Seeger, Stab/JG 2, Spitfire, south-east of Cassel, 1215 hrs.
Oblt Rudolf Pflanz, Stab/JG 2, Spitfire, location n/k, 1237 hrs.
Ofw Kurt Bühligen, 4/JG 2, Spitfire, location n/k, 1218 hrs.
Ofw Kurt Bühligen, 4/JG 2, Spitfire, location n/k, 1221 hrs.
Lt Erich Rudorffer, Stab II/JG 2, Spitfire, location n/k, 1230 hrs.
Hptmn Hans Hahn, Stab III/JG 2, Spitfire, St. Omer, 1208 hrs.
Lt Egon Mayer, 7/JG 2, Spitfire, location n/k, 1208hrs.
Stabs-Fw Franz Willinger, 8/JG 2, Spitfire, near Watten, 1210 hrs.
Hptmn Hans Hahn, Stab III/JG 2, Spitfire, St. Omer, 1212 hrs.
Lt Jakob Augustin, 8/JG 2, Spitfire, location n/k, 2035 hrs.
Uffz Heinz Scheibner, 1Erg/JG 2, Blenheim, Cherbourg, 1233 hrs.
Fw Otto Bach, 1Erg/JG 2, Spitfire, Cherbourg, 1233 hrs.
Uffz Walter Hasse, 1Erg/JG 2, Spitfire, Cherbourg, 1234 hrs.
Uffz Helmuth Augustin, 1 Erg/JG 2, Spitfire, Cherbourg, 1240 hrs.
Oblt Josef Priller, 1/JG 26, Spitfire, North of St. Omer, 1230 hrs.
Oblt Josef Priller, 1/JG 26, Spitfire, north-west of Boulogne, 1240 hrs.
Lt Robert Unzeitig, 1/JG 26, Spitfire, North of Cap Gris Nez, 1243 hrs.

11 July 1941
Ofw Kurt Bühligen, 4/JG 2, Spitfire, location n/k, 1455 hrs.
Lt Erich Rudorffer, Stab II/JG 2, Jagdgeschwader Spitfire, North of Boulogne, 1500 hrs.
Lt Walter Höhler, 7/JG 2, Spitfire, location n/k, 1508 hrs.
Hptmn Johannes Seifert, Stab I/JG 26, Spitfire, East of Wimereux, 1505 hrs.
Lt Horst Ulenberg, 2/JG 26, Spitfire, West of Cap Gris Nez, 1520 hrs.
Oblt Josef Priller, 1/JG 26, Spitfire, West of Calais, 1610 hrs.
Lt Horst Ulenberg, 2/JG 26, Spitfire, south-east, Dünkirchen, 1620 hrs.
Lt Hans-Jürgen Harder, 2/JG 26, Spitfire, North of Calais-Mardyck, 1623 hrs.
Fw Emil Babenz, 3/JG 26, Spitfire, 10 km, north-west of Gravelines, 4,000 m, 1630 hrs.
Hptmn Gerhard Schöpfel, Stab III/JG 26, Spitfire, location n/k, 1455 hrs.

APPENDIX 4

12 July 1941
Fw Karl Pfeiffer, 3/JG 2, Spitfire, North of Morlaix, 1055 hrs.
Lt Egon Mayer, 7/JG 2, Spitfire, location n/k, 1926hrs.
Lt Egon Mayer, 7/JG 2, Spitfire, location n/k,1928 hrs.

14 July 1941
Lt Wolfgang Flügel, 1Erg./JG 2, Spitfire, Cherbourg, 0759 hrs.
Hptmn Johannes Seifert, Stab I/JG 26, Spitfire, South of Dünkirchen, 1030 hrs.
Oblt Josef Priller, 1/JG 26, Spitfire, South of Dünkirchen, 1030 hrs.
Uffz Ernst Christof, 1/JG 26, Spitfire, 10 km off Dover, 1040 hrs.
Oblt Otto Meyer, 8/JG 26, Spitfire, location n/k, 1020 hrs.
Fw Günther Höfer, 1[F]/123, Spitfire, location n/k, 1425 hrs.

17 July 1941
Lt Julius Meimberg, 3/JG 2, Spitfire, North of Etaples, 1617 hrs.
Ltn. Hans Schneider, 1Erg/JG 2, Blenheim, Cherbourg, 1510 hrs.
Fw Otto Bach, 1Erg/JG 2, Blenheim, Cherbourg, time n/k.
Uffz Heinz-Günther Adam, 2/JG 26, Spitfire, South of Cassel, 2100 hrs.

18 July 1941
Oblt Walter Otte, 3/JG 26, Blenheim, South of Mardyck, 1125 hrs.
Lt Paul Schauder, 3/JG 26, Blenheim, between Gravelines and Dünkirchen, 1128 hrs.
Fw Erwin Leibold, 3/JG 26, Spitfire, between Mardyck and St. Pol, 1129 hrs.
Uffz Hans-Jürgen Fröhlich, 2/JG 26, Spitfire, 10–15 km north-west of Dünkirch, 1130 hrs.
Fw Ernst Jäckel, 2/JG 26, Stirling, south-east of Lille, 1140 hrs.
Ofw Walter Meyer, 6/JG 26, Spitfire, north-west of Dünkirchen, 1220 hrs.

19 July 1941
Lt Erich Rudorffer, 6/JG 2, Spitfire, south-east of Calais, 1425 hrs.
Lt Josef Hayartz, Stab I/JG 26, Spitfire, North of Dünkirchen (4-5 km out to sea), 1415 hrs.
Oblt Christian Eickhoff, 2/JG 26, Stirling, south-east of Bergues, 1425 hrs.
Oblt Josef Priller, 1/JG 26, Spitfire, 5 km off Dover, 1435 hrs.

20 July 1941
Ofw Max Martin, 8/JG 26, Curtiss P-40, Channel, West of Le Touquet, 1605 hrs.

BADER'S SPITFIRE WING

21 July 1941

Fw Günther Seeger, Stab/JG 2, Spitfire, 5 km south-east of Boulogne, 2045 hrs.
Uffz Friedrich Schellbach, 7/JG 2, Spitfire, location n/k, 0835 hrs.
Hptmn Hans Hahn, Stab III/JG 2, Spitfire, Gravelines, 0850 hrs.
Lt Egon Mayer, 7/JG 2, Spitfire, location n/k, 0852 hrs.
Hptmn Hans Hahn, Stab III/JG 2, Spitfire, Watten, 2045 hrs.
Hptmn Johannes Seifert, Stab I/JG 26, Stirling, Channel, 0840 hrs.
Oblt Werner Kahse, 1/JG 26, Spitfire, between Calais and Dünkirchen, 0845 hrs.
Hptmn Johannes Seifert, Stab I/JG 26, Spitfire, south-west of Ypern, 2025 hrs.
Uffz Gottfried Dietze, 2/JG 26, Spitfire, south-west Cap Gris Nez, 2100 hrs.
Ofw Walter März, 5/JG 26, Spitfire, West of Lille, 5,000 m, 0835 hrs.

22 July 1941

Oblt Rudolf Pflanz, Stab/JG 2, Spitfire, Hesdin, 1401 hrs.
Stabs-Fw Erwin Kley, 1/JG 2, Spitfire, location n/k, 1333 hrs.
Uffz Kuno Dollenmaier, 2/JG 2, Spitfire, location n/k, 1340 hrs.
Hptmn Hans Hahn, Stab III/JG 2, Spitfire, Calais, 1345 hrs.
Hptmn Hans Hahn, Stab III/JG 2, Spitfire, Calais, 1353 hrs.
Uffz Theodor Zingerle, 8/JG 2, Spitfire, location n/k, 1402 hrs.
Oblt Johann Schmid, Stab/JG 26, Spitfire, location n/k, 1900 hrs.
Oblt Josef Priller, 1/JG 26, Spitfire, 10 km West of Gravelines, 1340 hrs.

23 July 1941

Oblt Rudolf Pflanz, Stab/JG 2, Spitfire, location n/k, 1320 hrs.
Oblt Erich Leie, Stab/JG 2, Spitfire, 10 km, East of Calais, 1321 hrs.
Fw Günther Seeger, Stab/JG 2, Spitfire, 15 km North of Calais, 1325 hrs.
Oblt Rudolf Pflanz, Stab/JG 2, Spitfire, location n/k, 1327 hrs.
Oblt Erich Leie, Stab/JG 2, Spitfire, north-west of Calais, 1328 hrs.
Oblt Rudolf Pflanz, Stab/JG 2, Spitfire, location n/k, 1329 hrs.
Oblt Erich Leie, Stab/JG 2, Spitfire, West of Hesdin, 2035 hrs.
Oblt Rudolf Pflanz, Stab/JG 2, Spitfire, West of Hesdin, 2038 hrs.
Oblt Erich Leie, Stab/JG 2, Spitfire, West of Hesdin, 2039 hrs.
Fw Günther Seeger, Stab/JG 2, Spitfire, West of Hesdin, 2040 hrs.
Oblt Rudolf Pflanz, Stab/JG 2, Spitfire, location n/k, 2042 hrs.
Oblt Erich Leie, Stab/JG 2, Spitfire, south-west of Berck-sur-Mer, 2043 hrs.
Oblt Rudolf Pflanz, Stab/JG 2, Spitfire, location n/k, 2046 hrs.

APPENDIX 4

Oblt. Erich Leie, Stab/JG 2, Spitfire, 20 km West of Berck-sur-Mer, 2047 hrs.
Fw Günther Seeger, Stab/JG 2, Spitfire, 20 km south-west of Berck-sur-Mer, 2048 hrs.
Stabs-Fw. Erwin Kley, 1/JG 2, Spitfire, location n/k, 2050 hrs.
Fw. Karl Pfeiffer, 3/JG 2, Fortress I, La Pallice, 2151 hrs.
Uffz Gerhard Schmalenberg, 3/JG 2, Fortress I, La Pallice, 2156 hrs.
Lt Ulrich Adrian, 1/JG 2, Stirling, La Pallice, 2217hrs.
Lt Erich Rudorffer, 6/JG 2, Spitfire, West of Calais, 1318 hrs.
Ofw Kurt Bühligen, 4/JG 2, Spitfire, location n/k, 1323 hrs.
Ofw Kurt Bühligen, 4/JG 2, Spitfire, location n/k, 1327 hrs.
Lt Egon Mayer, 7/JG 2, Spitfire, location n/k,1314 hrs.
Lt Egon Mayer, 7/JG 2, Spitfire, location n/k, 1320hrs.
Uffz Karl Nowak, 9/JG 2, Spitfire, location n/k, 1325 hrs.
Oblt Werner Stöckelmann, Stab III/JG 2, Spitfire, location n/k, 1327 hrs.
Uffz Ernst Federle, 8/JG 2, Spitfire, location n/k, 1330 hrs.
Hptmn Hans Hahn, Stab III/JG 2, Spitfire, West of Hesdin, 2020 hrs.
Hptmn Hans Hahn, Stab III/JG 2, Spitfire, West of Hesdin, 2023 hrs.
Oblt Bruno Stolle, 8/JG 2, Spitfire, location n/k, 2035 hrs.
Uffz Karl Nowak, 9/JG 2, Hurricane, 30 km north-west of Berck-sur-Mer, 2055 hrs.
Obstlt Adolf Galland, Stab/JG 26, Spitfire, 40 km north-west of Gravelines, 1335 hrs.
Obstlt Adolf Galland, Stab/JG 26, Spitfire, Fruges, 7,000 m, 2010 hrs.
Obstlt Adolf Galland, Stab/JG 26, Spitfire, Fruges, 6,500 m, 2015 hrs.
Oblt Johann Schmid, Stab/JG 26,Spitfire, Fruges, 2015 hrs.
Lt Johann Aistleitner, 1/JG 26, Spitfire, 10 km North of Gravelines-Calais, 1400 hrs.
Fw Erwin Leibold, 3/JG 26, Spitfire, between Gravelines and Watten, 1400 hrs.
Oblt Josef Priller, 1/JG 26, Spitfire, 16 km north-west Gravelines-Calais, 1405 hrs.
Lt Kurt-Erich Wenzel, 1/JG 26, Spitfire, 8 km north-north-west Fort Grand Philippe, 1405 hrs.
Uffz Alfred Barthel, 5/JG 26, Blenheim, Ostende, 1409 hrs.
Lt Wolfgang Kosse, 5/JG 26, Blenheim, Ostende, 1420 hrs.
Hptmn Walter Adolph, Stab II/JG 26, Blenheim, Ostende, 1420 hrs.
Lt Paul Keller, Stab II/JG 26, Blenheim, Ostende, 1425 hrs.
Oblt Wilhem-Ferdinand Galland, 6/JG 26, Spitfire, north-west of Hesdin, 4,000 m, 2050 hrs.

BADER'S SPITFIRE WING

Ofw Max Leschnig, 5/ZG 76, Blenheim, location n/k, 1245 hrs.
Oblt Hotari Schmude, 5/ZG 76, Blenheim, location n/k, 1255 hrs.
Ofw Ludwig Schmidt, 5/ZG 76, Blenheim, location n/k, 1246 hrs.

<u>24 July 1941</u>
Uffz Walter Vock, 3/JG 2, Spitfire, North of Brest, 1417 hrs.
Fw Harry Mayer, 1/JG 2, Halifax, La Rochelle, 1420 hrs.
Hptm Karl-Heinz Krahl, Stab I/JG 2, Spitfire, North of Brest, 1423 hrs.
Uffz Friedrich Schumann, 2/JG 2, Hampden, location n/k, 1423 hrs.
Lt Julius Meimberg, 3/JG 2, Hampden, west-south-west of Ploudelengau, 1424 hrs.
Uffz Gerhard Schmalenberg, 3/JG 2, Stirling, 30 km West of Camaret, 1425 hrs.
Uffz Georg Deinzer, 3/JG 2, Spitfire, Brest, 1425 hrs.
Fw Erwin Richey, 3/JG 2, Hampden, location n/k, 1426 hrs.
Fw Wolfgang Liedig, 2/JG 2, Halifax, location n/k, 1435 hrs.
Ofw Gerhard Mund, 2/JG 2, Halifax, location n/k, 1440 hrs.
Lt Julius Meimberg, 3/JG 2, Hampden, location n/k, 1445 hrs.
Lt Herbert Horn, 3/JG 2, Wellington, west-south-west of Plougerneau, 1446 hrs.
Uffz Helmut Baudach, 1/JG 2, Halifax, location n/k, 500 m, 1450 hrs.
Lt Julius Meimberg, 3/JG 2, Wellington, Brest, 1500 hrs.
Lt Horst Walbeck, 3/JG 2, Wellington, 20 km north-west of Pabu, 3,000 m, 1500 hrs.
Uffz. Georg Deinzer, 3/JG 2, Wellington, North of Camaret, 1520 hrs.
Lt Herbert Horn, 3/JG 2, Wellington, location n/k, 1522 hrs.
Hptmn Karl-Heinz Krahl, Stab I/JG 2, Wellington, location n/k, 1525 hrs.
Oblt Horst Steinhardt, Stab I/JG 2, Wellington, 30 km North of Plouguerneau, 3,500 m, 1525 hrs.
Hptmn Karl-Heinz Krahl, Stab I/JG 2, Wellington, 20 km North of Brignogan, 1525 hrs.
Lt Rudolf Schleicher, 2/JG 2, Wellington, 1541 hrs.
Uffz Rudolf Alf, 2/JG 2, Wellington, location n/k, 1545 hrs.
Oblt Siegfried Bethke, 2/JG 2, Wellington, location n/k, 1550 hrs.
Ofw Rudolf Täschner, 1/JG 2, Halifax, location & time n/k.
Uffz. Heinz Scheibner, 1Erg/JG 2, Spitfire, Cherbourg, 1440 hrs.
Gefr Heinz Richter, Stab/JG 26, Spitfire, location n/k, 1950 hrs.
Oblt Josef Priller, 1/JG 26, Spitfire, 7 km north-west of Dünkirchen, 1445 hrs.

APPENDIX 4

Lt Hans-Georg Dippel, 2/JG 26, Hurricane, 15 km north-west of Calais, 1500 hrs.
Hptmn Walter Adolph, Stab II/JG 26, Spitfire, 15-20 km north-west of Gravelines, 5,000 m, 1455 hrs.
Lt Arthur Beese, Stab III/JG 26, Spitfire, location n/k, 1438 hrs.

25 July 1941
Uffz Rudolf Alf, 2/JG 2, Hudson, Brest, time n/k.

27 July 1941
Uffz Hans-Jürgen Fröhlich, 2/JG 26, Spitfire, Gravelines, 1438 hrs.

2 August 1941
Uffz Peter Gerth, 4(Eins)/JFS 5, Blenheim, South of Fécamp, 1217 hrs.

3 August 1941
Oblt Johann Schmid, Stab/JG 26, Spitfire, Calais, 1932 hrs.

5 August 1941
Lt Erich Rudorffer, 6/JG 2, Spitfire, North of Gravelines, 1005 hrs.
Lt Erich Rudorffer, 6/JG 2, Spitfire, Dünkirchen, 1905 hrs.
Hptmn Hans Hahn, Stab III/JG 2, Spitfire, Calais, 1844 hrs.

6 August 1941
Fw Otto Bach, 1Erg./JG 2, Spitfire, North of Cap de la Hague, 1618 hrs.

7 August 1941
Ofw Josef Wurmheller, Stab II/JG 2, Spitfire, location n/k, 0752 hrs.

Ofw Josef Wurmheller, Stab II/JG 2, Spitfire, location n/k, 1747 hrs.
Ofw Kurt Bühligen, 4/JG 2, Spitfire, location n/k, 1748 hrs.
Lt Wolfgang Wehrhagen, 4/JG 2, Spitfire, location n/k, 1755 hrs.
Fw Ludwig Spinner, 4/JG 2, Spitfire, Fruges, 6,500 m, 1809 hrs.
Ofw Josef Wurmheller, Stab II/JG 2, Curtiss P-40, location & time n/k.
Hptmn Hans Hahn, Stab III/JG 2, Spitfire, Calais, 1817 hrs.
Oblt Johann Schmid, Stab/JG 26, Spitfire, Campagne, 1120 hrs.
Obstlt Adolf Galland, Stab/JG 26, Spitfire, south-west of St Omer, 1123 hrs.
Oblt Johann Schmid, Stab/JG 26, Spitfire, south-east of Calais, 1130 hrs.
Obstlt Adolf Galland, Stab/JG 26, Spitfire, 10 km north-west of St Omer, 1740 hrs.

BADER'S SPITFIRE WING

Oblt Johann Schmid, Stab/JG 26, Spitfire, St Omer-Ardres, 1743 hrs.
Obstlt Adolf Galland, Stab/JG 26, Spitfire, North of Ardres, 1744 hrs.
Hptmn Johannes Seifert, Stab I/JG 26, Spitfire, Gravelines, 4,000 m, 1125 hrs.
Oblt Josef Priller, 1/JG 26, Spitfire, 5 km north-west of Calais, 1130 hrs.
Uffz Kurt Bohn, 3/JG 26, Spitfire, 10 km south-east Calais, 1130 hrs.
Oblt Josef Priller, 1/JG 26, Spitfire, 8 km West of Calais, 1820 hrs.
Oblt Walter Schneider, 6/JG 26, Spitfire, south-east of Deal, 0830 hrs.
Oblt Harry Koch, 5/JG 26, Spitfire, Guînes, 1120 hrs.
Oblt Walter Schneider, 6/JG 26, Spitfire, Gravelines, 1805 hrs.
Hptmn Gerhard Schöpfel, Stab III/JG 26, Spitfire, location n/k, 1140 hrs.
Hptmn Gerhard Schöpfel, Stab III/JG 26, Spitfire, south-west of Dünkirchen, 5,000 m, 1800 hrs.
Oblt Josef Haiböck, Stab III/JG 26, Spitfire, Boulogne, 4,000 – 4.500 m, 1805 hrs.

<u>9 August 1941</u>
Fw Helmut Baudach, 1/JG 2, Blenheim, location n/k, 1718 hrs.
Oblt. Johann Schmid, Stab/JG 26, Spitfire, 10 km East of St Omer, 1125 hrs.
Uffz Heinz Richter, Stab/JG 26, Spitfire, North of Dünkirchen, 1130 hrs.
Obstlt Adolf Galland, Stab/JG 26, Spitfire, north-west of St Pol, 1132 hrs.
Obstlt Adolf Galland, Stab/JG 26, Spitfire, North of Ardres, 5,000 m, 1744 hrs.
Oblt Johann Schmid, Stab/JG 26, Spitfire, Gravelines, 1744 hrs.
Oblt Johann Schmid, Stab/JG 26, Spitfire, Gravelines, 1745 hrs.
Lt Paul Schauder, 3/JG 26, Spitfire, 15 km North of Gravelines, 1756 hrs.
Ofw Walter Meyer, 6/JG 26, Spitfire, St Omer, 1125-30 hrs.
Lt Wolfgang Kosse, 5/JG 26, Spitfire, South of St. Omer, 3,000 m, 1140 hrs.
Lt Karl Borris, 6/JG 26, Spitfire, Campagne, 1830 hrs.
Ofw Erwin Busch, 9/JG 26, Spitfire, location n/k, 1125 hrs.
Hptmn Gerhard Schöpfel, Stab III/JG 26, Spitfire, East of Marquise, 1145 hrs.
Hptmn Gerhard Schöpfel, Stab III/JG 26, Spitfire, location n/k, 1759 hrs.

Appendix 5

Profiles of Me 109E, Me 109F & Spitfire Mk IIA (in appearance identical to the Mk VA).

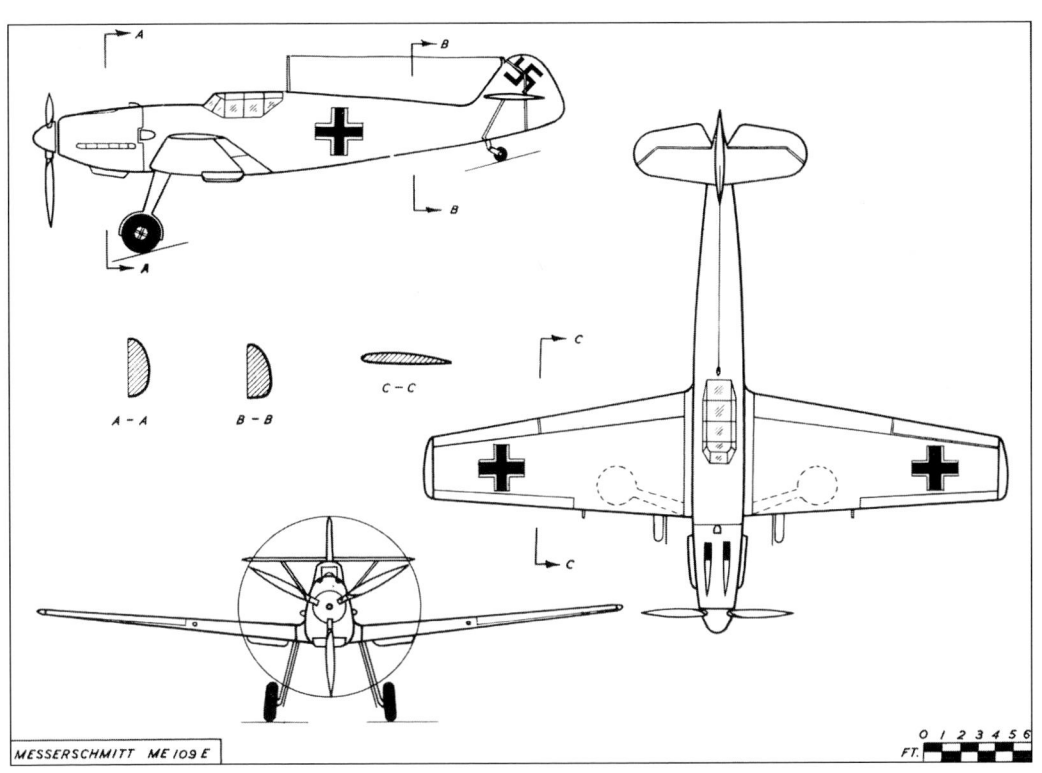

BADER'S SPITFIRE WING

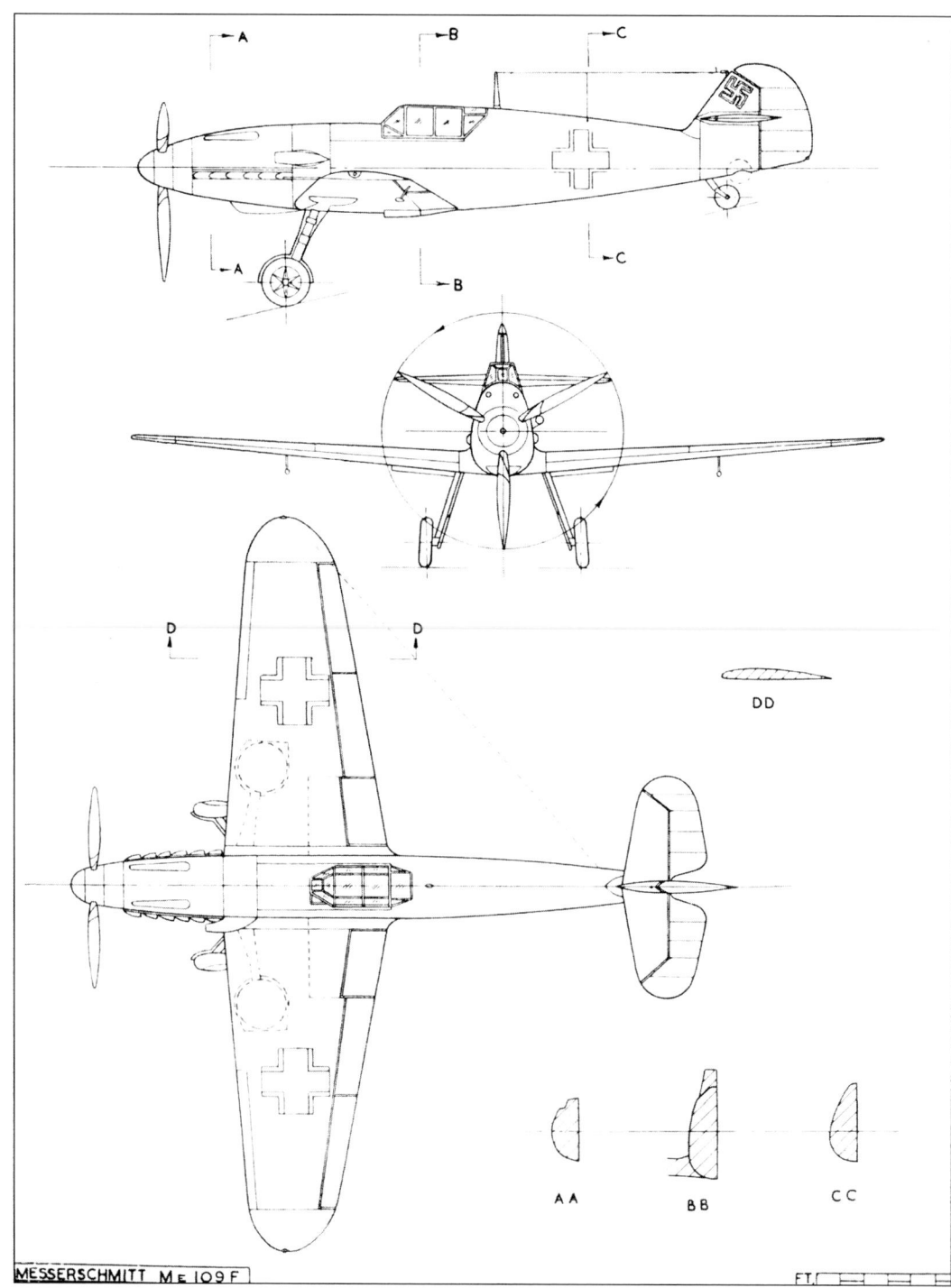

APPENDIX 5

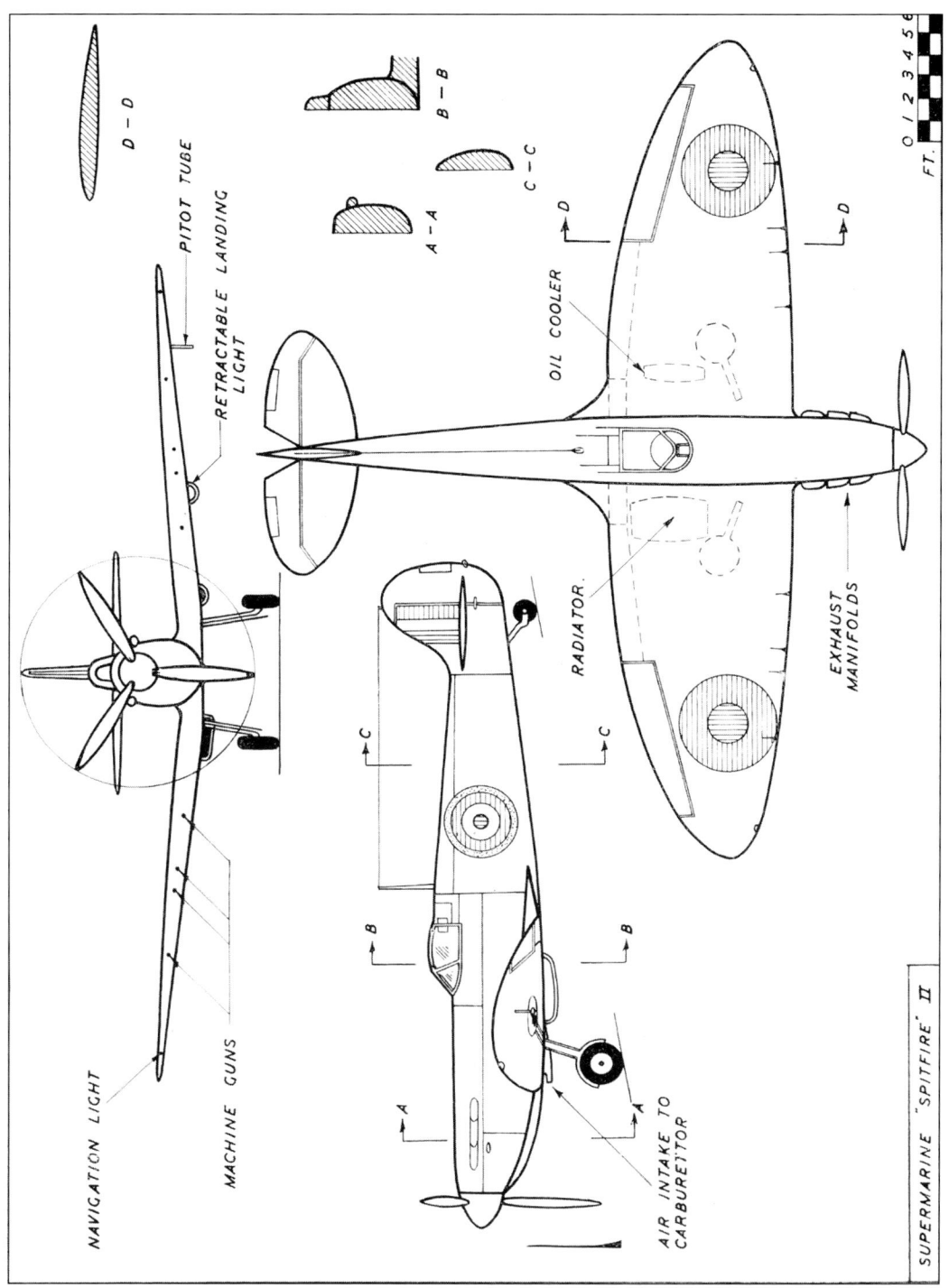

Acknowledgements

Firstly, I must thank those sadly now late Tangmere Wing survivors who contributed to my original research twenty-five years ago:

Air Marshal Sir Denis Crowley-Milling KCB CBE DSO DFC*
Air Vice-Marshal J.E. Johnson CBE DSO* DFC* DL
Air Commodore Sir Archie Winskill KCVO CBE DFC* AE
Air Commodore E.W. Merriman DFM CBE
Group Captain Sir Hugh Dundas KB DSO DFC* DL
Squadron Leader L.H. Casson DFC AFC
Squadron Leader F.A.O. Gaze DFC**
Squadron Leader Sir Alan Smith DFC
Squadron Leader W.J. Johnson DFC*
Flight Lieutenant R. Rayner DFC
Flight Lieutenant F. Twitchett AE
Flight Lieutenant P. Ward-Smith
Warrant Officer R.A. Morton
Warrant Officer D. Denchfield

Tangmere's supporting personnel:

Alan Baldwin, Arthur Berrowcliffe, Harold Clowes, 'Pop' Elvidge, Pat Goodenough, Dave Horne, Harry Jacks, Norman Jenkins, Harold Mead, George Reid, Douglas Roberts, P.A. 'Jack' Younie.

Also:

Lady Bader OBE.
Keith Delderfield, Douglas Bader Foundation.
Chris Johnson.

ACKNOWLEDGEMENTS

Mrs Jean Allom, widow of Wing Commander H.F. Burton DSO DFC.
The Baroness Hodgson CBE
Martin Woodhall, son of Group Captain A.B. Woodhall.
Brian Mabbett, brother of Sergeant S.W.R. 'George' Mabbett.
Air Commodore Graeme Pitchfork
Wing Commander N.P.W. Hancock DFC OBE, Honorary Secretary, Battle of Britain Fighter Association.
Wing Commander P.B. Lucas CBE DSO DFC
145 Squadron Association.
616 Squadron Association.
610 Squadron Association.
RAF Museum.
The National Archives.
MOD Air Historical Branch.
Dr Alfred Price.
C.J. Mckenzie.
Andy Long.
John Foreman.
Professor Bernard-Marie Dupont.
Georges Goblet.
Artur Dubreu.
Mark Hiller.
James West.

On the German side:

Gerhard Schöpfel, Johannes Naumann, Ottomar Kruse and Josef Niemark, all formerly of JG 26, and Frank Kamp.

The Douglas Bader Foundation was set up by his friends as a living memorial to Sir Douglas after his death in 1982, ensuring that his story and example would continue inspiring people, the amputee community especially, which the charity strives to support. More information can be found here, a worthy cause indeed: https://www.douglasbaderfoundation.com

    As always, Martin Mace and the Pen & Sword editorial and production team were a pleasure to work with.

Bibliography

The following Tangmere Wing pilots' flying log books were invaluable:

Group Captain Sir D.R.S. Bader (RAF Museum).
Air Marshal Sir Denis Crowley-Milling (610 Squadron).
Air Vice-Marshal J.E. Johnson (616 Squadron).
Group Captain Sir Hugh S.L. Dundas (616 Squadron).
Wing Commander H.F. Burton (616 Squadron).
Squadron Leader Sir Alan Smith (616 Squadron).
Flight Lieutenant R. Rayner (41 Squadron).

The following documents at The National Archive:

11 Group combat reports.
Pilots' individual combat reports.
Operations Record Books: 41, 145, 610 and 616 Squadrons.

Please see: www.nationalarchives.gov.uk

Private Archives and unpublished manuscripts:-

Bader Papers.
Johnson Papers.
Dilip Sarkar Archive (all photographs in this book are from the author's archive).
Woodhall, Group Captain A.B., *Soldier, Sailor, Airman Too*, unpublished manuscript.

The following programmes are available on YouTube:

Douglas Bader, *This is Your Life*: https://www.youtube.com/watch?v=4408_DJOu3I

BIBLIOGRAPHY

Johnnie Johnson, *This is Your Life*: https://www.youtube.com/watch?v=z2ZfHeS6KMU
RAF CASPS Historic Interview: Sir Hugh Dundas: https://youtu.be/znohBspDSjk
RAF CASPS Historic Interview: Johnnie Johnson: https://youtu.be/aPetW8IKfVk

Films

Danny Angel's *Reach for the Sky*, starring Kenneth More and Muriel Pavlow, is widely available as both a DVD and to stream online.

Published sources

Anon., *The Rise and Fall of the German Air Force, Air Ministry Pamphlet No 248*, Public Record Office, Key, 2001
Bader, Group Captain Sir D.R.S., *Fight for the Sky*, Sidgwick & Jackson, London, 1973
Badiansky, S., *Battle of Wits: The Complete Story of Codebreaking in World War II*, Simon & Shuster, London, 2018
Bekker, C., *The Luftwaffe War Diaries*, MacDonald, London, 1966
Brickhill, P., *Reach for the Sky*, William Collins, London, 1954
Caldwell, D., *The JG 26 War Diary Volume One 1939–1942*, Grub Street, London, 1996
Delve, K., Fighter Command 1936–1968: An Operational Record & Historical Record, Pen & Sword, Barnsley, 2007
Dundas, Group Captain Sir H.S.L., *Flying Start: A Fighter Pilot's War Years*, Stanley Paul Ltd, London, 1988
Foreman, J., RAF *Fighter Command Victory Claims of World War Two, Part Two, 1 January 1941 – 30 June 1943*, Red Kite, Walton-on-Thames, 2005
Foreman, J., *1941 Part Two – The Blitz to the Non-stop Offensive, The Turning Point*, Air Research Publications, Walton-on-Thames, 1994
Franks, N., *Fighter Command Losses of the Second World War – Revised Edition*, Midland Publishing, Hersham, 2008
Galland, General A., *The First and the Last*, Methuen, London, 1955
Johnson, AVM J.E., *wing leader*, Chatto & Windus, London, 1956
McCairns, J.A., *Lysander Pilot: Secret Operations with 161 Squadron*, Tangmere Military Aviation Museum, Chichester, 2018

Mead, H.T., *RAF & Ready... or How DID we win the war Dad?*, unpublished manuscript

Musciano, W., Messerschmitt *Aces*, Tab/Aero Books, New York, 1989

Obermaier, E., Der Ritterkreuz Trager Der Luftwaffe *1939-45, Volume I –* Jagdflieger, Verland Dieter, Berlin, 1966

Sarkar, D., *The Invisible Thread: A Spitfire's Tale*, Ramrod Publications, 1992

Sarkar, D., *A Few of the Many: Air War 1939-45, A Kaleidoscope of Memories*, Ramrod Publications, 1995

Sarkar, D., *Bader's Tangmere Spitfires: The Untold Story, 1941*, Haynes (PSL), 1996

Sarkar, D., *Douglas Bader*, Amberley Publishing, 2013

Shores, C., & Williams, C. *Aces High*, Grub Street, London, 1994

West, J. (ed), *Spitfires & Spots: Jeff West, Fighter Pilot Diaries 1941–1945*, privately published by James West, New Zealand, 2018

Wynn, *Men of the Battle of Britain*, Frontline Books (Pen & Sword), Barnsley, 2015

Other books by Dilip Sarkar
(in order of publication)

Spitfire Squadron: No 19 Squadron at War, 1939-41
The Invisible Thread: A Spitfire's Tale
Through Peril to the Stars: RAF Fighter Pilots Who Failed to Return, 1939-45
Angriff *Westland: Three Battle of Britain Air Raids Through the Looking Glass*
A Few of the Many: Air War 1939-45, A Kaleidoscope of Memories
Bader's Tangmere Spitfires: The Untold Story, 1941
Bader's Duxford Fighters: The Big Wing Controversy
Missing in Action: Resting in Peace?
Guards VC: Blitzkrieg 1940
Battle of Britain: The Photographic Kaleidoscope, Volumes I-IV
Fighter Pilot: The Photographic Kaleidoscope
Group Captain Sir Douglas Bader: An Inspiration in Photographs
Johnnie Johnson: Spitfire Top Gun, Part I
Johnnie Johnson: Spitfire Top Gun, Part II
Battle of Britain: Last Look Back
Spitfire! Courage & Sacrifice
Spitfire Voices: Heroes Remember
The Battle of Powick Bridge: Ambush a Fore-thought
Duxford 1940: A Battle of Britain Base at War
The Few: The Battle of Britain in the Words of the Pilots
Spitfire Manual 1940
The Last of the Few: Eighteen Battle of Britain Pilots Tell Their Extraordinary Stories
Hearts of Oak: The Human Tragedy of HMS Royal Oak
The Sinking of HMS Royal Oak In the Words of the Survivors (re-print of Hearts of Oak)
Spitfire Voices: Life as a Spitfire Pilot in the Words of the Veterans
How the Spitfire Won the Battle of Britain

Spitfire Ace of Aces: The True Wartime Story of Johnnie Johnson
Douglas Bader
Fighter Ace: The Extraordinary Life of Douglas Bader, Battle of Britain Hero (re-print of above)
Spitfire: The Photographic Biography
Hurricane Manual 1940
River Pike
The Final Few: The Last Surviving Pilots of the Battle of Britain Tell Their Stories
Arnhem 1944: The Human Tragedy of the Bridge Too Far
Spitfire! The Full Story of a Unique Battle of Britain Fighter Squadron
Battle of Britain 1940: The Finest Hour's Human Cost
Letters from The Few: Unique Memories of the Battle of Britain
Johnnie Johnson's 1942 Diary: The War Diary of the Spitfire Ace of Aces
Johnnie Johnson's Great Adventure: The Spitfire Ace of Ace's Last Look Back
Spitfire Ace of Aces – The Album: The Photographs of Johnnie Johnson
Sailor Malan – Freedom Fighter: The Inspirational Story of a Spitfire Ace
The Real Spitfire Pilot
Bader's Big Wing Controversy: Duxford 1940

Index

19 Squadron, 8, 32, 146, 174
41 Squadron, 9, 11, 167–73, 182, 225
56 Squadron, 9, 149
65 Squadron, 13, 15, 20, 22, 29–30, 47
66 Squadron, 7, 12, 52
74 Squadron, 9, 12–13, 37, 134, 175
92 Squadron, 9, 12, 19, 229
145 Squadron, 50, 78, 82–3, 88, 90, 92, 95, 101, 107–109, 111–12, 115–17, 119, 121, 130, 132–6, 138, 141, 144–8, 153, 157, 159, 164, 167, 227
219 Squadron, 104, 137
242 Squadron, 9, 32–3, 61, 82, 86, 95, 108, 111, 124, 165, 175, 215
302 Squadron, 13, 75–6
610 Squadron, 13, 50, 56, 58–60, 72, 75, 78, 83, 88–9, 91, 95, 97, 102–104, 107–109, 111–12, 115–16, 120–1, 129–30, 132, 134, 136, 138–9, 142, 144, 147, 153–4, 157, 159–60, 164–5, 167, 171, 182–3, 185, 188, 196, 198, 225
611 Squadron, 22, 85
616 Squadron, 25, 30–2, 50–6, 63, 65, 67, 75–8, 90–2, 101–102, 104, 108–109, 112, 114–16, 118–21, 123, 126, 128–30, 132, 134, 136, 138–9, 141, 143–6, 149–50, 153–7, 160, 164, 166, 169, 171–2, 179, 182, 184–5, 188, 202, 204, 206, 212, 215, 225, 229

Abbeville, 20, 44, 47, 75, 90
Acklington, 50
Airey, Leading Aircraftman Cliff, 68–9
Aitken, Wing Commander Max, 130
Anderson, Sergeant J.E., 153
Arthur, Flight Lieutenant C.I.R., 86, 130, 145

Bader, Group Captain Sir Douglas 'Dogsbody', vi–vii, 9, 32–3, 47, 50, 53–4, 56, 58–60, 68, 71–2, 78–9, 86, 89, 92, 95, 97, 104, 107–108, 110, 112–14, 118, 121, 123, 125–7, 129, 132, 139–46, 149–-51, 153, 155, 157, 159–61, 163–6, 170–2, 174–5, 179, 182–9, 191, 193, 195–201, 203, 206–207, 210–16, 219–21, 224–5, 227, 233, 235, 237

Baldwin, Alan, 29, 70, 137
Balthasar, Hauptmann Wilhelm, 37, 40, 42, 142
Barbarossa, Operation, 122
Barwell, Squadron Leader Dickie, 52, 154
Battle of Britain, 2, 4–5, 9, 22, 36–7, 40, 44, 50–3, 85, 167–8, 174–6, 215, 228, 235
Beardsley, Squadron Leader Bob, 9–11, 172, 174–5
Beaverbrook, Lord, 3, 5, 61
Beedham, Sergeant, 115, 121, 123, 142, 160, 173
'Big Wing', 7, 9, 26, 32, 51–3, 67, 174, 229
Biggin Hill, 12, 50, 154, 229
   Biggin Hill Wing, 125, 134, 175–6
Blackman, Sergeant H.C.D., 153
Bodie, Pilot Officer, 7
Boulton-Paul Defiant, 2
Bowen, Sergeant, 142
Breeze, Sergeant, 165
Brewer, Sergeant, 129–30, 172
Bristol:
   Beaufighter, 2–3, 51
   Blenheim, 2, 8–9, 12–13, 17, 67, 88, 115, 121–2, 128, 132, 134, 139, 142, 161, 163–6, 179, 210
Broadhurst, Group Captain Henry, 143, 173, 232
Brown, Pilot Officer Edward, 119–20
Burton, Squadron Leader H.F. 'Billy', 26, 30–1, 50–4, 56–9, 104, 113–14, 116, 125–7, 143, 150, 152, 154, 158, 162, 165, 179, 182, 186, 188–9, 191–2, 201, 229, 231–3

Camplin, Sergeant, 130
Casson, Flying Officer L.H. 'Buck', 52, 92, 121, 133, 136, 159, 166, 182, 185–6, 190–1, 193, 195, 201–202, 212, 219–21, 223
Christie, Flight Lieutenant, 7
Churchill, Winston, vii, 25, 175, 232, 237
Clarke, Flying Officer, 108
Clowes, Sergeant Harold, 141–2
Cox, Wing Commander David, 8, 22, 146
Crowley-Milling, Air Marshal Sir Denis, 32, 110, 120, 130, 142, 155, 157, 159, 185, 196, 206, 215

Davies, Sergeant, 130
Denchfield, Sergeant David, 2, 13, 20
Derby, Operation, 116
Doley, Sergeant Joe, 72, 147
Dornier,
   Do 17, 105, 132
Douglas, Air Marshal Sholto, 1–5, 7–8, 24, 32, 123, 143, 203, 225–7, 229
Dover, 46, 97, 112, 117, 123, 135, 154, 195
Dowding, Air Chief Marshal Sir Hugh, vi, 1, 36, 176
Draper, Flight Lieutenant Gilbert, 172
Duke, Squadron Leader Neville, 216
Dundas, Flying Officer Hugh 'Cocky', 52–4, 56, 90–1, 97, 101, 105, 129, 132, 135, 144, 146, 159–62, 166, 179, 182–3,

INDEX

185–6, 200–203, 206, 215, 221, 223, 234–5
Dunkirk, 19, 36, 43, 52, 115–16, 121, 129, 132, 134–5, 145, 147, 155–6, 159, 165, 174–5, 197
Duxford, 32, 89, 95, 174
　Duxford Wing, 235

Ellis, Squadron Leader John, 50–1, 75, 78
Elvidge, 'Pop', 136–8
Evill, Air Vice-Marshal, 203

Fighter Command, 3, 5, 7–9, 11, 24, 32, 36–7, 45, 97, 101, 112, 122, 126, 132, 134, 139, 142–4, 148, 153–6, 158, 163, 172, 179, 203–204, 216, 225, 227, 229, 234
Finlay, Squadron Leader Lionel Don, 167, 172
Finucane, Flying Officer 'Paddy', 22, 47

Galland, Major Adolf, 35, 37, 44–8, 111, 119–20, 129, 134, 204–205, 207, 212–13, 215
Gaunce, Squadron Leader L.M. 'Elmer', 167–8, 182–3
Gaze, Pilot Officer Tony, 72, 89, 95, 107, 116, 132, 138, 159
Gibbs, Squadron Leader Edward P. 'Gibbo', 76, 121, 129, 149–51
Gill, Flying Officer, 151
Goebbels, Joseph, 2
Grant, Sergeant R.J.C., 119, 130, 164
Gray, Pilot Officer, 155, 165

Hahn, Hauptmann Hans 'Assi', 41
Hawker Hurricane, 2, 9, 32, 36, 61
　Merlin, 17, 23, 32
Heath, Pilot Officer Barrie, 22
Heinkel,
　He 60, 92
　He 111, 52
Hepple, Pilot Officer Philip 'Nip', 28, 52, 121, 138–9, 154, 156, 160–2, 185, 188–90, 200–201, 204, 219
Hill, Pilot Officer, 15, 20
Hitler, Adolf, vii, 34, 36–7, 44, 61, 122, 225, 227
Holden, Flight Lieutenant Ken, 28, 52, 101, 108–110, 121, 130, 132, 135, 150, 159, 182–7, 198
Horner, Pilot Officer F.G., 121, 147
Hugill, Pilot Officer, 104, 120

Kell, Hauptmann Hermann, 41

Jagdgeschwader,
　JG 2, 38–41, 48, 88, 90, 118, 122, 129, 132–4, 139, 142–3, 148, 153–6, 158, 163, 172, 185, 225, 227
　JG 3, 13, 20, 40
　JG 26, 20, 42–4, 46–8, 111, 116–19, 122, 129, 132, 134–5, 138–9, 142–3, 148, 152–6, 158, 162–4, 172, 185, 193, 204–207, 210, 213, 219, 225, 227
　JG 27, 40
　JG 51, 97
　JG 53, 9, 44, 56
　JG 234, 43

Jenks, Wing Commander, 28, 121, 130
Johns, Captain W.E., 106
Johnson, Air Vice-Marshal Johnnie, 3, 26, 31–2, 51–2, 54, 58, 61–2, 69, 76, 78, 82, 101, 104, 113–14, 132, 137, 140, 142, 145, 149, 156–8, 160–2, 166, 173–4, 177, 179, 181, 186, 188, 195–6, 200–201, 203, 206, 215, 221, 224, 228–9, 234
Junkers,
    Ju 87, 108, 155
    Ju 88, 52, 72, 75–6, 85, 92, 232

Laguna, Squadron Leader Piotr, 51, 76, 134
Leather, Squadron Leader Jack, 50, 82–3, 86
Le Havre, 37, 88, 108, 116, 164
Lee-Knight, Flight Lieutenant, 111, 116, 132, 142, 144, 147, 167
Leigh-Mallory, Air Vice-Marshal Sir Trafford, 8–9, 32, 72, 89, 108, 114, 123, 167, 177, 210, 225, 229
Lucas, Wing Commander 'Laddie', 215
Luftwaffe, 2, 19, 34, 36–7, 40, 45–6, 85, 122, 143, 172, 212, 227, 232, 235

Mabbett, Sergeant S.W.R. 'Thug', 52, 90–1, 135, 161–3
Macbeth, Sergeant, 116, 132
MacDonald, Flight Lieutenant Peter, 108, 178
MacFie, Flight Lieutenant, 88, 90, 116, 144, 152

Machacek, Flying Officer, 116, 118, 135, 148
Maine, Sergeant, 97, 101
Mains, Sergeant, 138, 144
Malan, Squadron Leader A.G. 'Sailor', 12–13, 37, 101, 125, 134, 144, 154, 175–8
Marples, Flying Officer Roy, 92, 118, 121, 129–30, 159, 168–9, 184, 186, 190–1
Matzke, Oberleutnant, 117
McCairns, Sergeant James Atterby, 83, 107, 136, 145
McDevette, Sergeant Francis, 90
McFarlane, Sergeant James, 148
McKee, Sergeant, 225
Mead, Harold, 50–1, 59, 102
Merriman, Air Commodore E.W. 'Peter', 72, 115, 142, 147, 155, 160
Messerschmitt,
    Me 109, 11–13, 22–3, 32, 34–7, 42–8, 56, 59, 67–8, 83, 92, 95, 101, 104, 106, 109–10, 112, 115–18, 120–1, 125, 129, 132–3, 139, 142–3, 145–6, 149, 155, 163, 165–6, 172, 199–200, 205–206, 214–15, 221, 228
    Me 109E, 45, 47, 106, 118, 120, 129, 133, 139, 144, 157
    Me 109F, 31–2, 44, 106, 120, 125, 129, 132–3, 135, 138–9, 143–4, 147, 154–6, 159, 172
Michelmore, Squadron Leader E.J.C., 13
Mitchell, Sergeant, 172
Mölders, Oberleutnant Werner, 34–5, 45, 97, 101

INDEX

Morton, Sergeant Bob 'Butch', 23, 52, 56, 78, 88, 105, 130, 133, 142, 149, 151–2
Mungo-Park, Squadron Leader John, 134

Newling, Flight Lieutenant Michael, 121, 134, 145
Norris, Flight Lieutenant, 72, 75

Offenberg, Pilot Officer, 92
Operation Mondscheinsonate, 1
Owen, Flying Officer, 107

Park, Air Vice-Marshal Keith, 7
Peel, Squadron Leader J.R.A, 83, 152
Pike, Air Vice-Marshal Tom, 178
Pine, Pilot Officer Peter, 109, 148
Pingel, Hauptmann Rolf, 154
Pollock, Sergeant, 167
Portal, Air Chief Marshal Charles 'Peter', 5, 123, 225

RAF Cranwell, 52, 170
RAF Hawkinge, 12, 47, 101, 131, 133, 144, 146, 160, 201
Raine, Sergeant, 121, 130, 159, 165
Rayner, Flight Lieutenant Ron, 11, 170
Reid, George, 141, 206
Richthofen, Manfred Freiherr von, 34, 37
Robertson, Air Commodore E.D.M., 52
Robillard, Sergeant Larry, 121, 136, 138

Schlager, Unteroffizier Albert, 204–205, 219–20
Schöpfel, Hauptmann Gerhard, 44, 48, 193, 195, 206–207, 210
Scott, Pilot Officer, 120, 130, 133
Sellars, Sergeant Robert Lindon, 88
Smith, Squadron Leader Sir Alan 'Smithy', 12–13, 54, 62, 112, 136, 138, 145, 149, 155–6, 158–9, 215
Sperrle, General Hugo, 34, 37
Spitfire,
  Mk I, 32, 85
  Mk II, 85, 144
  Mk IIA, 31–2, 54, 60, 62–3, 159, 171
  Mk IIB, 32, 62, 109–10, 144
  Mk IIC, 137
  Mk V, 144
  Mk VA, 63, 147, 164, 171, 182
  Mk VB, 151–2, 159, 162, 164, 190
St Omer, 13, 16, 19–20, 47, 111, 115–17, 121, 123, 125, 130, 135–6, 140, 146, 148–9, 152–3, 155–7, 162–3, 171–2, 197–9, 204–205, 210, 212, 235
St Pierre, Flying Officer, 136
Stevens, Flight Lieutenant, 107

Tangmere, vii, 13, 28–32, 50–1, 53–4, 56, 63–4, 67, 70, 72, 76, 78, 83, 88–9, 95, 97, 101–102, 104, 106, 109, 113, 115–16, 118, 120–1, 123, 125–6, 128, 130, 132, 134–8, 140–2, 144–8, 150, 152–4, 156–61, 163–7, 170, 172–4, 178–9, 182–3, 196–7, 201, 204–206, 210, 212,

215, 219–21, 225, 227, 229, 231, 233–5, 237
Trenchard, Lord 'Boom', 5
Turner, Squadron Leader P.S. Stan, 82–3, 86, 88, 101, 111, 118, 130, 134, 141, 148, 157–8, 164, 167
Twitchett, Sergeant Frank, 83, 91, 95, 115, 117, 141, 165, 227

Ward-Smith, Flight Lieutenant Peter, 67, 153
Warden, Sergeant, 95
Wellum, Squadron Leader Geoffrey, 229
West, Sergeant-Pilot Jeff, 52, 75, 78, 82–3, 91, 104, 106–107, 112, 121, 128–9, 135, 143, 154, 159–60, 166–7, 171–3, 179, 187–8, 200–201, 215, 221
Winskill, Flight Lieutenant Archie, 140, 170, 172, 225
Woodhall, Group Captain A.B. 'Woody', 9, 53, 71–2, 89–90, 108, 113, 116, 123, 154, 174, 182–3, 195, 200, 202, 207, 225
Woodhouse, Squadron Leader 'Paddy', 78, 88–9, 97, 101, 104, 108, 225